MasterChef
Cookery course

Eating is sensorial. More than that, it's about interpreting the information that your senses give you.

Chef Andoni Luis Aduriz

you use your heart!

Fish, to taste right, must swim three times – in water, in butter and in wine.

Polish proverb

A clever cook can make good meat of a whetstone.

Erasmus

Anybody can make you enjoy the first bite of a dish, but only a real chef can make you enjoy the last.

François Minot

My wife, inviting me to sample her very first soufflé, accidentally dropped a spoonful of it on my foot, fracturing several small bones.

Woody Allen

than this!

What you'll learn...

Getting started
Stock up on staples, see how to choose fresh ingredients, get your essential equipment, and learn the principles of cooking to take you on your way.

Building blocks
This guide to the essential building blocks of cooking gives you a firm foundation in skill and confidence.

The recipes
These recipes have been selected to build on your new techniques and skills, and they will deliver delicious results time and time again.

Make it your own
Take these seasonal favourites, add some super tips from John and Gregg, and mix in your own flair to take your cooking to the next level.

Taking notes
Here's a space for you to record helpful notes on your journey to excellence – from successes and failures, to flavour pairings and recipe ideas. **412**

GETTING STARTED

Before you begin any cookery course you need to have the best tools and ingredients to hand. So get your store cupboard, fresh ingredient know-how, and kitchen equipment in order and you're ready to start your love affair with cooking.

The perfect store cupboard

Start with a well-stocked kitchen. Non-perishable ingredients are versatile key staples and add flavour to your cooking.

Store cupboard essentials

Pasta, rice, and grains These are long lasting, quick to cook, and require minimal embellishment. rice (risotto; brown; basmati) • pasta (spaghetti; macaroni; penne) • couscous • bulghur wheat

Pulses and beans Thrifty sources of protein and fibre, these nutritional powerhouses are invaluable standbys for quick suppers or soups. lentils (green; red) • beans (flageolet; cannellini; butter; kidney) • chickpeas

Condiments, powders, oils, and vinegars These work equally as well at the start of cooking – in marinades – as they do in finishing dishes. olive oil (light; extra virgin) • sunflower oil • sesame oil • vinegars (rice wine; cider; balsamic; white or red) • salt • honey • Dijon mustard • pickle • Tabasco • soy sauce • Thai fish sauce • bouillon • mustard powder • Worcestershire sauce

Cans and jars Canned and preserved goods are often strong in flavour and fresh tasting. chopped tomatoes • coconut milk • anchovies • tuna • pesto • chutney • jalapeños • capers • tomato purée

Dried fruit, nuts, and seeds Perfect to add to bread dough, breakfast dishes, and baked goods. raisins • apricots • dates • sesame seeds • ground almonds • whole nut selection

Baking ingredients Dozens of delicious bakes are conjured up with the help of these basics. flour (self-raising; plain) • vanilla extract • golden syrup • baking powder • bicarbonate of soda • sugar (demerara; soft brown; caster; icing) • jam

Dried spices and herbs Keep spices and herbs in airtight containers, replacing them frequently. chilli flakes • ground cinnamon • whole black peppercorns • cayenne pepper • cumin seeds • whole nutmeg • whole cloves • cinnamon sticks • ground ginger • cardamom pods • vanilla pods • garam masala • turmeric • ground coriander • Chinese five-spice powder • chilli powder • paprika • bay leaves • mixed herbs • fennel seeds • curry powder

Dried herbs and spices

Dried fruit, nuts, and seeds

Baking ingredients

7

Choosing fish and shellfish

All fish and shellfish should be super fresh when you buy, and ideally consumed on the day of purchase. Choose sustainable varieties.

Shellfish

All shellfish should show signs of life, most obviously movement. Never buy dead, uncooked shellfish as decomposition begins immediately after death and they may not be safe to eat. Buying shellfish may seem daunting, but there are some easy methods to help you choose the freshest possible.

Crab

Male crabs have large claws and yield more white meat than females. Distinguish the sex by looking at their tail flap: the male's is narrower and pointier than the female's.

Limbs Gently flexed, the limbs should snap back to position whether they're cooked or raw.

Shell Avoid any that are cracked or damaged. The shell should feel crisp and dry.

Weight A crab should feel heavy for its size and should not be seeping water.

The same rules apply when choosing lobster.

Oysters

Choose Pacific over native oysters in the summer months, as this is when natives are spawning. Store oysters cup-side down to prevent their natural juices from escaping.

Shell This needs to be tightly closed, clean, and bright. Avoid those with chipped shells. Don't let a greenish tinge on the shell put you off as this can be caused by a diet of a particular plankton.

The same rules apply when choosing scallops, mussels, clams, and cockles.

Fish

All fish should smell fresh and pleasant, not "fishy". There are signs of quality all over the body of a fish, as indicated by the sea bass, pictured opposite.

Eyes These should be full, bright, and clear – not sunken. As a fish loses condition, the pupil appears grey or milky, and the cornea opaque.

Scales These should be bright, shiny, and glistening, and firmly attached to the skin. None should be missing. Scales that look dull and dry indicate that the fish is no longer fresh and should be avoided.

Gills Look for bright red gills. As the fish loses condition, the colour fades to brown and the mucus becomes sticky.

Flesh Good-quality fresh fish may still show signs of rigor mortis (feel firm and rigid). This indicates that it has been out of the water for no more than 24–48 hours. The tail should also feel stiff. Pressing along the back of a fish is often the best way to check for freshness, as once a fish loses condition it will be soft and flabby.

The same rules apply when choosing all types of whole fish.

Other seafood

Prawns and crayfish Whether raw or cooked, these should smell fresh. They should have a moist shell. Avoid prawns with cracked shells.

Squid and octopus The tubular flesh of a good-quality specimen is white, turning pink as it begins to decompose.

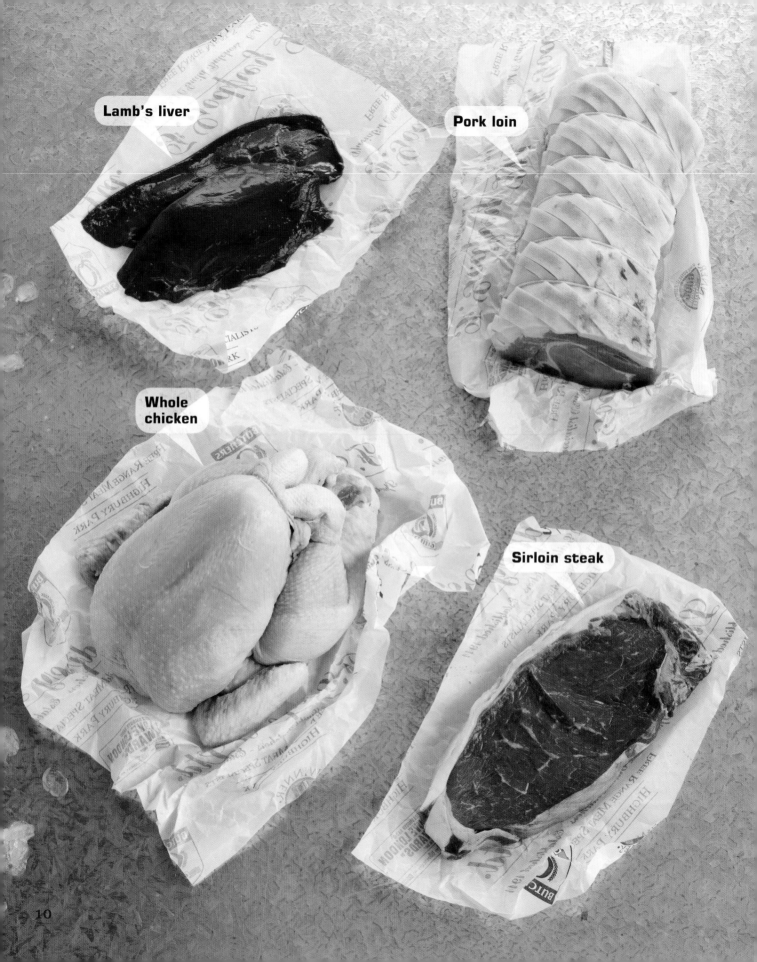

Choosing meat and poultry

For the best flavour, choose meat and poultry that have clear signs of freshness. Always choose the cut most suited to your recipe.

Pork

Pork should be pink. The fat should always be white and soft. Intensively farmed pork is the palest and leanest, and outdoor-reared pork will be a darker, firmer meat with tastier fat.

Meat Check the meat is pink – not white, grey, or red – with fine threads of marbling.

Beef

Beef that indicates its origin and breed is likely to be of better quality. All beef should smell pleasant and fresh.

Flesh Beef flesh should be red, not grey – the deeper red it is, the longer it's had to mature. Beef matured for 3–4 weeks is ideal. Most cuts should be marbled with fat, although silverside cuts will have little marbling as they are more lean. Avoid clammy beef steaks, notably when vacuum-packed.

Fat Look for steaks and sirloin joints with a generous layer of fat around their edge – this will help them to remain moist when cooking. Check that the fat is creamy white, not yellow. You may find that brisket cuts are too fatty and will need trimming before cooking.

Offal

All offal should smell fresh, and of little. For variety and quality, buy from a local butcher. Liver is probably the most popular of the wide variety of offal available. It should be a rich, deep red colour, although calf and lamb's liver will be paler than beef or pig's liver.

Flesh Liver should have no grey spots on the surface. Flesh should be smooth, supple, and glossy. It should never be dry or wrinkled.

Poultry

Intensively farmed poultry is cheaper than organic or free-range varieties, but it doesn't have the same flavour.

Skin Look for plump flesh, with taut skin. There should be no dry patches or tears. Avoid birds that exude a lot of liquid.

Colour Look for an even colour, with no dark patches (although the legs will look darker).

Legs Avoid birds with bruised or broken legs and check that there is no discolouration around the knee joints.

Scent All poultry should have a clean, fresh smell: a bad odour will indicate that it is past its best.

The same rules apply when choosing grouse, partridge, and pheasant.

Other meats and offal

Veal Good quality veal should be lean and firm with little creamy-white fat (veal is not as heavily marbled as beef). Avoid veal that is watery or that has grey bones.

Lamb All lamb should have a thin covering of white fat. It is not marbled, although when becoming mature it can have quite a lot of intramuscular and external fat.

Mutton This is darker than lamb with more fat that will require trimming.

Kidney This must smell fresh and be clean-looking. The membrane should be fine and silvery-white.

Choosing fruit

The quality of fruit can vary greatly. Use your sense of smell, touch, and a practised eye to choose the freshest produce.

Choose rough-skin **melons** with pronounced ribbing and a floral scent. Choose smooth-skin melons by pressing the stem end: it should give slightly. There should be no stem still attached.

Strawberries should be red – avoid any with white tips. The green hull should look fresh, not dry. They should have a heady sweet scent.

Choose **oranges** that are heavy for their size; check the skin for patches and reject soft-patched fruit.

A heady sweet scent is a sign of a ripe **peach**. Check there are no green patches on the skin. Don't just use colour as a signifier of ripeness – the blush is a genetic variation.

Avoid **apples** and **pears** with skin that wrinkles when gently pressed; check for deep colour in the skin, a sign of good flavour. They should feel firm and heavy for their size.

Grapes should be heavy for their size. The skin should be taut with a dusty "bloom". Avoid bright green grapes, and those with a ring of bruising around the stem.

Choosing vegetables

Choose fresh vegetables that are bright in colour with no yellowing.
They should smell fresh and be tight and firm to the touch.

Savoy cabbage should have tight heads of fresh leaves, and protective outer leaves. Avoid ones with dry or bruised stalks, or signs of slime or insect damage.

Artichokes should be heavy. Unblemished leaves should squeak when you press them.

Potatoes should be firm. Dirt is a good sign that they may be grown locally. Check the potatoes for cuts and damage, which accelerate decay.

Lettuce leaves should be firm and crisp; check the lettuce carefully for insect damage.

Mushroom stems should look fresh, not dried out. They should smell fresh and earthy, not sour. Avoid bruised mushrooms with wrinkly skin.

Check that the **onion** and **garlic** skin is taut against the flesh. Avoid bulbs with green sprouts. Check the base for mould.

Carrot and **beetroot** should have glossy leaves. Check that the root feels firm. Avoid any roots with hairy secondary roots. Check the skin for cracks and abrasions.

5 essential saucepans

There is a myriad of saucepans on the market. Here is a simplified guide to the saucepans you really need.

Bain-marie Perfect for recipes requiring gentle heat such as melted chocolate or egg-based sauces. Best in stainless steel.

Casserole A casserole dish is great to have on hand for slow cooking. Best made from cast iron with an enamel coating.

Saucepan Used for all-purpose cooking; get some in a few different sizes. Buy them made from copper or stainless steel with a copper or aluminium base.

Steamer A must-have for preparing vegetables. Buy in stainless steel with a glass lid as part of a set for best fit.

✚ SAUCEPAN CARE

Copper and even stainless steel can stain or corrode over time, so soak them in cold water immediately after use to remove food particles, and then hand-wash in warm, soapy water. Enamel-coated cast-iron pans can be washed the same way, but uncoated cast iron requires a little more care. Season a new cast-iron pan by baking in a coating of oil to protect the surface and prevent corrosion. Clean with boiling water, but forgo soap to protect the seasoning. Rub in a clean, thin film of oil before storing.

Stock pot Makes soups and boils big batches of pasta. Buy one with an aluminium or copper bottom to spread heat.

5 essential knives

Good-quality knives are a must. Here are the "top five" knives that every cook should own.

Bread knife To ensure clean, even slices from any type of bread, soft or crusty. A bread knife enables thick and thin slicing, reduces crumbs, and keeps the loaf intact.

Chef's knife A must-have for any kitchen. Each part of the blade, serves a different purpose. When cooking a complex dish, a chef's knife is up to every task.

All-purpose knife Another multi-purpose kitchen tool, this is perfect for small jobs where the heft of a chef's knife is not required, like chopping a handful of herbs.

➕ **KNIFE CARE**

High carbon stainless steel is considered the best material for knife blades, as the carbon content adds to durability and, unlike high carbon steel, contains enough chronium to resist discolouration. Titanium is also a good choice as it is light, durable, and corrosion resistant when properly cared for. Preserve the lifespan of knives and keep them sharp and safe by looking after them correctly. Store in a block or on a magnetic knife strip to protect the blade. Wipe clean immediately after use.

Serrated all-purpose knife Perfect for slicing anything with a tough exterior and a soft middle like avocados and lemons.

Paring knife This knife is useful for small tasks such as peeling, coring, and mincing fruit and vegetables, or for removing seeds.

5 essential pans

Here are five essential pans that will serve you well in the kitchen. Choose materials according to your budget.

Wok Perfect for stir-fries, but also good for braising and deep-frying. Some woks are made from carbon steel, which needs to be seasoned and cared for in a similar way to cast iron.

Skillet Must-have and multi-purpose, look for a skillet in coated cast iron, copper, or stainless steel with a heavy heat-conductive bottom.

Griddle pan Cast iron ridged pans are great for chargrilling; try flat ones for pancakes.

Roasting pan A must-have for slow cooking and oven roasting. It's best to find one made from stainless steel sandwiched around aluminium or copper.

Sauté pan Like a skillet, but with deep vertical sides, a sauté pan is best used for anything requiring high heat. Buy in copper or aluminium-based stainless steel.

✛ PAN MATERIALS

Each material serves a different purpose. Copper is one of the most conductive metals and spreads heat evenly and quickly. Stainless steel is durable, non-corrosive, prevents sticking and burning, and, unlike standard non-stick cookware, doesn't scratch. Buy one with a heavy copper or aluminium base to conduct heat efficiently. Cast iron retains heat and is perfect for anything that requires slow cooking. A good quality cast iron pan can last a lifetime, but requires a little care (see p14).

5 best of the rest

There is an astounding array of kitchen tools and gadgets available. Here are some choice pieces that will streamline your cooking.

Bakeware Baking tins (pictured), spring-form tins, tart tins, and pie dishes are versatile and are useful for all baked recipes. Buy durable, non-stick pans.

Handheld gadgets Handheld gadgets such as graters, peelers (pictured), mezzalunas, and juicers are very handy for preparing herbs, citrus fruits, and other ingredients. Best made from stainless steel, hand wash them. Store a mezzaluna in thick fabric to protect the blade.

Work-top gadgets These can simplify many a task. A food processor (pictured) or blender can chop, purée, and mix. A juicer can make juices from whole fruits and vegetables. Mixers transform the complexities of baking into quick tasks. Disassemble and clean each piece in warm soapy water.

Kitchen scales These are necessary for measuring the weight of flour and other baking and cooking ingredients. Ensure the scales are wiped clean with soap and water after use to protect the surface and eliminate kitchen bacteria.

Thermometer Use this to determine whether meat is thoroughly cooked. Thermometers should only be used in microwaves and ovens if they are designed to. Instant-read ones should be used only for a few seconds at a time and not left in food while cooking.

Principles of cooking

The behaviour and direction of heat affects food in different ways, giving you several choices when cooking. Learn about the major cooking methods with this guide.

Dry-heat cooking

Cooking techniques that transfer heat without the use of water are dry-heat methods, including those using oil and fats. Dry-heat cooking typically involves high temperatures of more than 150°C (300°F). Cooking times are often short, but there are exceptions when slow-roasting meat and baking rich fruit cakes.

Baking and roasting

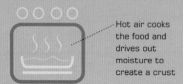
Hot air cooks the food and drives out moisture to create a crust

In both baking and roasting, dry heat envelops the food to cook it, but the goals are subtly different. Roasting usually involves higher temperatures to caramelize the surface of the food, but aims to keep it moist inside – a coating of fat often acts as a barrier to keep the succulence in. When baking, natural moisture evaporates slowly as steam to cook the food or to make it rise and form a crust.

Deep-frying

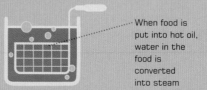
When food is put into hot oil, water in the food is converted into steam

Deep-frying is submerging food in hot, liquid oil. The oil should be between 160°C (325°F) and 200°C (400°F). The larger the size of the food, the lower the temperature should be. If the oil is too hot, foods will be raw in the centre, and if the oil is not hot enough the food will absorb oil. As the temperature rises, the food gets a crisp coating. Foods deep-fried at the right temperature absorb surprisingly little oil.

Pan-frying and sautéing

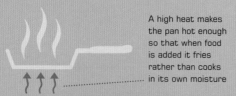
A high heat makes the pan hot enough so that when food is added it fries rather than cooks in its own moisture

Pan-frying and sautéing are both high-heat cooking methods that use a small amount of hot oil, butter, or other fat. The hot fat cooks the food while keeping its texture and flavour intact. Pan-frying uses more fat and requires the food to be turned only once or twice. Sautéing uses less fat, so the food must be moved or tossed in the pan to cook it evenly.

Grilling

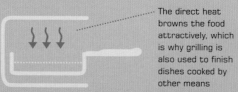
The direct heat browns the food attractively, which is why grilling is also used to finish dishes cooked by other means

Grilling uses a direct heat source above or under the food – usually with a flame or an electric coil. The browning that occurs with direct heat adds flavour, but foods that cook fairly slowly, such as chicken, should either be grilled under a cooler heat or moved a little distance from the heat source, to stop them burning before they cook all the way through.

Moist-heat cooking

This describes the various cooking methods that use wet heat or water-based liquids – whether it's steam, water, stock, wine, or milk. The temperatures involved are usually lower than dry-heat cooking, since the boiling point of water is 100°C (212°F), and therefore includes some of the gentler cooking methods.

Boiling

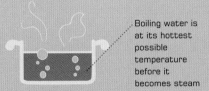

Boiling water is at its hottest possible temperature before it becomes steam

Boiling occurs when water reaches 100°C (212°F) and produces large bubbles that continuously rise and break the surface. Some foods, like rice, pasta, and eggs, cook evenly in boiling water, but as the agitation of the bubbles can damage food or turn it stringy or dry, the heat is usually reduced to a simmer after reaching boiling point.

Steaming

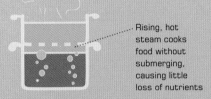

Rising, hot steam cooks food without submerging, causing little loss of nutrients

Steaming involves cooking food over a small amount of rapidly boiling water. The food is placed inside a covered, perforated steamer compartment, allowing the food to be cooked by the heat of the rising steam. Steaming is often favoured for delicate ingredients because there is no agitation, enabling the food to retain more nutrients.

Stewing and braising

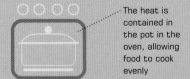

The heat is contained in the pot in the oven, allowing food to cook evenly

Stewing and braising are both slow-cooking moist-heat techniques where the cooking liquid becomes an integral part of the dish. For stewed dishes, the food is added to a pot (meat is often seared beforehand to add flavour), covered with liquid, and simmered slowly at a relatively low temperature on either a stove or in the oven. The steam generated by the liquid is insulated by the covered pot, causing the food to cook more evenly. A perfect temperature is key: if the liquid boils it may become greasy, and if it is not hot enough the food will take too long to cook. Braising is very similar but cooks larger, often whole, cuts of meat and uses less liquid – often only partially covering the ingredients. Pot-roasting is one method of braising. Both techniques are great for tough cuts of meat, as they allow muscle fibres to absorb moisture from the cooking liquid and steam.

Poaching

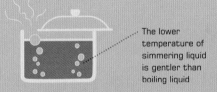

The lower temperature of simmering liquid is gentler than boiling liquid

Poaching uses "pre-boiling", simmering liquid to cook food. The liquid can then be used as part of the dish or discarded. To ensure the food cooks evenly, whole fish and pieces of meat should be placed in cold poaching liquid, and then heated up. Quick-cooking smaller-sized foods, such as fish steaks, should be plunged into already simmering liquid.

Cooking terminology

Searing means cooking food quickly over a high heat in oil or butter so that it colours all over and forms a caramelized crust.
Simmering produces bubbles rising in a steady stream. Much smaller than those in boiling water, the bubbles are just visible.
Reducing means to boil a liquid rapidly so that a proportion evaporates leaving a deeper, more concentrated sauce.

BUILDING BLOCKS

Your cookery course starts here. This guide to the essential building blocks – the key techniques, the mother sauces, and the key staples – gives you a firm foundation in skill and confidence.

5 KEY TECHNIQUES

Get to grips with core cooking techniques. Detailed lessons in these versatile methods will give your cooking a thorough grounding. Additional advice gives you the expert edge.

ROASTING
The dry heat of an oven caramelizes and enhances the flavours of meat, poultry, and vegetables. Follow the steps for a perfect roast chicken.

STEWING
Tenderize cuts of meat and poultry by simmering them in a flavoured broth. Master the long, slow cooking of the classic French beef stew, *pot-au-feu*.

FRYING
Quick and easy frying methods give foods a lovely golden brown exterior. Pan-fry a steak following detailed steps, understanding how to test for "doneness".

POACHING
Immersing foods in simmering water poaches them – an ideal method for delicate foods like eggs, which may be damaged by other methods of cooking.

BAKING
A gentle heat concentrates flavours, evaporating moisture and allowing bakes to rise. A simple Victoria sponge cake is a delicious introduction to this art.

The key techniques
Roasting

The dry, all-round heat of an oven browns and caramelizes the surface of food, enhancing flavour.

Principles of roasting

Meat or poultry must be at **room temperature**, so remove from the refrigerator 30 minutes before roasting (if frozen, be sure to thaw completely). During cooking, keep the meat moist by **basting** it at least once with the drippings in the roasting tin or another liquid. Roast birds or joints should always **rest** before serving – leave for 20–30 minutes in a warm place. For meat and poultry roasting timings, please refer to the tables on pp428–9.

Roasting recipes to try are **Roast partridge** (p174); **Roast rack of lamb** (p186); **Roast rib of beef** (p188); **Roast leg of pork** (p196); **Roast pork belly** (p198); **Roast baby leeks** (p256); and **Roast potatoes** (p258).

shopping list for a roast chicken

Practise the technique of roasting with a classic chicken roast. It can be tricky to perfect, but ensuring you have the best ingredients will help.

One free-range, corn-fed **organic chicken**

A drizzle of **olive oil** (optional)

2 tbsp softened unsalted **butter**

1 **lemon** (optional)

A pinch of freshly ground **black pepper**

A handful of fresh **thyme** (optional)

A pinch of **sea salt**

the perfect technique

Roast a chicken for 20 minutes per 450g (1lb), plus 10–20 minutes extra. If you like, a halved lemon placed inside the chicken's cavity adds flavour, as do whole garlic cloves in the roasting tin. Rubbing with olive oil instead of butter will help make the skin extra crisp.

1 Preheat the oven to a high heat, about 240°C (475°F/Gas 9). Put the chicken, breast-side up, in a roasting dish or tin on top of prepared vegetables (if using). Rub the butter (or oil) all over the bird. Season well. Place in the oven and immediately turn the heat down to 200°C (400°F/Gas 6).

2 Scatter over the sprigs of thyme, if using, then leave to roast. Baste the chicken once, about halfway through the roasting, or several times: remove from the oven and carefully tilt the dish slightly so that all the juices run to one end, then spoon the juices all over the chicken.

2 hrs
1.35kg/3lb chicken

preparing
10 mins

roasting
20 mins per 450g/1lb chicken

If the juices run clear, it's done. If not, roast for 10 more minutes, then check again.

3 Turn the oven up to 220°C (425°F/Gas 7) for the last 15 minutes of cooking, to crisp the skin further. To check if the chicken is cooked, push a skewer into a meaty part such as the leg.

4 When the chicken is cooked, remove from the oven, transfer to a carving board (using two carving forks is the easiest way to do this), cover with foil, and rest for 20–30 minutes.

5 Tilt the roasting tin so the juices collect at one end. Using a large shallow spoon, skim the fat off the top of the juices and transfer to a bowl. Use the juices left in the tin for the gravy.

A precise way to check if a chicken is cooked is to use a thermometer. At the end of the cooking time, insert one into the thickest part of the thigh, not near the bone. Internal temperature should be 75°C (170°F); white breast meat will be cooked at 71°C (160°F).

6 To carve the chicken, first remove the legs. Use a carving fork to hold the chicken steady on the board, then pull the leg away from the bird and cut down between the body of the bird and the thigh on one side to sever the ball and socket joint.

7 To divide the leg into two pieces, cut through the joint to separate the thigh and drumstick. Remove the wing on the same side, taking some breast meat with it, then carve the rest of the breast into slices. Repeat on the other side of the chicken. Serve on a warmed platter.

plus 10–20 mins extra

resting
30 mins

The key techniques

Stewing

Stewing is the process of simmering meat and poultry very gently in a flavoured liquid, giving an extra moist result. It also tenderizes tough meat cuts and older poultry.

Principles of stewing
If meat is to be **cut up**, pieces should be no smaller than 2.5cm (1in). **Browning** the meat first will add rich colour and flavour to the stew. During cooking, the liquid should **simmer**, rather than boil. Once the meat is tender, stop cooking. If you want to **reduce the liquid** by boiling, remove the meat first. If time permits, for juiciness, leave meat to **cool in the liquid** (reheat for serving).

Stewing recipes to try are **Coq au vin** (p160); **Venison casserole** (p168); **Pot-roast pheasant** (p170); **Irish stew** (p180); **Lamb shanks braised in red wine** (p182); and **Lamb and apricot tagine** (p184).

shopping list for pot-au-feu

A classic *pot-au-feu* recipe stews several cuts of beef with a mixture of vegetables in a delicious stock flavoured with garlic and cloves.

6 peeled **carrots** and 3 washed and peeled **leeks**, chopped

3 litres (5¼ pints) cold **water**

800g (1lb 12oz) **beef brisket** or **flank**

6 **turnips**, peeled and chopped

400g (14oz) **sirloin steak**

6 **parsnips**, peeled and chopped

1 **onion**, peeled and chopped

bouquet garni (see p65)

4 **cloves**

400g (14oz) **chuck steak**

4 **garlic cloves**, crushed

3 **celery sticks**, washed and chopped

salt and freshly ground **black pepper**

the perfect technique

Cut the vegetables into 5–8cm (2–3in) lengths – big pieces are less likely to become mushy during the long, slow cooking. You could replace the beef with a large chicken, whole or in joints, omitting the parsnips and turnips. Chicken will need to rest in the stock after cooking – keep the vegetables warm in a low oven.

1 Place the beef brisket in a large flameproof casserole and pour in the cold water. Set over medium heat and bring just to simmering point. Skim off the scum, then partially cover, reduce the heat to low, and leave to simmer for 1 hour.

During the first half hour, remove the lid every 10 minutes or so to skim off any scum.

4 hr 32 mins

preparing	stewing
20 mins	4 hrs 10 mins

2 Stud the onion with the cloves and add it to the casserole with the garlic, bouquet garni, and some salt and black pepper.

3 Add the sirloin and chuck steak. Bring back to a simmer, then partially cover the pot and leave to simmer gently for 2 hours.

4 Add the celery and leeks and simmer for 10 minutes, then add the carrots, turnips, and parsnips. Cook for a further hour.

Pot-au-feu is traditionally served with poached marrow bones. Poach 4 sections of veal bone in lightly salted water for 20 minutes. Drain the bones and add them to the platter, with toasted bread on which to spread the marrow.

5 Remove the meat and vegetables with a large slotted spoon (discard the bouquet garni and onion) and arrange them on a large warmed platter (pictured opposite). Strain the cooking liquid through a sieve into a large saucepan.

6 Skim the fat off the broth (laying sheets of kitchen paper over the surface and removing them as soon as they are saturated is another option). Reheat, check the seasoning, and pour a little over the meat and vegetables. Serve hot.

serving

2 mins

The key techniques
Frying

Cooking over heat in hot fat or oil is known as frying. Great for tender foods, it is a quick method that produces a crisp, golden brown exterior.

Principles of frying

Whether sautéing, shallow- or deep-frying, or stir-frying, the fat in the pan needs to be **hot**. Don't **overcrowd** the pan – this will lower the temperature and the food will stew rather than fry. For stir-frying, cut all the ingredients into **equal-sized** pieces so they will cook in the same time.

Frying recipes to try are **Chargrilled asparagus** (p118); **Haddock and herb fishcakes** (p128); **Pan-fried pollock** (p132); **Seared tuna** (p138); **Fish and chips** (p146); **Pan-fried duck breast** (p166); **Liver and bacon with onions** (p206); **Chilli and tofu stir-fry** (p224); **American blueberry pancakes** (p280).

knowing your steaks

Frying is ideal for tender beef steaks, as well as lamb steaks and chops, chicken fillets, and small whole fish or fillets.

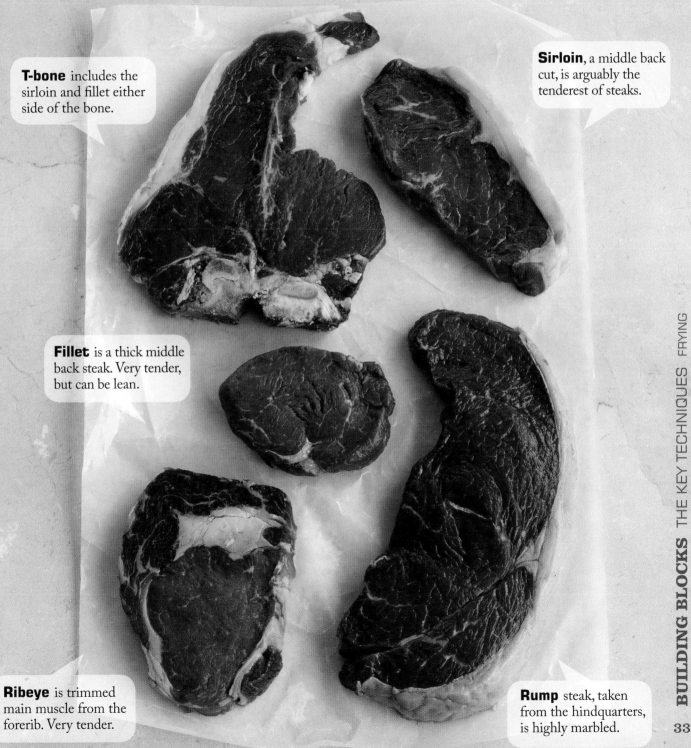

T-bone includes the sirloin and fillet either side of the bone.

Sirloin, a middle back cut, is arguably the tenderest of steaks.

Fillet is a thick middle back steak. Very tender, but can be lean.

Ribeye is trimmed main muscle from the forerib. Very tender.

Rump steak, taken from the hindquarters, is highly marbled.

the perfect technique

Remove the steaks from the refrigerator 30 minutes before cooking, so that they are at room temperature. Cooking times depend on the thickness of the steaks and your taste: timings for 3cm (1½in) steaks – as used here – are given in the guide to cooking to perfection. Rest the steaks before serving.

1 Preheat a heavy-based frying pan over high heat until very hot. Add 1–2 tbsp butter or oil to the pan, heating until it shimmers (as shown here); or if preferred, spray both sides of the steaks with oil. Lay the steaks in the pan away from you (to avoid fat splashing). Ensure each steak is in contact with the pan by pressing it down all over with a slotted spatula.

2 Turn the heat down slightly to avoid the fat burning, then leave the steaks untouched for 1–2 minutes before lifting them with the tongs to check the underside (as pictured). This process of browning on a very hot surface is called searing. Turn the steaks over onto the uncooked side.

43 mins

getting to room temperature
30 mins

3 Season the browned sides with salt and pepper. Leave the steaks to cook for a few minutes (how long depends on how you like your steak, see guide below), then flip them over and season the other browned sides. Continue frying the steaks, flipping them every 1–2 minutes, until they are cooked to your liking. Remove from the pan and leave to rest on a warmed plate for 3–5 minutes before serving.

Testing for "doneness"

To check the cooked stage of a steak, you can press lightly with a finger – the more it is cooked, the harder it will feel, so a rare steak will have a lot of give. Try the "heel of your thumb" test. Touching your thumb and little finger together, press the fleshy base of your thumb: this is an indication of well done (it's quite firm). At the other end of the spectrum, press thumb and index finger together for an indication of rare – the heel of your thumb feels quite soft.

To make a quick sauce, deglaze the frying pan with a little splash of red wine or stock, and whisk in a little butter.

cooking to perfection

Bleu *2–3 mins* Cook just until seared. The steak feels very soft when pressed, and the interior is reddish purple. The steak feels like the heel of your thumb when your hand is completely relaxed.

Rare *6–8 mins* Drops of blood appear on the surface and the steak feels spongy. The interior is red. The steak feels like the heel of your thumb when your thumb is pressed to the index finger.

Medium *10–12 mins* Drops of juice are just visible. The steak offers resistance and its centre is pink. It feels like the heel of your thumb when your thumb is pressed to the middle finger.

Well done *12–14 mins* Drops of juice are clearly visible and the steak feels firm. It is uniformly brown. It feels like the heel of your thumb when it is pressed to the little finger.

frying (for a rare 3cm/1½in thick steak)

8 mins

resting

5 mins

The key techniques
Poaching

Foods immersed in simmering liquid are described as poached – ideal for delicate fish, eggs, and whole fruit, as it helps them to keep their shape.

Principles of poaching

For most foods, keep the **heat low** (so the poaching liquid just bubbles gently) and the poaching time to a **minimum**. This will prevent the food from breaking up and ensure a moist result. Because poaching times for fish are short, fish stock and **court bouillon** (see p135) are often used as they add extra flavour. When poaching fruit, choose **firm whole fruit** that is not too ripe.

Poaching recipes to try are **Fish pie** (p124); **Poached skate with black butter** (p134); **Bouillabaisse** (p144); **Pears in Marsala** (p278).

know your eggs

Poached eggs are simple yet sublime, tenderly set with a deliciously runny yolk – a prime example of the poaching technique at its best.

Rich-flavoured **duck** eggs have large yolks and watery whites.

Hen eggs' colour doesn't denote quality or flavour, only breed. Readily available, they are delicious poached.

Luxurious **quail**'s eggs have a high yolk-to-white ratio.

Ostrich eggs equal 24 hen eggs in size. Great for sharing, poaching brings out their delicate flavour.

Seasonal **goose** eggs have a strong flavour.

the perfect technique

For poached hen eggs, the more boiling water there is, the less the temperature drops when the eggs are added, so use a large pan. There is no need to swirl the water before adding the eggs, but a teaspoon of vinegar in the water will speed coagulation. Use the freshest eggs for the best results.

1 Bring a large heavy-based pan of water to the boil over medium heat. Turn the heat down to low, so that the water is barely moving. Break the egg into a cup, then slide it gently into the water without breaking the yolk (as pictured).

3 mins

cooking
3 mins

2 With a large slotted spoon, draw the egg white in around the yolk to envelop it. Adjust the heat so it is at a gentle boil, then poach the egg for 2–3 minutes or until the white is set; the yolk will still be soft.

3 Carefully lift the egg out of the water with the slotted spoon.

4 Place it on kitchen paper or a clean tea towel to drain briefly.

5 If you want a very neat finish, trim all around the edge of the egg white with a small sharp knife. Serve immediately.

testing for freshness

In a glass of cold water, a very fresh egg will lie horizontally on the bottom.

If an egg is in a vertical position on the bottom, it is slightly older, but still fresh.

As eggs age they become lighter and will float. These are not fresh enough to poach.

Keep poached eggs in a bowl of warm water until you are ready to use them. Or, if you are going to use them cold, put them in a bowl of cold water. Keeping the eggs in water keeps the whites supple.

Baking

Prolonged cooking in the dry heat of an oven has a delicate effect on foods, perfect for whole fish and creating delicious golden-crusted cakes and breads.

Principles of baking

Baked foods are cooked at a **gentle** heat. Be sure the oven is fully **heated** before starting. **Measure** ingredients accurately. **Cakes** are baked at moderate temperature to give them time to rise and set, and **pastry** at high temperature so it sets quickly. Baking tart cases blind prevents a soggy bottom (see p272). **Biscuits** and **cookies** are soft after baking, so allow to firm up before moving to a rack.

Baking recipes to try are **Feta filo pie** (p216); **Tarte tatin** (p284); **Profiteroles** (p300); **Sourdough bread** (p318); **Fruit cake** (p332); **Macaroons** (p338); **Chocolate cake** (p340).

shopping list for a Victoria sponge

A light, delicate Victoria sponge is the quintessential baked cake.
Only butter will do, with the freshest eggs and real vanilla extract.

175g (6oz) **self-raising flour**

2 tsp **vanilla extract**

175g (6oz) golden **caster sugar**

2 tbsp **milk**

250g (9oz) **icing sugar**, plus extra for dusting

300g (10oz) soft unsalted **butter**

3 large **eggs**

the perfect technique

You can use the sponge mixture to make fairy cakes; just use cake cases and reduce the cooking time accordingly. Try new flavourings – add lemon zest in place of vanilla, or sandwich with whipped cream and jam. Before you start, be sure the butter is soft but not oily, and eggs are at room temperature.

1 Preheat the oven to 180°C (350°F/Gas 4). Line the bases of two 18cm (7in) round cake tins with baking parchment: draw around the tin on the paper with a pencil, cut out, and place pencil-marked side down in the tin.

2 Cream together 175g (6oz) of the butter and the golden caster sugar using a hand-held electric mixer, or a tabletop mixer, until pale, light, and very fluffy. Scrape down the sides of the bowl a few times.

| 1 hr 15 mins | lining the tin 5 mins | beating the mixture 10 mins | baking 20 mins |

3 Beat the eggs in a small bowl, just to break them up, then add to the creamed mixture a little at a time, beating well after each addition. Towards the end, if the mixture looks like it might curdle, add 1 tbsp of the flour. Beat in 1 tsp vanilla extract. Add the sifted flour and milk and fold in.

Use a large metal spoon to fold in the flour gently but thoroughly.

The reason cakes sink is excess liquid in the mixture – the proportion of butter and sugar is too high for the amount of egg and flour in the recipe. If your cake emerges from the oven dry and crumbly, it may be that too much flour was used. To save the cake from the bin, moisten it by brushing it with warm sugar syrup.

4 Divide the mixture equally between the tins and spread out evenly using a spatula. Bake for 20 minutes or until the cakes are well risen, golden brown, and springy to the touch.

5 Allow the cakes to cool for 5–10 minutes in the tins, then turn them out onto a wire rack. Peel off the lining paper. Turn the cakes right-side up on the rack, then leave to cool completely.

6 To make the butter icing, cream together the remaining 125g (4oz) soft butter with the icing sugar and 1 tsp vanilla extract until fluffy.

7 Sandwich the two cakes together with the icing: turn one of the cakes upside down on a plate and spread over the icing (pictured opposite). Set the other cake on top. Dust the surface of the cake with sifted icing sugar.

ooling
30 mins

icing
10 mins

5 MOTHER SAUCES

The classic mother
sauces originate
in French cooking.
They form the basis
of many recipes
and have inspired
endless variations.
Master the sauces,
understanding their
unique consistencies
and flavours.

TOMATO
Rich classic tomato sauce is made primarily with the ripest tomatoes, and given texture and flavour with onion and garlic cloves.

BÉCHAMEL
The classic white sauce, béchamel is made by whisking milk into a white roux. Consistent stirring is required to create that creamy, smooth texture.

HOLLANDAISE
Cooked over a bain marie, smooth, rich hollandaise is an emulsion of egg yolk and butter, seasoned with salt, pepper, and a drizzle of lemon juice.

VELOUTÉ
Velouté is a white sauce made from a light stock that has been thickened with a buttery roux. Its name roughly translates as "velvety", after its delicate texture.

ESPAGNOLE
A thick, strong-flavoured brown sauce made from a dark roux that is boiled with vegetables, pieces of beef, and seasonings until it reduces down.

The mother sauces
Tomato

This versatile sauce can add a tangy flavour and rich colour to many kinds of dishes. Easy to make, fresh ingredients are key to its success.

shopping list

Very few ingredients are needed for a good tomato sauce, so they must be the best. Choose ripe, fragrant tomatoes with an intense colour.

1–2 tbsp medium-strength **olive oil**

Salt and freshly ground **black pepper**

Handful of **basil** leaves (optional)

1–4 **garlic** cloves, finely chopped

900g (2lb) **tomatoes** (ripe plum tomatoes like San Marzano have the best flesh–juice ratio)

1 medium yellow or red **onion**

the perfect technique

Chop the onion and garlic as finely as possible, sweating them softly to gain flavour and the best consistency. This classic sauce can be adapted – try adding a tablespoon of chopped fresh basil or a teaspoon of chilli powder.

1 Cut a small cross in the base of each tomato, then place them in a heatproof bowl. Pour over boiling water to cover. Leave for only about 1 minute, then use a slotted spoon to remove all the tomatoes from the water, otherwise they will start to cook.

2 Use a small knife to peel off the skin (as pictured). If the tomatoes are still very hot, hold them with a clean cloth while peeling off the skin. Roughly chop the tomatoes, making sure you keep all the juice and pips as well.

| 55 mins | preparing the tomatoes 10 mins | chopping 5 mins | sweating 5 mins | cooking 30 mins |

3 Cut the onion in half lengthways. Peel off the skin, leaving the root intact. Make cuts into the onion halves from root to tip. Turn the onion and slice in the opposite direction, to dice. (You can make narrow or wide cuts as the recipe requires.)

4 Bash the garlic cloves with the flat side of the knife to loosen the skin, then peel it off. Hold the cloves together to chop them finely.

Add the garlic to the onions. Cook for 1–2 minutes or until soft.

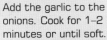

5 Heat 1–2 tbsp of olive oil in a saucepan. Add the onions and sweat them over very low heat, until translucent, for about 5 minutes.

6 Add the chopped tomatoes to the pan and stir well to mix everything together. Season with salt and pepper to taste.

7 Bring to the boil, then lower the heat and cook gently for about 30 minutes so that all the flavours come together and the sauce reduces slightly. Stir from time to time.

8 Strain the sauce through a coarse sieve into a bowl, using the back of a ladle to press out as much liquid from the ingredients as possible.

straining

5 mins

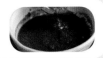

The mother sauces
Béchamel

The king of white sauces, béchamel is endlessly versatile. It is the basis for other sauces and is used in many recipes, from soufflés to lasagne.

shopping list

Béchamel is made by combining flour and butter (a roux), then adding milk that has been subtly flavoured with aromatics.

500ml (16fl oz) whole **milk**

40g (1½ oz) **plain flour**

½ peeled **onion**

40g (1½ oz) **butter**

salt and freshly **ground black pepper**

1 **bay leaf**

1 blade of **mace**

the perfect technique

This classic sauce is very easy to make. Flavour by stirring in 2 tbsp finely chopped parsley or 1 tbsp Dijon mustard at the end, or enrich with 4 tbsp double cream or crème fraîche. For a mornay sauce, remove from the heat and add 75g (3oz) grated Cheddar or Gruyère and a pinch of mustard powder.

1 Put the milk in a pan with the bay leaf, onion, and mace. Heat gently until just boiling, then take off the heat. Leave to infuse for about half an hour. Strain the milk through a sieve into a jug.

45 mins	preparing	infusing the milk
	5 mins	30 mins

2 Melt the butter in a heavy-based saucepan over low heat. Add the flour and mix well with a wooden spoon, or whisk to make a smooth roux.

3 Cook the roux over low heat, stirring constantly, for 1–2 minutes or until foaming. Don't allow the roux to darken at all.

4 Gradually add the strained milk to the roux. Beat well with the spoon or whisk while adding the milk so that no lumps form.

When all the milk has been added, bring the sauce to the boil. Keep stirring and cook until the sauce thickens.

5 Season the sauce with salt and pepper, then taste it and add more if needed.

6 Reduce the heat and simmer gently for 3–4 minutes, stirring occasionally. The sauce should be smooth and creamy. This makes a coating sauce (see tip for thin and thick sauces).

Quantities in the roux determine the consistency – reduce quantities for a thin sauce and increase for a thick, binding sauce. Whatever the thickness, if the sauce starts to go lumpy, whisk vigorously or transfer the mixture to a blender and blitz until smooth.

making a roux	stirring
5 mins	5 mins

Hollandaise

Buttery hollandaise is ideal with poached dishes. It is notoriously tricky, but slowly adding the butter over a low heat helps prevent separation.

shopping list

This delicate yet rich emulsified sauce is created from egg yolks and unsalted butter, flavoured with just lemon juice, salt, and pepper.

juice of half a **lemon**

2 **eggs** at room temperature

100g (3½oz) chilled unsalted **butter**

salt and freshly ground **black pepper**

the perfect technique

Hollandaise is the basis of many delicious variations – try stirring in 100g (3½oz) of chopped watercress leaves, ½ tsp saffron threads, or ½ tsp Dijon mustard. Add 50g (1¾oz) beurre noisette for a sauce to serve with fish. Or fold in a dollop of whipped cream and serve with chicken or vegetables.

1 Cut the butter into small cubes. Carefully crack the eggs and separate the yolks from the whites. You need only the yolks for the hollandaise, so keep the whites in a container in the refrigerator for another recipe.

2 Place the yolks in a heatproof bowl and whisk with a splash of cold water until pale and frothy. Set the bowl over a saucepan of simmering water placed on low heat. Make sure that the water does not touch the base of the bowl.

13 mins

preparing
5 mins

whisking
6 mins

3 Add a cube of butter and whisk until it melts and is incorporated into the yolks. Repeat this process with the remaining butter. If the mixture starts to get too hot, remove the bowl from the saucepan and allow to cool a bit before continuing.

Lift up the whisk: the sauce should make a trail like a ribbon on the sauce in the bowl and remain there for a few seconds before sinking.

If the sauce curdles, there are two remedies – remove from the heat, whisk in an ice cube to lower the temperature; or strain the curdled sauce into a clean heatproof bowl, set it over the pan of water, and gradually whisk in another egg yolk with a splash of water.

4 When all the butter has been added, whisk until the sauce reaches the ribbon stage (see inset, above). Remove the bowl from the pan, add fresh lemon juice, and whisk to combine. Season with salt and pepper. Serve immediately.

making mayonnaise – a close relative

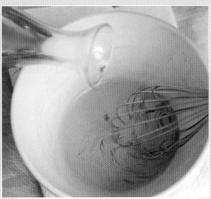

1 Place 2 egg yolks in a bowl. Add 1 tsp Dijon mustard and a few drops of lemon juice. Season. Whisk until well blended.

2 Start adding 200ml (7fl oz) olive oil, drop by drop at first. Whisk constantly. After adding 2 tbsp oil the mixture will start to thicken.

3 Pour in the rest of the oil in a thin stream, whisking all the time. When all the oil has been incorporated, taste and season.

stirring in lemon juice

2 mins

The mother sauces
Velouté

Velouté begins as a roux, to which a light stock is gradually added. It simmers for up to an hour to achieve its velvety, creamy perfection. It is commonly served with poultry or fish dishes.

shopping list

A good velouté depends on the quality of the stock used to make it. Home-made is the best choice, or a good ready-made chilled stock.

20g (¾oz) **plain flour**

400ml (14fl oz) **chicken** or **veal stock**

1–2 tbsp **double cream**

20g (¾oz) unsalted **butter** plus a few cubes to finish (optional)

salt and freshly ground **black pepper**

the perfect technique

The basis for classic sauces allemande and suprême, velouté is rarely served without flavouring as it can be varied so easily. Stir ½ tbsp curry paste in with the cream for delicate spice; whisk in 2–3 tbsp tomato purée or some fine spinach purée; or add 1 tbsp chopped tarragon – wonderful with white fish.

A last-minute addition will lift a sauce lacking in flavour: add a splash of wine or Champagne to a velouté made with fish stock, or port or Madeira to one made with chicken or veal stock.

50 mins	boiling the stock	making a roux	simmering
	3 mins	5 mins	40 mins

1 Place the white stock in a saucepan over medium heat and bring to the boil, skimming off any scum if necessary. Keep hot while you make the roux in a heavy-based saucepan.

2 Melt the butter over low heat. Add the flour and stir it into the butter. Cook, stirring, for 2 minutes or until the roux is a pale straw colour.

Keep whisking until the sauce thickens, then reduce the heat.

3 Remove from the heat and gradually pour in the hot white stock, stirring constantly. Return the saucepan to the heat and bring the mixture to the boil, whisking constantly.

4 Simmer gently for 30–40 minutes, stirring occasionally. Skim the sauce frequently to remove scum that rises to the surface – removing impurities will leave the sauce almost translucent.

5 For a glossier final consistency, you could pass the sauce through a fine sieve into a clean saucepan (pictured opposite). Reheat.

6 Add the double cream. For an extra rich sauce, remove from the heat and whisk in a few cubes of cold butter. Season to taste with salt and freshly ground black pepper.

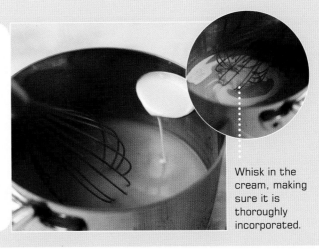

Whisk in the cream, making sure it is thoroughly incorporated.

whisking in cream
2 mins

The mother sauces

Espagnole

This robust sauce has a deep, mellow flavour and rich red-brown colour. Typically used as the base for demi-glace and other sauces, it can also be served as it is with any roast meat or poultry.

shopping list

The darker the stock used, the richer the flavour of the espagnole sauce will be – use brown veal stock for poultry and beef stock for meat.

50g (1¾oz) **plain flour**

2.4 litres (4 pints) rich **meat stock**

4 tbsp **vegetable oil**

1 **celery** stick, finely chopped

2 tbsp **tomato purée**

2 **onions**, peeled and finely chopped

1 **carrot**, peeled and finely chopped

25g (¾oz) chilled unsalted **butter**

2 small **tomatoes**, halved

125g (4½oz) **smoked bacon**, diced

freshly ground **black pepper**

bouquet garni

pinch of **salt**

the perfect technique

For a good espagnole, the roux must be thoroughly cooked so it browns without burning. Long simmering then darkens the sauce. Given the cooking time and complexity, it's worth making a large quantity to freeze.

1 Bring the rich meat stock to the boil in a large saucepan. Reduce the heat and simmer for about 1 hour, skimming off the scum from the surface, until it reduces to half its original volume.

2 Meanwhile, heat the oil in another pan over medium heat. Add the bacon and cook for 2 minutes or until the fat runs. Add the onion, carrot, and celery (as pictured). Lower the heat and cook gently, stirring, for 5–10 minutes or until they are softened.

4 hr 15 mins	preparing	boiling stock and making the roux		simmering
	10 mins	1 hr		3 hrs

3 Sprinkle the flour over the bacon and vegetables and stir with a wooden spoon until blended. Cook for 4–5 minutes, stirring frequently, until the roux turns a rich dark brown (take care that it doesn't burn). Add the tomato purée.

4 Remove the pan from the heat. Add about three quarters of the hot stock to the vegetables and roux, a ladleful at a time, stirring to blend well. Return the pan to the heat and bring to the boil, stirring constantly until the sauce thickens.

5 Add the tomatoes and bouquet garni to the sauce and stir in. Reduce the heat and leave to simmer for 2–3 hours, stirring occasionally and skimming off scum from the surface. Reheat the remaining stock and add it to the espagnole. You should end up with a glossy sauce that coats the back of a wooden spoon lightly.

A bouquet garni is a bunch of fresh thyme, parsley stalks, and bay leaves used to flavour stews and sauces. Secure with string or a tie in a piece of muslin.

6 Strain the sauce through a fine sieve (but do not press down on the solids in the sieve). Reheat the sauce for serving, then season to taste and stir in the butter.

straining
5 mins

5 KEY STAPLES

Master these staples
and enhance your
everyday cooking.
You may have cooked
these before, but have
you cooked them to
perfection? When you
have, you'll know the
difference, and the
possibilities are endless.

RICE

Prevalent in many cuisines, the best way to cook fluffy, delicate rice is heavily debated – try these two methods and decide which one works for you.

PASTA

Dried pasta is a great storecupboard staple, but making fresh pasta is far easier than many people think. Follow simplified steps to making tagliatelle.

SALAD

Fresh ingredients are key to a simple green salad, but so is a methodical approach. Find out how to prepare a perfect salad and a simple dressing.

PIE

Master the art of pastry preparation with a method for a simple double-crusted shortcrust apple pie – a technique that could be easily adapted for savoury pies.

BREAD

Bread is a trusted staple almost anywhere in the world. Discover how to create a crusty, meltingly light white loaf that will inspire you to bake, not buy.

The key staples

Rice

Well-cooked rice is integral to many recipes. As a side dish it can temper spice and balance flavours.

Principles for rice

Long-grain Two methods are used – see over the page.

Basmati Best soaked for 30 minutes before cooking; follow the absorption method.

Risotto Add stock gradually while stirring for 20–25 minutes.

Sticky Best soaked for at least 4 hours before cooking; steam for 15–20 minutes.

Pudding Best simmered with milk in oven for 1–1¼ hours.

Rice recipes to try are **Kedgeree** (p126); **Beef Stroganoff** (p190); **Risotto primavera** (p236); **Paella** (p238); **Massaman curry** (p240); and **Rice pudding** (p276).

knowing your rice

The five most common types of rice have short, medium, or long grains. These determine the most suitable cooking methods.

Basmati long-grain is nutty and aromatic. Ideal with curries.

Short-grained **sticky** rice can be easily moulded. Serve with southeast Asian dishes.

Long-grain rice becomes tender and fluffy but keeps its shape.

Rounded short-grain **risotto** rice absorbs liquid without turning too soft.

Short grains of **pudding** rice contain more starch. Served for desserts.

the perfect technique

Allow about 85–100g (3–3½oz) rice per person to accompany a main course. There are two popular methods for cooking long-grain white rice – both result in perfectly fluffy, tender grains. Try both and see which works for you.

Never stir any long-grain rice while it is cooking because this could rupture the cells in the grain, making it sticky.

15 mins

boiling

15 minutes

absorption method

the absorption method

1 Measure the volume of rice you are going to cook. Place the rice in a saucepan and cover with twice the volume of cold water.

2 Add salt. Bring to the boil, then lower the heat, cover the pan, and cook until all the water has been absorbed, which will take about 10 minutes. Avoid lifting the lid.

3 When the rice is cooked there will be tiny dimples on the surface. If any water remains after this time, take the lid off and let the rice dry briefly. Fluff up the grains of rice with a fork before serving.

the excess water method

1 Bring a saucepan of salted water to the boil. The quantity of water should be five to six times the volume of rice you are cooking.

2 When the water boils, add the rice. Bring back to the boil and simmer with the lid off for 12–15 minutes or until the rice is tender.

3 As soon as the rice is cooked, remove the pan from the heat. Drain the rice in a sieve and rinse with boiling water, then serve.

15 mins

boiling

15 minutes

excess water method

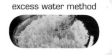

Pasta

Versatile pasta forms the basis of many favourite dishes. Dried pasta is a store-cupboard staple, but it is worth making fresh pasta for its flavour.

Principles for pasta

Use a lot of **water** – up to 10 times the weight of the pasta. Bring to the boil, then add 1 tsp **salt** per litre (1¾ pints) followed by the pasta. Fresh pasta cooks very quickly; test as soon as the water comes back to the boil: it should be **tender**. Dried pasta will need up to 12 minutes. During cooking, **stir** occasionally to prevent the pasta from sticking together. To **test**, lift out a piece and bite it: it should be a little firm (**al dente**).

Pasta recipes to try are **Macaroni cheese** (p212); **Spaghetti bolognese** (p226); **Crab ravioli** (p228); **Cannelloni** (p230); **Pasta with rocket pesto** (p232); and **Lasagne** (p234).

knowing your pasta shapes

The shapes shown below cover the major pasta types. Traditionally in Italy, pasta shapes are matched to particular sauces and dishes.

Pasta groups

Spirals work well in salads and creamy sauces.

From small macaroni to larger rigatoni, bake sturdy **tubes**. Alternatively, you could serve with a heavy meat ragù or arrabiata sauce.

Small farfalline **bows** are popular in soups and delicate sauces. Larger bows suit simple tomato sauces. Try to cut vegetables in sauces to suit the size of the bows.

Quick and versatile, thin **ribbon** pasta is best with oil- or tomato-based sauces. Thicker ribbons suit more robust chunky sauces. Both thicknesses suit seafood dishes.

Filled pasta requires simple seasoning or melted butter to allow the filling flavours to shine.

Perfect for layering, lasagne **sheets** can have curled edges for a decorative finish.

Fun, dense **other shapes** – from ear-shaped to shell-shaped – suit rich meat sauces.

Spiral fusilli

Tube penne

Ribbon tagliatelle

Ribbon spaghetti

Filled ravioli

Filled tortellini

Sheets lasagne

Shaped conchiglie

the perfect technique

Pasta may be served as a first course (as in Italy) or as a main dish. Use this fresh pasta immediately, or wrap it in greaseproof paper and cling film and keep in the refrigerator for a couple of days. Freeze for up to a month.

1 Sift 400g (14oz) strong plain flour onto the work surface. Make a well in the centre. Put 4 large eggs and 1 tbsp olive oil into the well.

2 Using the fingers of one hand, gradually draw in the flour to make a stiff dough.

3 Knead the dough for 5–8 minutes or until it feels very smooth and elastic.

When the dough is elastic, wrap in cling film and leave in a cool place for 1 hour.

1 hr 32 mins	kneading 10 mins	resting 1 hr

Flatten the dough with the palm of your hand.

4 Unwrap the dough and pull off a small piece, about the size of an egg. Roll into a ball, then flatten it. Turn the flattened dough on the floured work surface to coat both sides with flour.

5 Roll the dough through a pasta machine to make a paper-thin sheet: start on the thickest setting, folding, turning 90 degrees, and repeating the process (to stretch the gluten), then rolling it on progressively thinner settings. Repeat with the rest of the dough, a piece at a time.

6 To make tagliatelle or spaghetti, fit the appropriate cutting rollers onto the machine and feed a sheet of dough through. It helps to support the strands over your hand as they come out of the machine.

Bear in mind that the pasta will continue to cook between colander and plate, particularly if it's combined with a hot sauce, so drain it when it is just tender to the bite (or the firmer al dente if cooking dried pasta).

7 Set a large pan of water over high heat and bring to the boil. When the water is boiling vigorously, add salt and lower the pasta into the pan. Stir gently to make sure the strands are not sticking together, then cook for 1–2 minutes. As soon as the pasta is tender, remove from the heat.

8 Drain in a large colander, retaining a little of the cooking water in the pan, then tip the pasta back into the pan. This water will prevent the pasta from drying out before the sauce is added, and will thin the sauce so it coats the pasta.

shaping and cutting
20 mins

cooking
2 mins

Green salad

Delicious and cooling, a fresh green salad makes a great side dish for almost anything.

Principles of salads

The leaves are the heart of the salad, so don't overwhelm them with other ingredients. **Wet salad** leaves will be less crisp and will dilute the dressing, so take time to dry them thoroughly. For a subtle **garlic** flavour, rub the bowl with a halved clove before putting in the salad. If adding **tomatoes** or other juicy fruits or vegetables, do this just before tossing the salad.

Other kinds of salad and dressing recipes to try are **Caesar salad** (p246); **Tomato and mozzarella salad** (p248); **Salade niçoise** (p250); **Coleslaw** (p252); and **Tabbouleh** (p254).

shopping list

There's a wide range of salad greens now available, varying in colour, texture, leaf shape, and flavour, so a green salad need never be dull.

Crisp **lettuce** such as **Cos** or **romaine**

200ml (7fl oz) mild **olive oil**

Firm, crisp **cucumber**

Attractive, red-tinged **lettuce** such as **oak leaf**

Spring onions

5 tbsp **white wine vinegar**

Tangy, delicate **lamb's lettuce**

Salt and freshly ground **black pepper**

the perfect technique

A successful green salad relies on a good balance of the freshest ingredients. Vary the vinaigrette by adding finely chopped herbs such as chives or tarragon, or for more of a punch try 4 puréed anchovies and 1 tsp capers.

Shake well to mix and emulsify the ingredients.

1 To make the vinaigrette, place the white wine vinegar in a small jar with the olive oil and some salt and pepper. (This makes more than you need for one salad, but it keeps well.)

2 The vinaigrette can be kept in the tightly covered jar in the refrigerator for up to 3 months. Shake well before use.

22 mins	mixing vinaigrette	washing	chopping
	5 mins	5 mins	10 mins

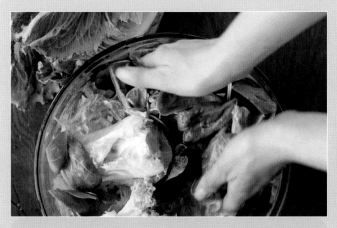

3 Separate the salad leaves and break up large ones into smaller pieces. Immerse in a bowl or sink of cold water and swish them around with your fingers to rinse well.

4 Dry the salad leaves in a salad spinner. If you don't have a spinner, pat the leaves dry gently but thoroughly with kitchen paper or a clean tea towel.

Holding the sticks together, cut across for chunky dice.

5 Cut the cucumber in half lengthways and remove the seeds with the tip of a teaspoon. Cut the cucumber into shorter lengths, then cut these lengthways into sticks.

6 Trim off the ends of the spring onions and remove any old or discoloured outer leaves. Slice the spring onions on the diagonal into small pieces.

7 Place the salad leaves in a large salad bowl with the cucumber and spring onions. Drizzle over about 4 tbsp of the vinaigrette and toss until the leaves are coated.

Always toss a green salad with its dressing just before serving so there is no time for the dressing to wilt the leaves.

tossing

2 mins

Pie

A fine pie – light, crisp pastry encasing a sweet or savoury filling – is every cook's goal. Quick mixing and chilling the pastry dough are vital.

Principles of pies

Using a **food processor** to make shortcrust pastry keeps contact with warm hands to a minimum. Roll out pastry on a cold surface – marble is ideal. Take care not to stretch the pastry when **lining the tin**; it will shrink back during baking. For a double-crust pie, press the edges together well to seal. A steam hole in the lid will keep the pastry crisp. Be sure the **oven** has reached the right temperature before putting in the pie to bake.

Pie recipes to try are **Chicken pot pie** (p156); **Steak and mushroom pie** (p192); **Pork pies** (p210); **Feta filo pie** (p216); and **Lemon meringue pie** (p308).

shopping list for an apple pie

You could replace half the butter with lard, but all-butter shortcrust is favoured by modern bakers for its crumbly and delicate texture.

75g (2½oz) **caster sugar**, plus extra for sprinkling

400g (14oz) **plain flour**

1kg (2¼lb) cooking **apples** such as braeburn or golden delicious

½ tsp **baking powder**

1 tbsp **cornflour**

200g (7oz) chilled **unsalted butter**, cut into small pieces

½ tsp **salt**

the perfect technique

Serve this apple pie hot with chilled double cream, ice cream, or custard. You could use the same rich shortcrust pastry to make other delicious fruit pies such as pear and walnut, or rhubarb and ginger. Beef and ale pie, chicken and leek pie, and game and red wine pie are some savoury ideas for fillings.

1 Sift the flour, baking powder, and salt into a mixing bowl. Rub the butter into the flour with the tips of your fingers until the mixture resembles coarse breadcrumbs. Work deftly and gently to avoid warming the mixture.

2 Slowly add about 4 tbsp cold water, stirring with a round-bladed knife to bring the dough together. Once the water has been added, knead the dough briefly into a ball. Preheat the oven to 220°C (425°F/Gas 7).

Flatten the ball gently, then wrap it in cling film and chill for 30 minutes while you prepare the fruit.

1 hr 45 mins	preparing the pastry 15 mins	chilling the pastry, preparing the fruit 30 mins	rolling out the pastry 15 mins

Peel, quarter, core, and slice the apples.

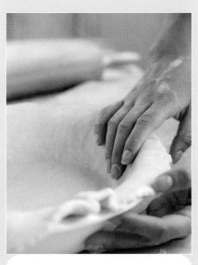

Invert the pie dish on the pastry and cut around it.

3 Place the apples in a bowl. Mix the cornflour with the sugar, sprinkle over the apples, and toss to coat the apple slices evenly.

4 Roll out half of the pastry on a lightly floured surface and use to line a 24cm (9½in) rimmed pie dish. Trim off the excess pastry.

5 Roll out the remaining pastry to a round or oval about 5mm (¼in) thick and larger than the pie dish. Cut a strip about 2.5cm (1in) wide from around the edge, then cut out the pastry lid.

6 Dampen the rim of the dish, then fit the strip of pastry on the rim, pressing firmly. Spoon in the apple filling. Dampen the pastry strip, then lay the pastry lid over the filling and press to seal to the dampened pastry strip.

7 Trim off the excess pastry to give the edge a neat finish.

Re-roll the pastry trimmings and cut out pastry leaves or other decorative shapes. Attach these to the pastry lid with a little water.

8 Crimp the pastry edge. Decorate the top with pastry leaves (see tip). Make a small hole in the centre of the lid.

9 Brush with water and sprinkle with caster sugar. Set on a baking sheet and bake for 10 minutes, then reduce the oven to 190°C (375°F/Gas 5) and bake for a further 30 minutes or until golden brown.

decorating the pie
5 mins

baking
40 mins

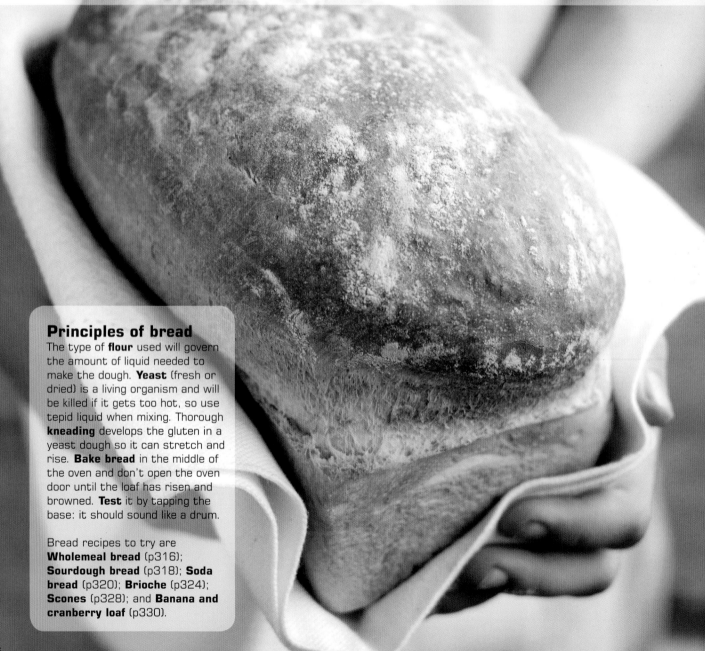

 The key staples

Bread

Whether it is risen with yeast or other raising agents, or unleavened and flat, bread is truly the staff of life almost everywhere in the world.

Principles of bread

The type of **flour** used will govern the amount of liquid needed to make the dough. **Yeast** (fresh or dried) is a living organism and will be killed if it gets too hot, so use tepid liquid when mixing. Thorough **kneading** develops the gluten in a yeast dough so it can stretch and rise. **Bake bread** in the middle of the oven and don't open the oven door until the loaf has risen and browned. **Test** it by tapping the base: it should sound like a drum.

Bread recipes to try are **Wholemeal bread** (p316); **Sourdough bread** (p318); **Soda bread** (p320); **Brioche** (p324); **Scones** (p328); and **Banana and cranberry loaf** (p330).

knowing your flour

These are flours used for baking bread. Wheat flour is much used for bread, owing to its protein content, which gives a dough its elasticity.

Spelt is a high-protein flour ground from a type of wheat. Bread is nutty, sweet, and nutritious.

Rye contains less protein, so wheat flour is often added to a rye dough to make the loaf less dense.

Brown flour with malted wheat grains has good flavour and texture.

Wholemeal is ground from the entire wheat kernel. This inhibits rising so wholemeal is often mixed with white flour.

Strong white flour for making bread has a higher protein content than flours used for cakes, biscuits, and pastry.

the perfect technique

A simple white loaf with a golden crust is hard to beat, but you can knead flavourings into the dough before its second rise – some finely chopped fresh rosemary with 1 tbsp of olive oil will make a wonderfully fragrant bread, or try adding a handful of raisins and toasted hazelnuts for a fruitier loaf.

1 Put 750g (1lb 10oz) strong white flour, 15g (½oz) dried yeast, and 2 tsp salt in a large glass bowl. Make a well in the centre of the dry ingredients and pour in 450ml (15fl oz) tepid water. Gradually draw the flour into the liquid, mixing with a wooden spoon until all the flour is incorporated.

Continue mixing with the spoon or your hands until the dough comes away from the sides of the bowl. If it is very sticky, add a bit more flour.

2 Lightly flour a work surface. Turn the soft dough out of the bowl onto the surface. Now start kneading gently: fold the dough over onto itself (as pictured), then push or pull it out to stretch it. Continue this kneading action for about 10 minutes or until the dough is smooth and feels firm and elastic.

5 hr 2 mins

kneading	rising		kneading
20 mins	2 hrs		2 mins

3 Lightly grease the large bowl. Shape the dough into a ball and place it in the bowl. Cover with oiled cling film and leave the dough to rise at room temperature for 1–2 hours or until it has doubled (see far right).

4 Remove the cling film from the bowl and knock back the dough (by punching it once or twice) to deflate it. Turn it out onto the lightly floured surface and knead for a couple of minutes. Shape into an oval.

5 Place in a greased 1kg (2¼ lb) loaf tin, seam-side down. Cover the tin with greased cling film, or a damp clean tea towel, and leave to rise again in a warm place for 1½–2 hours or until the dough reaches the top of the tin.

6 Preheat the oven to 230°C (450°F/Gas 8). Remove the cloth or cling film from the loaf, sprinkle with a little flour, and bake for 30–40 minutes or until well risen with a golden firm crust. Turn out onto a wire rack to cool.

A lower temperature will mean a slower rise, so if you'd rather make the dough the night before baking, leave it covered in the refrigerator after its first knead. It will have doubled in size by the morning, ready to shape.

rising

2 hrs

baking

40 mins

THE RECIPES

You're now ready to develop your expertise
with these carefully selected recipes,
designed to build on your cooking skills.
Perfect everything from Bouillabaisse
to pavlova, trusting in the fail-safe tips
and clear and concise techniques to
help you along the way.

STARTERS

This selection of starters and light bites cannot fail to impress. Every modern classic will give you the opportunity to improve your cooking skills – from preparing shellfish expertly to perfecting the texture of a pâté.

Leek and Potato Soup

This method asks you to remove the potatoes after simmering and mash them with butter. Stirred back in, they add a thick, creamy texture.

Serves 4

Ingredients
1kg (2¼lb) potatoes
500g (1lb 2oz) leeks
1 large onion, chopped
1.5 litres (2¾ pints) vegetable
    stock, or water mixed
    with 2 tsp yeast extract
salt and freshly ground
    black pepper
50g (1¾oz) butter

1 Peel the potatoes, but leave them whole. Wash the leeks thoroughly and cut into shreds. Put the potatoes, shredded leeks, onion, and stock (or water with yeast extract) in a large pan. Season lightly. Bring to the boil, then reduce the heat, cover, and simmer for 30 minutes, or until the potatoes are tender.

2 Using a slotted spoon, lift the potatoes out of the pan and mash with the butter. Return the mashed potatoes to the pan and stir thoroughly, then simmer for a further 25–30 minutes, stirring occasionally. Ladle into warmed bowls and add a good grinding of pepper to each.

⚠ Rescue it!
The suggested simmering time creates a deliciously creamy consistency. If you've simmered too long (or if you prefer it a little thinner), simply add a little extra stock or water to thin it down as it simmers.

1 hr 20 mins

preparation	cooking
20 mins	1 hr

Carrot and Orange Soup

A light, refreshing soup with a hint of spice. For the smoothest result, be sure all the vegetables are completely tender before puréeing.

Serves 4

Ingredients

2 tsp olive oil or sunflower oil
1 leek, washed and sliced
500g (1lb 2oz) carrots, sliced
1 potato, approx. 115g (4oz), chopped
½ tsp ground coriander
pinch of ground cumin
300ml (10fl oz) orange juice
500ml (16fl oz) vegetable or chicken stock
1 bay leaf
salt and freshly ground black pepper
2 tbsp chopped coriander, to garnish

1 Heat the oil in a large saucepan, add the leek and carrots, and cook over low heat, stirring frequently, for 5 minutes or until the leek has softened. Add the chopped potato, ground coriander, and cumin, then pour in the orange juice and stock. Stir well. Add the bay leaf.

2 Increase the heat and bring the soup to the boil, then cover and simmer for about 40 minutes or until all the vegetables are very tender.

3 Allow the soup to cool slightly, then transfer to a blender or food processor and process until smooth, working in batches if necessary.

4 Return to the saucepan. Add a little extra stock or some water if the soup is too thick, and season with salt and pepper to taste. Bring back to a simmer, then ladle into warmed serving bowls and sprinkle with chopped coriander.

Vegetable stock
Coarsely chop 3 each large carrots, onions, and celery sticks plus 2 leeks. Put them in a large pan with 1.7 litres (3 pints) water and bring to the boil, skimming off the foam. Add 10 crushed black peppercorns, a bunch of flat-leaf parsley, 2 bay leaves, and ½ tsp salt. Simmer, partially covered, for 45 minutes. Strain. Keep refrigerated.

50 mins

preparation
10 mins

cooking
40 mins

French Onion Soup

A bit of brandy stirred into the soup just before serving gives an extra dimension of taste. Serve piping hot to enjoy it at its best.

Serves 4

Ingredients

30g (1oz) butter
1 tbsp sunflower oil
675g (1½lb) onions,
   thinly sliced
1 tsp sugar
salt and freshly ground
   black pepper
120ml (4fl oz) red wine
2 tbsp plain flour
1.5 litres (2¾pints) hot
   beef stock
4 tbsp brandy
8 croûtes (see the
   technique below)
1 garlic clove, halved
115g (4oz) Gruyère or
   Emmental cheese, grated

1 Melt the butter with the oil in a large, heavy-based pan over low heat. Add the onions and sugar, and season with salt and pepper. Turn to mix well, then press a piece of damp greaseproof paper on top of the onions. Cook, uncovered, stirring occasionally, for about 40 minutes or until they are a rich, dark brown colour. Take care not to let them stick and burn.

2 Remove the greaseproof paper and stir in the wine. Increase the heat to medium and stir for 5 minutes while the onions glaze. Sprinkle in the flour and stir for 2 minutes, then pour in the stock and bring to the boil. Reduce the heat to low, cover with a lid, and leave to simmer for 30 minutes. Taste and season with more salt and pepper, if necessary.

3 Preheat the grill to high. Ladle the soup into 4 flameproof bowls and stir 1 tbsp of brandy into each. Rub the croûtes with the cut sides of the garlic and place one in each bowl. Sprinkle with the cheese. Grill for 2–3 minutes or until the cheese is bubbling and golden. Serve at once.

Making croûtes
Large croûtons are known as croûtes. To make them, cut a day-old baguette into 1cm (½in) thick slices and toast until golden. Alternatively, place them on a baking sheet and bake in an oven preheated to 180°C (350°F/Gas 4) for 15 minutes.

1 hr 35 mins

preparation	cooking	garnish
10 mins	1 hr 20 mins	5 mins

New England Clam Chowder

The clams for this creamy American soup must be alive when you buy them, with intact shells, and cooked on the day of purchase.

Serves 4

Ingredients

36 live clams, well scrubbed
1 tbsp vegetable oil
115g (4oz) thick-cut, rindless
    streaky bacon rashers, diced
2 floury potatoes, such as King
    Edward, peeled and cut into
    1cm (½in) cubes
1 onion, finely chopped
2 tbsp plain flour
600ml (1 pint) whole milk
salt and freshly ground
    black pepper
120ml (4fl oz) cream
2 tbsp finely chopped
    flat-leaf parsley

1 Discard any open clams, then shuck the rest (see the technique below), reserving the juices. Add enough water to the juices to make 600ml (1 pint). Chop the clams. Heat the oil in a large, heavy-based saucepan and fry the bacon rashers over medium heat for 5 minutes or until crisp. Remove with a slotted spoon and drain on kitchen paper.

2 Add the potatoes and onion to the pan and fry for about 5 minutes or until the onion has softened. Add the flour and stir for 2 minutes. Stir in the clam juice and milk and season with salt and pepper to taste. Cover with a lid, lower the heat, and simmer for about 20 minutes or until the potatoes are tender. Add the clams and simmer gently, uncovered, for a further 5 minutes. Serve hot.

3 Stir in the cream and reheat without boiling. Serve sprinkled with the bacon and parsley.

Shucking clams

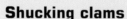

1 Hold the clam in a thick towel and insert the tip of a round-ended knife into the opening, then twist the knife upwards to open the clam.

2 Slide the knife inside, keeping it close to the underside of the top shell. Sever the muscle to free the clam; repeat with the bottom shell.

50 mins

preparation
15 mins

cooking
35 mins

Chicken Consommé

It's surprisingly easy to make a clear consommé using an egg white "raft" to filter out impurities. Be sure to start with a good chicken stock.

Serves 4

Ingredients

2 large egg whites
1 tbsp passata, or
   1 tsp tomato purée
1 chicken leg, skinned and
   boned, then minced
   or finely chopped
1 onion, chopped
1 carrot, chopped
1 leek, chopped
1 garlic clove, chopped
1 tbsp chopped parsley
2 litres (3½ pints) cold
   chicken stock
salt and freshly ground
   black pepper
chervil, to garnish

1 To make the clarification mixture, see the technique below. Combine the stock with the clarification mixture in a deep, narrow saucepan. Heat slowly, uncovered, until the stock comes to the boil. Gently stir from time to time to distribute the egg white mixture and prevent it from sticking.

2 Once the stock reaches boiling point, turn the heat down and leave to simmer gently for at least 1 hour, without stirring. During simmering, a white crust will form on top of the stock. When the crust is hard, poke a gap through it to check on the clarity of the liquid beneath.

3 When the liquid is clear, widen the gap in the crust and ladle the consommé into a muslin-lined sieve set over a clean container. Season the strained consommé with salt and pepper to taste. If necessary, reheat the consommé, then garnish with chervil and serve.

Clarifying with egg whites

1 Whisk the egg whites just enough to loosen them and form a few bubbles. Next, add the passata or tomato purée and mix well.

2 Place the chicken, vegetables, garlic, and parsley in a bowl, add the egg white mixture, and mix thoroughly together. Chill well.

THE RECIPES STARTERS SOUPS

1 hr 35 mins

preparation
15 mins   plus chilling

cooking
1 hr 20 mins

100

Gazpacho

The traditional inclusion of soaked stale bread adds body
and a creamy texture to this chilled tomato soup.

Serves 4

Ingredients

2cm (¾ in) thick slice of stale
    bread, crusts removed
1kg (2¼lb) tomatoes, skinned,
    deseeded, and chopped
1 small cucumber, chopped,
    plus extra to serve
1 small red pepper, deseeded
    and chopped, plus extra
    to serve
2 garlic cloves, crushed
4 tbsp sherry vinegar
120ml (4fl oz) extra virgin
    olive oil, plus extra to serve
salt and freshly ground
    black pepper
1 hard-boiled egg, yolk and
    white chopped separately

1 Soak the bread in cold water for 2 minutes. Drain off excess water, then put the bread in a food processor or blender with the tomato flesh, cucumber, red pepper, garlic, and sherry vinegar. Process until smooth. Pour in the olive oil and process again. Dilute with a little water if too thick. Season with salt and pepper to taste.

2 Transfer the soup to a bowl or other container, cover with cling film, and chill for at least 1 hour.

3 When ready to serve, finely chop the extra cucumber and red pepper. Place the cucumber, red pepper, and egg yolk and white in individual bowls, and arrange on the table, along with a bottle of olive oil. Ladle the soup into bowls and serve, letting each diner add their own garnishes.

1 hr 15 mins

preparation	chilling		chopping
10 mins	1 hr		5 mins

Lobster Bisque

Simmering the crushed lobster shells with vegetables, herbs, and wine gives rich colour and flavour to this creamy soup.

Serves 4

Ingredients

1 lobster, approx. 1kg (2¼ lb), cooked
50g (1¾oz) butter
1 onion, finely chopped
1 carrot, finely chopped
2 celery sticks, finely chopped
1 leek, washed and finely chopped
½ fennel bulb, finely chopped
1 bay leaf
1 sprig of tarragon
2 garlic cloves, crushed
75g (2½oz) tomato purée
4 tomatoes, roughly chopped
120ml (4fl oz) Cognac or brandy
100ml (3½fl oz) dry white wine or vermouth
1.7 litres (3 pints) fish stock
120ml (4fl oz) cream
salt and freshly ground black pepper
pinch of cayenne
juice of ½ lemon
chives, to garnish

1 Split the lobster body in half and remove the meat. Twist off the claws and legs, break at the joints, and remove the meat. Cut all the lobster meat into small pieces and set aside in the refrigerator. Crack all the shells with the back of a knife, then chop the shells into rough pieces.

2 Melt the butter in a large pan over medium heat. Add the vegetables with the herbs and garlic and cook, stirring occasionally, for 10 minutes or until softened. Add the lobster shells, tomato purée, tomatoes, Cognac, white wine, and fish stock and stir well. Bring to the boil, then simmer for 1 hour.

3 Leave to cool slightly, then ladle (in batches) into a blender or food processor. Process in short bursts to crush the shells into very small pieces. Strain through a coarse sieve, pushing through as much liquid as you can, then pass through a fine sieve into a clean pan.

4 Bring to the boil. Add the reserved lobster meat and the cream, then season to taste, adding the cayenne and lemon. Serve in warmed bowls, garnished with chives.

Making fish stock

1 Put raw bones of white fish in a pan of cold water with sliced onion, carrot, leek, celery, and bay leaves. Bring to the boil, skimming off scum.

2 Add parsley stalks, thyme sprigs, and black peppercorns, then simmer for 25–30 minutes; do not boil. Cool for a few minutes before straining.

1 hr 55 mins

preparation	
45 mins	plus chilling

cooking
1 hr 10 mins

Hummus

You can make this dip very quickly with canned chickpeas or those packed in water in jars, or more traditionally using cooked dried chickpeas.

Serves 4

Ingredients

400g can or jar chickpeas
3 tbsp tahini
juice of 3 lemons
3 garlic cloves, chopped
salt
warm pitta bread, to serve

To garnish

olive oil
paprika or cayenne pepper
chopped flat-leaf parsley

1 Drain the chickpeas, reserving 4–6 tbsp of the liquid from the can or jar, and rinse them well. Set aside 2–3 tbsp chickpeas for the garnish. Put the remaining chickpeas in a blender or food processor with 3 tbsp of the reserved liquid.

2 Add the tahini, lemon juice, and garlic. Blitz until smooth and creamy, stopping the machine and scraping down the sides of the processor bowl once or twice; add a little more of the liquid from the can if the hummus is too thick. Season with salt to taste.

3 Transfer the hummus to a small serving bowl, swirling it attractively. (It can be kept, covered, in the refrigerator for up to 24 hours before serving.) Drizzle a little olive oil over the top and garnish with the reserved whole chickpeas, paprika, and parsley. Serve at room temperature with warm pitta bread.

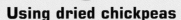

Using dried chickpeas

Cover 115g (4oz) dried chickpeas generously with cold water, then leave to soak overnight. Drain, discarding the soaking water, then tip into a pan and add four times their volume of fresh cold water. Bring to the boil and cook for 10 minutes. Skim off any scum, then reduce the heat, partly cover, and simmer for 2–3 hours or until the chickpeas are tender. Drain, reserving 4–6 tbsp of the cooking liquid, then continue making the hummus as shown in the method above.

10 mins

preparation

10 mins

Smoked Mackerel Pâté

Lemon juice and yoghurt add a subtle, balancing sharpness
to rich, oily mackerel in this simple pâté.

Serves 4

Ingredients

3–4 smoked mackerel fillets,
    approx. 300g (10oz) in total,
    skinned
300g (10oz) cream cheese
juice of 1–2 lemons
1–2 tbsp Greek-style yoghurt
freshly ground black pepper

To serve

thinly sliced brown or granary
    bread, toasted
1 lemon, cut into wedges

1 Using your hands, break up the mackerel into chunks and
place in a blender or food processor. Run the machine
until the fish is in small pieces.

2 Spoon in the cream cheese and blend again until a smooth
paste forms. Gradually add the lemon juice, blending
between each addition. Taste as you go, adding more lemon
juice as required.

3 Add the yoghurt and plenty of black pepper and blend
until the pâté is completely smooth. Spoon into a serving
dish or four individual ramekins. Serve with thinly sliced brown
or granary toast, plus lemon wedges for squeezing over, and
a peppermill for grinding.

Juicing a lemon

Lemons at room temperature will yield more juice
than lemons taken straight from the refrigerator.
You'll also get more juice from a lemon if you roll it
on the work surface, gently pressing it down with
your palm, before you cut it in half for juicing.

5 mins

preparation
5 mins

Chicken Liver Pâté

A pâté made with chicken livers is rich and smooth in texture.
Sautéed diced apples add contrast in texture and flavour.

Serves 6

Ingredients

200g (7oz) butter
2 dessert apples, peeled,
  cored, and diced
500g (1lb 2oz) chicken livers,
  trimmed
salt and freshly ground
  black pepper
4 shallots, finely diced
2 garlic cloves, finely chopped
4 tbsp Calvados or Cognac
wholemeal toast

To garnish

50g (1¾oz) butter
1 dessert apple, cored
  and cut into 6 rings
2 tbsp caster sugar
6 sprigs of mint (optional)

1 Melt 2 tbsp of the butter in a frying pan. Add the apples and sauté, stirring frequently, for 5–7 minutes or until tender. Transfer the apples to a bowl and set aside.

2 Melt another 2 tbsp butter in the frying pan. Add the chicken livers and season with salt and pepper. Fry, stirring, for 2–3 minutes or until browned. Add the shallots and garlic and cook, stirring, for a further 2 minutes.

3 Pour the Calvados or Cognac into the pan and bring to the boil. Stand back and hold a lighted match to the side of the mixture to set the alcohol alight. Baste the chicken livers for 20–30 seconds or until the flames subside. Leave to cool.

4 Tip the liver mixture into a food processor and process until smooth. Using a hand-held electric mixer, cream the remaining butter in a bowl until soft. Add the liver mixture and the sautéed apples to the butter. Mix well with a spoon or spatula. Season to taste. Spoon into six ramekins and smooth the tops. Cover and chill for 2–3 hours or until firm.

5 For the garnish, melt the butter in a frying pan, add the apple, and sprinkle with half the sugar. Turn and sprinkle with the remaining sugar. Fry for 2–3 minutes on each side or until caramelized. Set an apple ring and a mint sprig, if using, on top of each ramekin and serve with toast.

Preparing the livers
Using a small knife, trim off any green patches as well as the membrane and the strings or fibres around the centre of each liver. This will ensure that they will purée smoothly.

3 hrs
55 mins

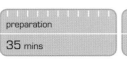
preparation	cooking	chilling	frying
35 mins	15 mins	3 hrs	5 mins

Pâté de Campagne

Sealing the terrine mould with a flour paste and then cooking in a bain-marie ensures that this pâté retains all its flavourful juices.

Serves 8–10

Ingredients

1 thick slice cooked ham, approx. 125g (4½oz), cut into 1cm (½in) wide strips
2 tbsp brandy
salt and freshly ground black pepper
15g (½oz) butter
1 onion, very finely chopped
2 garlic cloves, finely chopped
2–3 sprigs of thyme, leaves picked and chopped
125g (4½oz) chicken livers, trimmed and chopped
625g (1lb 6oz) minced pork
250g (9oz) minced veal
¼ tsp ground allspice
pinch of grated nutmeg
pinch of ground cloves
2 eggs, beaten
250g (9oz) streaky bacon rashers
1 bay leaf
45g (1½oz) plain flour, mixed with 2–3 tbsp water to a paste

To serve
crusty bread
gherkins

1 Combine the ham, brandy, and some seasoning in a bowl. Cover and leave to marinate for 1 hour.

2 Melt the butter in a frying pan and cook the onion for 3–5 minutes until soft and brown. Transfer to a bowl and cool. Add the garlic, thyme, chicken livers, minced pork and veal, spices, and seasoning. Mix well. Add the eggs and marinade from the ham. Beat the mixture for 1–2 minutes or until it comes away from the sides of the bowl.

3 Preheat the oven to 180°C (350°F/Gas 4). Use two-thirds of the bacon rashers to line the bottom and long sides of a 30 x 7.5 x 7.5cm (12 x 3 x 3in) terrine mould. Spoon half of the meat mixture into the terrine. Arrange the ham strips lengthways on the top and cover with the remaining meat mixture. Smooth the top. Fold over the ends of the bacon at the sides, then top with the remaining bacon and the bay leaf. Cover with the lid and seal with the flour paste.

4 Set the mould in a roasting tin and add boiling water to the tin to come halfway up the sides of the mould. Bake for 1¼–1½ hours, or until a metal skewer inserted into the terrine for 30 seconds is hot to the touch when withdrawn. Cool slightly, then press (see the technique below). Before turning out of the mould, scrape off any surface fat. Cut into thick slices and serve with crusty bread and gherkins.

Pressing a pâté
While the pâté is still warm, remove the lid, cover the pâté with foil, and set weights (about 500g/1lb 2oz) on top. Cool, then chill for a day so the flavours mellow.

26 hrs 50 mins

preparation	marinating	preparation	cooking	chilling
5 mins	1 hr	15 mins	1 hr 30 mins	24 hrs

Guacamole

Avocados will brown once cut, and mashing speeds this up. If you need to keep this dip before serving, press cling film directly onto the surface.

Serves 6

Ingredients

3 large, ripe avocados
juice of ½ lime
½ small onion, finely chopped
1 ripe tomato, deseeded
    and chopped
1 red chilli, deseeded and
    finely chopped
10 sprigs of coriander, chopped,
    plus extra to garnish
salt
tortilla chips, to serve

1 Prepare the avocados by removing and discarding the stones and skin (see the technique below). Place the avocado flesh in a mixing bowl and mash with a fork to create a chunky mixture.

2 Add the lime juice, followed by the onion, tomato, and chilli. Mix well, keeping the mixture chunky, then stir in the chopped coriander and season with salt to taste.

3 Pile the guacamole into a serving bowl and garnish with coriander. Serve immediately with tortilla chips.

Stoning and peeling an avocado

1 Slice the avocado lengthways in two, cutting all the way round the central stone, then separate the two halves by twisting gently.

2 Strike the stone with the blade of a large knife to embed it, then lift the knife to remove the stone.

3 Cut each avocado half in half again. Use a paring knife to lift off the skin gently.

20 mins

preparation

20 mins

Gravadlax

Salmon cured this way has a firm texture: a blanket of salt and sugar, with lemon and dill, draws out moisture and weights compress the fillets.

**Makes 2 fillets
of cured salmon**

Ingredients

85g (3oz) caster sugar
30g (1oz) dill, chopped
1 tbsp lemon juice
75g (2½oz) fine sea salt
1 tsp freshly ground
  black pepper
2 thick fillets of salmon,
  approx. 500g (1lb 2oz) each,
  scaled and pin-boned (see the
  pin-boning technique on p123)

1 To make the curing mixture, combine the caster sugar, chopped dill, lemon juice, sea salt, and pepper in a small bowl. Mix together well.

2 Use the mixture to cure the salmon fillets (see the technique below).

3 Remove the cured salmon from the refrigerator, unwrap, and pat dry with kitchen paper. To serve, use a long, sharp knife to slice the salmon very thinly, slicing at an angle and starting from the tail end; discard the skin. The cured salmon can be kept in the refrigerator for 3–4 days or frozen for up to 2 months.

Curing in salt

1 Lay one fillet, skin-side down, in a non-metallic shallow dish or tray. Spread the curing mixture evenly over the whole fillet.

2 Place the other fillet on top. Wrap tightly in cling film and weigh them down with a plate and cans of food. Place in the refrigerator.

3 Cure the salmon for 48 hours, turning the paired fillets every 12 hours and draining off the fluid so the fish firms up evenly.

48 hrs
10 mins

preparation	chilling
10 mins	48 hrs

Chargrilled Asparagus with Hollandaise

A rich sauce is perfect with chargrilled or grilled asparagus. Take care not to overcook – the spears should be tender, but still firm, not floppy.

Serves 4

Ingredients
500g (1lb 2oz) asparagus spears
1 tbsp extra virgin olive oil
1 quantity Hollandaise sauce (see Building Blocks, p56)
freshly ground black pepper

1 Prepare the asparagus (see the technique below). Heat a ridged cast-iron grill pan and brush with the oil. When very hot, add the asparagus and chargrill for 5–6 minutes, depending on the thickness of the spears, until lightly charred and just tender. Turn the spears once during cooking.

2 Alternatively, preheat the grill to high. Arrange the asparagus spears in one layer in the grill pan and drizzle over the oil. Grill the asparagus, turning the spears over once, for 5–6 minutes or until browned and just tender.

3 Divide the asparagus among serving plates and spoon the warm sauce over them. Sprinkle with some pepper and serve immediately.

How to prepare asparagus
Use a sharp knife to cut the tough, woody ends from the spears, or snap off the ends. Then, use a vegetable peeler to shave off a thin layer of skin from the stalks, starting just below the tips.

22 mins

preparation
10 mins

cooking
10 mins

MAINS

Main course dishes are often the focal point of a homecooked meal. Some of these classic recipes are more challenging than others, but clear directions and tips will help you to perfect them all.

Ceviche

A brief pickling of raw fish conserves its freshness. The acid in the pickle whitens the fish flesh and stiffens the texture, making it seem "cooked".

Serves 4

Ingredients

450g (1lb) very fresh, firm-
fleshed fish fillets, pin-boned
and skinned (see the
technique below)
1 red onion, thinly sliced
juice of 2 lemons or limes
1 tbsp olive oil
½ tsp pimentón picante
1 chilli, finely chopped
salt and freshly ground
black pepper
2 tbsp finely chopped
flat-leaf parsley
crusty bread, to serve

1 Wrap the fish in cling film or foil and put it in the freezer for 1 hour to firm up the flesh; this will make it easier to slice. With a sharp knife, slice the fish into very thin slivers.

2 Spread the onion evenly over the bottom of a shallow, non-metallic dish. Pour over the lemon or lime juice and olive oil, then sprinkle with the pimentón and chilli.

3 Place the fish on the onion and gently turn the slivers to coat with the marinade. Cover and leave to marinate in the refrigerator for at least 20 minutes, or preferably 1 hour. Season with salt and pepper to taste, sprinkle with parsley, and serve with crusty bread.

Pin-boning and skinning a fish fillet

1 Run your thumb along the fillet to make the line of tiny pinbones stand up, then pull them out with tweezers pulling towards the head.

2 Use a long, flexible knife for skinning. At the tail (the thinnest part of the fillet), make a slanting cut between the flesh and the skin.

3 Grip the cut end of the skin firmly. With the knife at a 30° angle to the taut skin, slice off the flesh neatly. Discard the skin.

2hr 20 mins

freezing	preparation	marinating
1 hr	20 mins	1 hr

Fish Pie

Once you've perfected a potato-topped fish pie, you can vary it to your taste, with different fish – fresh, smoked, or canned – and flavourings.

Serves 6

Ingredients

625g (1lb 6oz) potatoes,
    peeled and cut into chunks
salt and freshly ground
    black pepper
1 litre (1¾ pints), plus
    4 tbsp hot milk
150g (5½ oz) butter, plus
    extra for greasing
10 black peppercorns
2 bay leaves
1 small onion, quartered
750g (1lb 10oz) skinned
    haddock fillets, cut across
    into pieces
60g (2oz) plain flour
5–7 sprigs of flat-leaf parsley,
    leaves picked and chopped
125g (4½ oz) cooked,
    peeled prawns
3 eggs, hard-boiled and
    coarsely chopped

1 Cook the potatoes in boiling salted water for 15–20 minutes or until tender. Drain thoroughly, then mash with the 4 tbsp hot milk, 60g (2oz) butter, and salt and pepper to taste. Set aside.

2 Pour the remaining milk into a large saucepan and add the peppercorns, bay leaves, and onion. Bring to the boil, then remove from the heat. Cover and leave in a warm place to infuse for about 10 minutes.

3 Add the fish to the milk, cover, and simmer for 5–10 minutes or until it will flake easily when tested with a fork. Use a slotted spoon to transfer the fish to a plate; reserve the cooking liquid. Cool, then flake the fish.

4 Melt the remaining butter in a saucepan over medium heat. Whisk in the flour and cook until foaming, then strain in the fish cooking liquid, still whisking. Cook, stirring constantly, until the sauce boils and thickens. Simmer for 2 minutes. Season and stir in the parsley.

5 Preheat the oven to 180°C (350°F/Gas 4). Ladle a third of the sauce into a buttered 2 litre (3½ pint) pie dish. Spoon the flaked haddock on top in an even layer. Cover with the remaining sauce, then scatter on the prawns and chopped hard-boiled eggs. Spread the mashed potatoes on top to cover completely.

6 Bake for 20–30 minutes or until the potato topping is tinged with brown and the sauce is bubbling up around the edge. Serve hot.

Perfect mash

For best results, cut the potatoes into equal chunks so they cook evenly, and be sure they are tender before mashing with hot milk, butter, and seasoning. Then beat with a wooden spoon or hand-held electric mixer over medium heat for a few minutes until fluffy.

1 hr 15 mins

preparation
45 mins

cooking
30 mins

Kedgeree

Cold-smoked fish needs to be cooked before eating. For this kedgeree, the fish poaching liquid is used to cook the rice, which gives it a lot of flavour.

Serves 4

Ingredients

300ml (10fl oz) whole milk
400g (14oz) smoked pollock
 or haddock fillet
1 bay leaf
1 tbsp olive oil
30g (1oz) butter
1 large onion, thinly sliced
 from tip to root
2 tsp mild curry powder
175g (6oz) basmati rice, rinsed
 in cold water and drained
2 tbsp chopped coriander
4 large eggs, soft boiled
 and halved
1 tbsp finely chopped lovage,
 to garnish (optional)
4 lemon wedges
freshly ground black pepper

1 Put the milk and 300ml (10fl oz) water in a shallow pan with the fish and bay leaf. Cover and bring to a gentle simmer. By the time the liquid is simmering, the fish should be cooked through. If not, turn the fillet over in the hot liquid and leave it, off the heat, for 2–3 minutes to finish cooking.

2 Using a slotted spoon, remove the fish to a plate; discard the bay leaf and reserve the poaching liquid. Flake the fish, discarding the skin and picking out any bones.

3 Heat the olive oil with half the butter in a large saucepan. Add the onion and cook gently for 8–10 minutes or until translucent. Stir in the curry powder and then the rice. Add 300ml (10fl oz) of the poaching liquid. Bring to the boil, then cover the pan, turn the heat to low, and cook for 15 minutes. Remove from the heat and fluff up the rice with a fork.

4 Fold the flaked fish into the rice along with half the chopped coriander and the remaining butter.

5 Spoon the kedgeree into four warmed plates or wide bowls. Top each with two soft-boiled egg halves and sprinkle with the remaining coriander plus the optional lovage. Add a wedge of lemon and a grinding of pepper and serve.

Soft-boiling eggs

For this recipe, slightly set yolks are preferred, so cook them for longer than usual. Use a pan large enough to hold the eggs in a single layer. Cover them with water. Bring to the boil, then reduce the heat and simmer for 3 minutes. Peel the eggs once they are cool enough to handle.

45 mins

preparation
15 mins

cooking
30 mins

Haddock and Herb Fishcakes

This method uses dried breadcrumbs, which impart a crispier and crunchier coating to the fishcakes than fresh breadcrumbs.

Serves 6

Ingredients

300g (10oz) smoked haddock
   fillet, skinned and any
   bones removed
140g (5oz) mashed potato
½ tsp Dijon mustard
3 spring onions, finely chopped
grated zest and juice of ½ lemon
30g (1oz) chopped flat-leaf
   parsley
salt and freshly ground
   black pepper
45g (1½oz) plain flour
1 egg, beaten
85g (3oz) dried breadcrumbs
   (see the technique below)
sunflower oil, for frying

To serve

lemon wedges
mayonnaise
watercress

1 Preheat the oven to 190°C (375°F/Gas 5). Place the smoked haddock in a baking dish with 2–3 tbsp water, cover with foil, and bake for 15 minutes. Remove from the oven and leave to cool, then drain and flake into pieces.

2 Place the mashed potato, mustard, spring onions, lemon zest and juice, and parsley in a large bowl. Add the flakes of smoked haddock and mix well, keeping the flakes of fish as large as possible. Season with salt and pepper to taste.

3 Divide the mixture into 12 equal portions and shape each into a round cake. Place the flour in a small dish, the beaten egg in another dish, and the breadcrumbs in a third. Roll each fishcake in the flour to coat all over, then dip into the egg and finally coat evenly with breadcrumbs.

4 Heat oil for shallow-frying in a large frying pan. Add the fish cakes (cooking in two or three batches) and fry for 5–7 minutes, turning once, until crisp and golden all over (brown the edges too, holding the fish cakes with tongs). Drain on kitchen paper and serve hot with lemon wedges, mayonnaise, and watercress.

Making dried breadcrumbs

Break up day-old bread into a food processor and process to fine crumbs. Spread out the crumbs on a baking sheet and bake in a preheated 150°C (300°F/Gas 2) oven for about 20 minutes or until golden; stir once or twice to make sure the crumbs dry and colour evenly. Allow to cool before using.

40 mins

preparation
10 mins

cooking
30 mins

Whole Baked Sea Bream

Small whole fish are extra succulent when baked in a parcel. Make sure you use well-flavoured tomatoes, as they make all the difference.

Serves 4

Ingredients

4 small sea bream, approx.
　350g (12oz) in total, scaled,
　gutted, and trimmed
1 tbsp seasoned flour
5 tbsp extra virgin olive oil,
　plus extra for greasing
1 onion, finely chopped
2 celery sticks, thinly sliced
2 garlic cloves, chopped
8 plum tomatoes, roughly
　chopped
5 tbsp dry white wine
salt and freshly ground
　black pepper
pinch of sugar
2 tbsp chopped flat-leaf parsley

1 Preheat the oven to 190°C (375°F/Gas 5). Slash the sea bream 3–4 times on each side. Dust with the seasoned flour and arrange on a large sheet of oiled foil in a baking tray.

2 Heat the olive oil in a frying pan, add the onion, celery, and garlic, and cook over low heat for 2–3 minutes or until softened. Add the tomatoes and wine and cook for a further 3–4 minutes. Season and stir in the sugar.

3 Spoon the tomato sauce over the sea bream and wrap in the foil (see the technique below). Bake for 15–20 minutes or until the flesh of the fish along the backbone is white and opaque (check with the tip of a sharp knife).

4 Lift each fish onto a warmed serving plate and sprinkle with parsley. Serve immediately.

Baking whole fish

Wrap the fish and the spooned mixture tightly in the foil, sealing the parcel well. Bake for 15–20 minutes for small fish. If you adapt the recipe for a larger fish, cook for 35–40 minutes.

40 mins

preparation	cooking	baking
10 mins	10 mins	20 mins

Pan-fried Pollock with Spinach and Pine Nuts

A member of the cod family, pollock has firm, white,
flaky flesh, which makes it ideal for pan-frying.

Serves 4

Ingredients

4 pollock fillets, approx.
150g (5½oz) each,
scaled and pin-boned (see the
pin-boning technique on p123)
salt and freshly ground
black pepper
2 tbsp olive oil
1 onion, finely chopped
handful of plump raisins
handful of pine nuts, toasted
1–2 tsp capers, rinsed and
gently squeezed dry
2 large handfuls of spinach
leaves

1 Season the fish with salt and pepper – salting the fish (ideally with sea salt) before cooking firms the flesh by removing moisture – then pan-fry (see the technique below). To check if the fish is cooked, use the tip of a round-ended knife to move the flesh away gently from the skin at the thickest part; it should come away with ease.

2 Remove the fish fillets from the pan and keep warm. Carefully wipe out the pan with kitchen paper, then add the remaining oil and heat it.

3 Sauté the onion for about 5 minutes or until soft and translucent. Add the raisins, pine nuts, and capers and cook for a further 2–3 minutes, breaking up the capers with the back of a fork. Add the spinach and cook, stirring and tossing, until just wilted. Taste and add seasoning, if needed.

4 Divide the wilted spinach mixture among four warmed plates and place the fish fillets on top. Serve hot.

Pan-frying fish fillets

1 Heat half the oil in a non-stick frying pan. Add the fish, skin-side down, and leave to cook for 2–3 minutes, depending on thickness.

2 Turn the fillets over and cook the other side for 2–3 minutes, or longer if the fillets are thick. Keep the heat medium-high.

3 Turn the fish over again. It should be an even golden colour on both sides. Check if the fish is cooked, then remove from the pan.

25 mins

preparation
10 mins

cooking
15 mins

THE RECIPES MAINS FISH AND SEAFOOD

133

Poached Skate with Black Butter

Here skate wings are poached in an aromatic liquid called court bouillon, which is also used for cooking vegetables, offal, and delicate meats.

Serves 2

Ingredients

court bouillon, for poaching
  (see the technique below)
2 skate wings, approx.
  175g (6oz) each, skinned
60g (2oz) unsalted butter
2 tbsp white or red wine
  vinegar
2 tsp capers
2 tsp chopped flat-leaf
  parsley
boiled new potatoes, to serve

1 Pour the court bouillon into a wide pan. Lower the skate wings into the liquid and bring to the boil, then reduce the heat and poach for 10–12 minutes. The skate is cooked when the thick part of the cartilage at the "shoulder" of the wing can be pulled away easily. Lift the skate wings onto warmed plates and pat dry with kitchen paper; keep hot. Discard the court bouillon.

2 Melt the butter in a frying pan. When it sizzles, keep cooking until it turns nut brown. Take care not to let it get too dark or start smoking (although it is called "black", it should not be cooked to that colour). Stir in the vinegar, capers, and parsley. Immediately pour the furiously sizzling sauce over the skate wings and serve with new potatoes.

Court bouillon
Put 3 litres (5¼ pints) water, 1 each chopped onion, carrot, and celery stick, 300ml (10fl oz) white wine, and a bay leaf into a large pan. Bring to the boil, then simmer for 15 minutes. Remove from the heat and cool for a few minutes before using.

45 mins

preparation
15 mins

cooking
30 mins

Grilled Halibut with Beurre Blanc

Halibut has a delicate flesh that is low in fat, so a rich, buttery sauce like beurre blanc is perfect with simply grilled halibut steaks.

Serves 2

Ingredients
2 halibut steaks, approx.
    140g (5oz) each
melted butter, for brushing
sprigs of dill, to garnish

For the beurre blanc
115g (4oz) unsalted butter,
    cut into small chunks
1 shallot, finely chopped
5 tbsp fish stock
1 tbsp white wine vinegar
salt and freshly ground
    black pepper
lemon juice, to taste
peas, to serve

1 Preheat the grill to high, or heat a ridged cast-iron grill pan over high heat. Brush the halibut steaks with melted butter, then cook under the grill or on the grill pan for 3–4 minutes on each side. When cooked, the fish will just flake away from the bone when tested with a fork. Transfer to warmed plates and keep hot.

2 To make the beurre blanc sauce, see the technique below. Once all the butter has been added, the sauce should be creamy and fairly thick. Remove from the heat, season, and add lemon juice to taste. Pour the sauce over the halibut, garnish with dill, and serve with peas.

Making beurre blanc

1 Melt a quarter of the butter in a small saucepan, add the shallot, and cook for 2–3 minutes or until it has softened.

2 Add the stock and vinegar, bring to the boil, and simmer until the liquid has reduced to about 3 tbsp. Reduce the heat to low.

3 Gradually add the remaining butter, whisking vigorously. It is important to keep the sauce hot, but don't allow it to boil.

20 mins

preparation	cooking
5 mins	15 mins

Seared Tuna with Black Sesame Seed Crust

Firm, meaty tuna is best lightly cooked. Quickly searing thin steaks and then resting them ensures they will be moist with a crisp crust.

Serves 4

Ingredients
6 tbsp olive oil
1 garlic clove, finely chopped
1 small, hot red chilli, finely chopped
2 tbsp black sesame seeds, plus extra for sprinkling (optional)
salt
4 thin tuna steaks, approx. 600g (1lb 5oz) in total
2 radishes
juice of 1 lemon
½ bunch of chives, snipped into 5cm (2in) lengths

1 Mix together 4 tbsp of the oil, garlic, chilli, sesame seeds, and a sprinkling of salt on a large flat dish. Rinse the tuna steaks and pat dry with kitchen paper, then place on the sesame seed mixture. Carefully press them into the sesame seeds so that they stick. Turn and coat the other side. Arrange the steaks on the dish, side by side, cover, and leave to macerate in the refrigerator for at least 1 hour.

2 Meanwhile, cut the radishes into matchsticks. Put them into a bowl and toss with half the lemon juice to prevent them from browning.

3 Heat the remaining oil in a frying pan over high heat. Place the tuna steaks in the pan and sear for about 20 seconds on each side. Transfer to a plate and leave to rest for 5 minutes.

4 Put a tuna steak on each of four serving plates and drizzle over the remaining lemon juice. Drain the radishes and scatter them over the fish together with the chives and extra sesame seeds, if using.

Cooking tuna
Tuna steaks are best pan-fried or grilled quickly, and not overcooked, to prevent them from ending up dry. Thicker steaks – up to 2.5cm (1in) – need only 2–4 minutes on each side over high heat: the flesh inside the crisp exterior will be rare (deep pink) or medium rare (pink and no longer translucent).

1 hr 16 mins

preparation	macerating	cooking	resting
10 mins	1 hr	1 min	5 mins

Trout en Papillote

Baking fish in paper produces succulent, moist flesh because it is cooked in its own steam. During baking, the parcel browns and puffs up.

Serves 4

Ingredients

25g (scant 1oz) butter, softened
1 tbsp chopped flat-leaf parsley
grated zest of ½ lemon
1 red onion, sliced
4 sea trout fillets
4 slices of lemon
4 slices of orange
drizzle of olive oil
salt and freshly ground black pepper

1 Preheat the oven to 190°C (375°F/Gas 5). Mix together the butter, parsley, and lemon zest. Cut out four heart shapes from baking parchment and prepare the trout for baking en papillote (see the technique below). Place the parcels on a baking tray and bake for 10–12 minutes, depending on the thickness of the fillets.

2 To check if the fish is cooked, don't open the parcels, but insert a metal skewer through the paper into the fish; leave for 15 seconds and then withdraw. The tip of the skewer should be piping hot.

3 Lift each parcel carefully and place on a warmed serving plate. Serve immediately, opening the parcels at the table so everyone can enjoy the appetizing aromas with the first breath of steam.

Baking en papillote
Lay a few slices of onion on one half of each heart shape and top with the fillet, a quarter of the flavoured butter, a slice each of lemon and orange, and a drizzle of oil. Season well. Fold the other half of the heart over the fillet, leaving space inside the parcel, then fold over the edges several times to seal tightly.

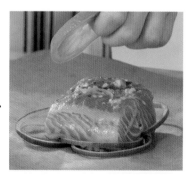

22 mins

preparation
10 mins

baking
12 mins

Moules Marinières

Mussels should be alive when you buy them and should be closed – tap them and discard any that do not close. Cook them promptly after purchase.

Serves 4

Ingredients

60g (2oz) butter

2 onions, finely chopped

3.6kg (8lb) mussels, prepared
  (see the technique below)

2 garlic cloves, crushed

600ml (1 pint) dry white wine

4 bay leaves

2 sprigs of thyme

salt and freshly ground
  black pepper

2–4 tbsp chopped flat-leaf
  parsley

1 Melt the butter in a large, wide, heavy-based pan, add the onions, and fry gently until lightly browned. Add the mussels, garlic, wine, bay leaves, and thyme. Season with salt and pepper to taste. Bring to the boil, then cover the pan and cook for 5–6 minutes or until the mussels have opened, shaking frequently.

2 Remove the mussels with a slotted spoon, discarding any that remain closed. Transfer them to warmed bowls, cover, and keep warm.

3 Strain the cooking liquid into a saucepan and bring to the boil. Check the seasoning and add the parsley, then pour over the mussels and serve at once.

Preparing mussels

1 Scrub the mussels under cold, running water in the sink. Rinse and remove any barnacles with a knife. Discard any mussels that are open.

2 To remove the "beard", pinch the dark stringy piece between your fingers, pull it away from the mussel, and discard.

35 mins

preparation
20 mins

cooking
15 mins

Bouillabaisse

A bouillabaisse, or stew, should contain a good variety of fish.
If you like, fillet the fish and use the bones to make the fish stock.

Serves 4

Ingredients
4 tbsp olive oil
1 onion, thinly sliced
2 leeks, thinly sliced
1 small fennel bulb, thinly sliced
2–3 garlic cloves, finely chopped
4 tomatoes, skinned, deseeded,
   and chopped
1 tbsp tomato purée
250ml (8fl oz) dry white wine
1.5 litres (2¾ pints) fish stock
   or chicken stock
pinch of saffron threads
strip of orange zest
1 bouquet garni
salt and freshly ground
   black pepper
1.35kg (3lb) mixed white and oily
   fish and shellfish, such as
   gurnard, John Dory, monkfish,
   red mullet, raw king or tiger
   prawns, and mussels
2 tbsp Pernod
8 croûtes, to serve (see p97)

For the rouille
125g (4½ oz) mayonnaise
1 bird's-eye chilli, deseeded
   and roughly chopped
4 garlic cloves, roughly chopped
1 tbsp tomato purée
½ tsp salt

1 Heat the oil in a large pot over medium heat. Add the onion, leeks, fennel, and garlic. Fry, stirring, for 5–8 minutes or until the vegetables are soft but not coloured. Stir in the tomatoes, tomato purée, and wine.

2 Add the stock, saffron, orange zest, and bouquet garni. Season with salt and pepper. Bring to the boil, then reduce the heat, partially cover, and simmer the broth for 30 minutes, stirring occasionally.

3 Meanwhile, combine the rouille ingredients in a blender and blend until smooth. Transfer to a bowl, cover, and keep in the refrigerator until required.

4 Cut the fish into chunks, discarding heads and bones. Peel and de-vein the prawns (see the technique below). Scrub and de-beard the mussels.

5 Remove the zest and bouquet garni from the broth. Add the chunks of firm fish and simmer gently, covered, for 2–3 minutes. Add the mussels and simmer for another 2–3 minutes, then add the chunks of delicate fish and the prawns and simmer for a further 2–3 minutes or until all the fish is cooked and flakes easily, the prawns are pink and opaque, and the mussels have opened (discard any that remain closed).

6 Stir in the Pernod and season with salt and pepper to taste. Spread the croûtes with rouille and place two in the bottom of each bowl. Ladle the soup on top and serve.

De-veining prawns
After peeling large prawns, you may see a thick, black intestinal "vein" running along the curved side. If you want to remove it (it can be a bit gritty), use a small knife to make a shallow cut along the curved side, then rinse out the vein under cold running water.

1 hr 5 mins

preparation
20 mins

cooking
45 mins

Fish and Chips

Skin on or off the fillets is down to personal taste, though purists say it should be removed. A flour coating helps the batter stick to the fish.

Serves 4

Ingredients
1kg (2¼lb) floury potatoes, such as Maris Piper, peeled and cut into thick chips
vegetable oil, for deep-frying
4 haddock fillets, 175–225g (6–8oz) each, pin-boned and skinned (see pin-boning technique on p123)
4 tbsp seasoned flour
tartare sauce, to serve

For the batter
115g (4oz) plain flour
1 tsp baking powder
salt and freshly ground black pepper
250–300ml (8–10fl oz) pale ale

1 Soak the potatoes in cold water for 10 minutes, then drain and dry thoroughly. Set aside.

2 To make the batter, sift the flour, baking powder, and ½ tsp salt into a bowl. Make a well in the centre and add half the ale. Gradually mix the flour into the liquid, then slowly stir in more ale to make a batter with the consistency of single cream. Season with salt and pepper. Set aside.

3 Half fill a large pan or deep-fat fryer with oil and heat to 160°C (325°F). Fry the potatoes, a small batch at a time, for 3–5 minutes or until soft but not brown. As each batch of potatoes is fried, remove with a slotted spoon and drain on kitchen paper.

4 Increase the temperature of the oil to 180°C (350°F). Dust the fish with seasoned flour. Using tongs, dip the fish into the batter to coat completely, then lift out, letting excess batter drip back into the bowl, and lower into the hot oil. Fry for 7–10 minutes or until the batter is golden brown. Lift the fish onto kitchen paper and keep hot.

5 Fry the chips a second time for 2–3 minutes or until brown and crisp. Drain on kitchen paper and sprinkle with salt. Serve the fish and chips hot, with tartare sauce.

Heating oil for deep-frying
For deep-frying fish, the oil must be at the correct temperature, usually 180°C (350°F). If it is too hot, the coating will turn brown before the fish is cooked. If it isn't hot enough, the coating will absorb oil and become soggy, and will not brown. If you don't have a deep-frying thermometer, drop a cube of bread into the oil to check the temperature: it will turn golden brown in 60 seconds at 180°C (350°F).

1 hr

preparation
30 mins

cooking
30 mins

Week-End à la mer

BAR
BRASSERIE
GLACIER

Bienvenue
à la buvette
de la plage

Salmon en Croûte

Baking salmon en croûte ("in a crust" of pastry) retains all its flavour and juices. You can assemble it up to 12 hours before baking.

Serves 4

Ingredients

85g (3oz) watercress
  leaves, very finely chopped
115g (4oz) cream cheese
salt and freshly ground
  black pepper
400g (14oz) puff pastry
plain flour, for dusting
600g (1lb 5oz) salmon fillet,
  pin-boned, skinned,
  and halved (see the pin-boning
  technique on p123)
oil, for greasing
beaten egg or milk, to glaze

1 Preheat the oven to 200°C (400°F/Gas 6). Place the watercress in a bowl, add the cream cheese, and season generously. Mix together well.

2 Roll out the pastry on a lightly floured surface (see the technique below) to an oblong 3mm (⅛in) thick. It should be 7.5cm (3in) longer than the salmon pieces and more than twice as wide. Trim the edges. Transfer to a lightly oiled baking tray.

3 Place one piece of salmon in the middle of the pastry. Spread with the watercress cream and set the other piece of salmon on top. Lightly brush the pastry edges with water, then fold the two ends over the fish. Fold in the sides so they overlap slightly and press together.

4 Decorate with shapes cut from the pastry trimmings, if you like. Brush with the beaten egg and make two or three small holes in the top of the pastry case to allow steam to escape during baking.

5 Bake for 30 minutes or until the pastry is well risen and golden. Remove from the oven and allow to stand for a few minutes before slicing to serve.

Rolling out puff pastry

If using home-made pastry, be sure it is well chilled; thaw ready-made pastry, following the instructions on the packet. Place the pastry on a lightly floured surface and use a floured rolling pin to roll out away from you, using short, sharp strokes. You can also buy ready-made puff pastry sheets, which may need to be rolled out to reach the required size.

55 mins

preparation	cooking
25 mins	30 mins

Dressed Crab

For the best results, buy the crab live and cook it for 15 minutes per 500g/1lb 2oz in salted water or court bouillon (see p135).

Serves 2

Ingredients

1 brown crab, approx. 1.3–2kg
(3–4½lb), cooked
splash of oil
2–3 tbsp fresh white
breadcrumbs
English mustard powder
cayenne pepper
Worcestershire sauce
freshly ground black pepper
lemon wedges, to serve

To garnish
1 egg, hard boiled
chopped flat-leaf parsley

1 To prepare the crab for picking out the meat, see the technique below. Crack the central body section and discard the soft gills from the side, then pick out the white meat with a spoon or skewer. Extract the meat from the claws and legs. Scoop the soft brown meat from the body shell, discarding the head sac and mouth.

2 Trim off the edge of the body shell opening, then wash the shell well and brush with a little oil. Mix the brown meat with enough breadcrumbs to bind. Add mustard, cayenne, Worcestershire sauce, and pepper to taste. Flake the white meat into a bowl, taking care to discard any tiny chips of shell and cartilage.

3 Neatly arrange both white and brown meat in the cleaned shell. Garnish with chopped egg white, sieved egg yolk, and parsley. Serve with wedges of lemon.

Preparing a crab

1 Hold the cooked crab on its back and firmly twist the claws and legs to break them from the body.

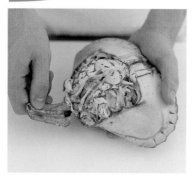

2 On the underside of the body, lift the triangular tail flap, twist it off, and discard. Lever the central body section out of the shell.

3 Gently break the shell of the claws, taking care not to crush them. Crack the leg shells or snip along the side using shears.

40 mins

preparation
40 mins

Roast Lobster

Here is a simple but very impressive celebration dish. If possible, poach the lobsters yourself to ensure they aren't overcooked and dry.

Serves 4

Ingredients

2 lobsters, cooked (see the technique below)
4 tbsp extra virgin olive oil
4 tbsp finely chopped flat-leaf parsley
2 garlic cloves, crushed
3–4 tbsp fresh breadcrumbs
salt and freshly ground black pepper
lemon halves, to serve

1 Preheat the oven to 190°C (375°F/Gas 5). Using a large, heavy chef's knife, split each lobster evenly in half, cutting through the centre of the head and down the body or tail; each half will have a claw. Remove the intestinal "vein" that runs along the back of the lobster, inside the shell, as well as the stomach sac situated behind the eyes. Put the lobster halves, cut-side up, on a large baking tray.

2 Heat the olive oil in a small saucepan, add the parsley and garlic, and sizzle for 30 seconds. Stir in the breadcrumbs and season with salt and pepper to taste.

3 Spoon the parsley mixture evenly over the lobster flesh. Roast for 7–10 minutes or until the lobsters are piping hot. Remove from the oven and arrange on a large, warmed serving dish with lemon halves. Serve hot.

Cooking a live lobster

Bring a very large pot of heavily salted water to the boil (there should be enough water to cover the lobster generously). When it is rapidly boiling, add the lobster and cover the pot. As soon as the water returns to the boil, reduce the heat to a simmer and start timing, allowing 8–10 minutes per 500g (1lb 2oz), poaching until the shells are completely red. It's better to undercook lobster if it is going to be cooked further by roasting.

preparation	cooking	baking
15 mins	5 mins	10 mins

30 mins

Chicken and Parsley Pot Pie

Here's a great way to use up leftover roast chicken and ham. The pies can be kept in the refrigerator overnight before glazing and baking.

Serves 4

Ingredients

150g (5½oz) frozen broad
  beans, or 400g can
  sweetcorn, drained
50g (1¾oz) butter
1 onion, finely chopped
50g (1¾oz) plain flour,
  plus extra for dusting
450ml (15fl oz) hot milk
1 tsp Dijon mustard
300g (10oz) cooked chicken,
  cut into chunky bite-sized
  pieces
150g (5½oz) cooked ham,
  cut into cubes
3 tbsp finely chopped curly
  or flat-leaf parsley
1 tbsp finely chopped
  marjoram leaves (optional)
salt and freshly ground
  black pepper
300g (10oz) shortcrust or puff
  pastry, or use shop-bought
  butter puff pastry
1 egg, beaten

1 Put the broad beans in a bowl and pour over boiling water to cover. Leave for 5–8 minutes, then drain. Set aside.

2 Melt the butter in a large pan over low heat, add the onion, and cook for 5–7 minutes or until soft and translucent. Remove from the heat and stir in the flour. Pour in a little milk, stirring, then put the pan back on low heat. Gradually add the rest of the milk, stirring well. Bring to the boil, then reduce to a simmer and cook for 2–3 minutes.

3 Remove from the heat and stir in the mustard, chicken, ham, herbs, and broad beans or sweetcorn. Season with salt and pepper to taste. Divide the mixture among four 300ml (10fl oz) pudding basins or one 1.2 litre (2 pint) basin.

4 Roll out the pastry on a lightly floured surface. Cut out four small lids, or one larger lid, 4cm (1½in) bigger than the basin(s). Wet the rims of the basin(s), then drape a lid over the top of each basin and press to seal to the rim. Make a steam hole in the top of each lid. Brush with half the beaten egg and chill for 20 minutes.

5 Meanwhile, preheat the oven to 200°C (400°F/Gas 6). Brush the rest of the egg over the pies, then bake for 25–30 minutes or until golden; a large pie may take a little longer. Serve hot.

⚠ Rescue it!

If the milk isn't getting absorbed smoothly when you are stirring it in, switch to a balloon whisk and beat vigorously while adding the rest of the milk.

1 hr
10 mins

preparation	chilling	cooking
20 mins	20 mins	30 mins

Chicken Tikka Masala

This is an easy version of a popular dish. Marinate and grill the chicken to give it a tandoori-baked flavour before adding it to a creamy sauce.

Serves 4

Ingredients

8 chicken thighs, skinned and boned (see the technique below)

2 garlic cloves, coarsely chopped

2.5cm (1in) piece of fresh root ginger, coarsely chopped

juice of 1 lime

1 red chilli, deseeded

2 tbsp coarsely chopped coriander leaves, plus extra to garnish

2 tbsp vegetable oil

1 red onion, chopped

1 tsp ground turmeric

1 tsp ground cumin

1 tbsp tomato purée

300ml (10fl oz) double cream

1 tbsp lemon juice

salt and freshly ground black pepper

1 Place the chicken thighs in a single layer in a shallow dish. Put the next five ingredients and 1 tbsp of the oil in a food processor or blender and process to a paste. Spread over the chicken, then leave to marinate for 2 hours.

2 Heat the remaining oil in a frying pan, add the onion, and fry until softened and starting to colour. Stir in the turmeric and cumin and fry for 2–3 minutes. Set aside.

3 Preheat the grill to high. Lift the chicken from the dish, reserving any marinade left behind, and place on a foil-lined grill rack. Grill for 2–3 minutes on each side or until almost cooked and slightly scorched at the edges.

4 Stir the tomato purée, cream, lemon juice, and reserved marinade into the onion mixture in the frying pan. Bring to the boil, stirring to mix well. Place the chicken in the pan and baste with the sauce, then simmer for 5 minutes or until the chicken is cooked through. Season with salt and pepper to taste and sprinkle with coriander to serve,

Boning a chicken thigh

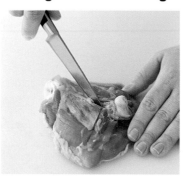

1 Place the thigh, skin-side down, on a chopping board. Using a sharp knife, cut through the flesh to expose the thigh bone.

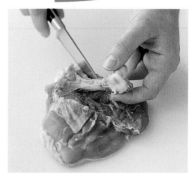

2 Keeping the knife close to the bone, cut around it to free it from the flesh. Discard or use for stock. To remove the skin, pull it off.

2 hrs 45 mins

preparation	marinating	cooking
20 mins	2 hrs	25 mins

Coq au Vin

For the best flavour, use a boiling fowl for this traditional dish.
Start the recipe a day ahead to allow time for marinating.

Serves 4–6

Ingredients

2kg (4½lb) chicken, jointed
   into 8 pieces
1 tbsp vegetable oil
15g (½oz) butter
125g (4½oz) piece of
   bacon, diced
18–20 baby onions, peeled
250g (9oz) mushrooms,
   quartered
3 tbsp plain flour
500ml (16fl oz) chicken
   stock or water
1 garlic clove, finely chopped
2 shallots, finely chopped
1 bouquet garni
salt and freshly ground
   black pepper

For the marinade

1 onion, thinly sliced
1 celery stick, thinly sliced
1 carrot, thinly sliced
1 garlic clove, peeled
6 black peppercorns
375ml (13fl oz) red wine
2 tbsp olive oil

1 Put the marinade ingredients, except the oil, in a pan. Bring to the boil and simmer for 5 minutes. Cool. Place the chicken pieces in a large bowl and pour over the marinade. Spoon the olive oil on top. Cover and leave to marinate in the refrigerator for 12–18 hours, turning the pieces occasionally.

2 Remove the chicken pieces from the marinade and pat dry with kitchen paper. Strain the marinade through a sieve set over a bowl; reserve both the liquid and vegetables. Heat the oil and butter in a heavy flameproof casserole until foaming. Add the bacon and fry until browned. Remove with a slotted spoon. Add the chicken and sauté for 10 minutes on each side or until golden brown. Remove.

3 Add the baby onions to the casserole and sauté until browned. Lift out with a slotted spoon and reserve. Add the mushrooms and sauté for 2–3 minutes. Remove with the slotted spoon and reserve.

4 Discard all but about 2 tbsp of fat from the casserole. Add the reserved marinade vegetables and cook over low heat for 5 minutes or until softened. Sprinkle over the flour and cook, stirring, until lightly browned. Stir in the reserved marinade, the stock, garlic, shallots, bouquet garni, and some salt and pepper. Bring to the boil. Replace the chicken pieces in the pot, cover, and simmer over low heat for 45–60 minutes or until just tender.

5 Transfer the chicken to a plate and keep warm. Pour the sauce into a bowl; scoop out and reserve a few pieces of carrot. Wipe out the casserole, then add the baby onions. Strain the sauce over them, pressing to extract the liquid from the vegetables. Simmer over low heat for 10 minutes.

6 Add the mushrooms and reserved carrots and continue to simmer for 2–3 minutes or until the sauce is reduced and thickened. Return the chicken pieces and bacon to the pot and reheat gently for 3–4 minutes. Serve hot.

20 hrs 15 mins

preparation	marinating		cooking
30 mins	18 hrs		1 hr 45 mins

Spatchcocked Chicken

If you split open and flatten a chicken, you can cook it whole over hot coals or under the grill. It will be perfectly juicy with a crisp skin.

Serves 4–6

Ingredients

1–2 tsp olive oil
grated zest of 1 lemon,
   plus juice of 2 lemons
1 tsp paprika
½ tsp salt
1 tsp freshly ground
   black pepper
1 chicken, approx. 1.8–2kg
   (4–4½lb), spatchcocked
   (see the technique below)
1 tbsp dried oregano

1 Put the oil, lemon zest and juice, paprika, salt, and pepper in a bowl or shallow dish and mix together well. Add the chicken and turn it over so it is coated with the marinade. Cover the bowl tightly and leave to marinate in the refrigerator for 1 hour.

2 Prepare a charcoal fire in the barbecue, or preheat the grill to moderate. Sprinkle the oregano liberally all over the chicken, then place over medium coals, or under the grill. Cook for 20–25 minutes on each side or until the chicken is golden and cooked through. During cooking, move the chicken on the barbecue or adjust the heat of the grill, as necessary, to prevent charring.

3 Remove the chicken to a carving board and leave to rest in a warm place for 15 minutes before pulling out the skewers and cutting the chicken into serving pieces.

Spatchcocking a bird

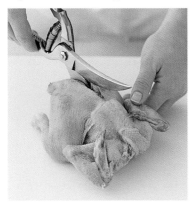

1 Place the bird, breast down. Using poultry shears, cut along both sides of the backbone to remove it. Turn the bird over.

2 Press down firmly to crush the breastbone and flatten the bird. Cut slits into the legs and thighs to ensure even cooking.

3 Push a metal skewer diagonally through the left leg to the right wing, then another skewer through the right leg to the left wing.

2 hrs 15 mins

preparation	marinating		grilling		standing
10 mins	1 hr		50 mins		15 mins

Stuffed Chicken Breasts with Mushroom and Thyme

Chicken breasts can be dry, but cutting a pocket and filling it with a savoury mixture will add moisture as well as good flavour.

Serves 4

Ingredients

25g (scant 1oz) mixed dried mushrooms such as shiitake, oyster, or porcini
handful of thyme sprigs, leaves picked
splash of chilli oil (optional)
salt and freshly ground black pepper
4 large skinless chicken breast fillets
1 tbsp olive oil
mashed potato, to serve

1 Put the dried mushrooms in a bowl, pour over boiling water to cover, and soak for at least 15 minutes. Drain the mushrooms, reserving the soaking liquid, and chop. Put them back in the bowl and add half the thyme leaves, the chilli oil (if using), and some salt and pepper. Mix together.

2 Stuff the chicken breasts with the mixture (see the technique below). Sprinkle with the remaining thyme leaves and seasoning. Heat the olive oil in a large frying pan over medium-high heat. Place the breasts in the pan and cook undisturbed for 6–8 minutes, then turn over and cook the other side for about the same time or until cooked through. Remove and keep warm.

3 Strain the reserved soaking liquid from the mushrooms into the pan. Bring to the boil and reduce by half. Spoon the reduced liquid over the chicken breasts and serve with creamy mashed potato.

Stuffing chicken breasts

1 Cut a pocket about 4cm (1½in) deep in each breast, starting at one side and cutting in centrally to ensure even cooking.

2 Stuff the pocket with the mushroom mixture, not packing it too full. Secure the opening with a wooden cocktail stick.

1 hr 10 mins

soaking		preparation	cooking	boiling
30 mins		15 mins	15 mins	10 mins

Five-spice Pan-fried Duck Breast

Duck breasts have a thick layer of fat under the skin. Scoring the skin allows the fat to melt so it bastes the meat and runs off on to the pan.

Serves 4

Ingredients

4 duck breasts, approx.
   150g (5½oz) each
2–3 tsp five-spice paste
knob of butter
2 tbsp freshly squeezed
   orange juice
1 tsp soft brown sugar
250g packet ready-cooked
   noodles
handful of finely chopped
   coriander

1 Using a sharp knife, score the skin of each breast in a crisscross pattern. Cut through the fat, but not into the flesh. Rub the duck breasts with the five-spice paste.

2 Melt the butter in a frying pan over high heat. Put the duck breasts in the pan, skin-side down, and cook for about 10 minutes or until the skin is golden and crisp. Carefully pour off the fat from the pan, then turn the breasts over and cook for a further 8 minutes or until cooked to your taste (see below).

3 Remove the duck breasts from the pan and place on a chopping board, covering with foil. Pour away any remaining fat from the pan, then add the orange juice and sugar. Simmer for 1–2 minutes, stirring and scraping up any browned bits from the bottom of the pan with a wooden spoon.

4 Add the noodles and toss them in the orange sauce for a couple of minutes. Remove from the heat and stir through the coriander. Slice the duck breasts and arrange on warmed plates. Add the dressed noodles and serve.

Rare, medium, or well done
Unlike chicken and turkey, duck breasts do not have to be cooked through. Although they will be well done if roasted on a whole bird, the tender, lean breasts are delicious when cooked separately just to rare or medium.

30 mins

preparation
5 mins

cooking
25 mins

Shallot, Chestnut, and Venison Casserole

Coating the pieces of venison with flour enhances their browning, giving this casserole a rich colour and extra, toasty flavour.

Serves 8

Ingredients

50g (1¾oz) dried mushrooms, such as shiitake, oyster, or porcini

1 tbsp plain flour

handful of thyme leaves

salt and freshly ground black pepper

1.1kg (2½lb) boned leg or shoulder of venison, cut into bite-sized pieces

knob of butter

3 tbsp olive oil

250g (9oz) bacon lardons or diced pancetta

250g (9oz) shallots, peeled and left whole

2 glasses of red wine

250g pack ready-cooked chestnuts

1 litre (1¾pints) hot vegetable stock

3 sprigs of rosemary

1 Preheat the oven to 150°C (300°F/Gas 2). Soak the dried mushrooms in 300ml (10fl oz) warm water for at least 15 minutes. Meanwhile, put the flour, thyme, and some salt and pepper in a mixing bowl. Add the venison and toss well to coat.

2 Heat the butter with 2 tbsp of the oil in a large flameproof casserole. Add the venison and cook over medium heat, stirring frequently, for 6–8 minutes or until the pieces are lightly browned. Remove with a slotted spoon and set aside. Add the bacon lardons or pancetta to the casserole and stir for 5 minutes or until browned and crisp. Remove with a slotted spoon and set aside with the venison.

3 Add the remaining oil to the pot, then add the shallots and cook over medium-low heat for 8 minutes or until they turn golden. Return the venison and lardons to the pot, season with pepper to taste, and pour in the wine. Bring to the boil and boil for 2 minutes, scraping up all the browned bits from the bottom of the pot.

4 Drain the mushrooms, reserving the liquid, and add to the casserole. Strain the liquid into the pot. Add the chestnuts, stock, and rosemary and stir everything together. Cover with a lid and transfer to the oven. Cook for 2 hours or until the meat is tender, topping up with hot water if necessary (see below). Check the seasoning and serve hot.

⚠ Rescue it!

If the mixture seems to be sticking to the pan while the casserole is in the oven, give the contents of the pot a good stir and check that there is still sufficient liquid to keep the meat covered. If not, top up with hot water.

2 hrs 50 mins

soaking	preparation	cooking
20 mins	5 mins	2 hrs 25 mins

Pot-roast Pheasant

Unless they are young and tender, most lean game birds benefit from a moist cooking method such as pot–roasting rather than roasting.

Serves 4

Ingredients

2 tbsp olive oil
60g (2oz) butter, chilled
2 pheasants, approx.
   750g (1lb 10oz) each
salt and freshly ground
   black pepper
250g (9oz) chestnut mushrooms
2 tbsp chopped thyme
1 large onion, finely chopped
100g (3½oz) rindless streaky
   bacon, chopped
750ml (1¼pints) red wine

To serve

mashed potato and swede
a green vegetable such as
   French beans

1 Preheat the oven to 190°C (375°F/Gas 5). Heat half the oil with half the butter in a large frying pan. Add the pheasants, one at a time if necessary, and brown them all over. Transfer to a large casserole and season them with some salt and pepper.

2 Add the mushrooms and thyme to the frying pan and cook for 5 minutes or until the mushrooms are browned. Transfer them to the casserole.

3 Heat the remaining oil in the frying pan, add the onion and bacon, and cook, stirring, for 5 minutes or until the onion has softened. Add the onion, bacon, and wine to the casserole. Cover it and place in the oven. Cook for 1½ hours or until the pheasants are cooked through: you should be able to pull a leg away from the bird easily. Transfer the pheasants to a carving board and leave to rest in a warm place.

4 Strain the liquid from the casserole into a saucepan (reserve the mushrooms and bacon). Skim off any fat, then bring to the boil and boil for 10 minutes or until reduced by a third. Whisk in the remaining butter to make the gravy glossy. Carve the pheasant and divide among warmed plates with the mushrooms, bacon, and hot gravy. Serve hot with the mashed potato and swede and the beans.

2 hrs	preparation	cooking	roasting	boiling
	10 mins	10 mins	1 hr 30 mins	10 mins

Rabbit Provençal

Herbes de Provence includes wild thyme, savory, and fennel. As with all dried herbs, make sure to use them quickly or they will lose their flavour.

Serves 4

Ingredients

2 shallots, chopped
250ml (8fl oz) dry white wine
4 tbsp olive oil
2 tbsp herbes de Provence
1 rabbit, approx. 1.4kg (3lb), cut into 8 pieces (see the technique below)
1 tbsp plain flour
250ml (8fl oz) chicken stock
thyme leaves, to garnish

For the tomatoes

6 plum tomatoes, approx. 500g (1lb 2oz) in total, each cut into 3 slices
1 tbsp olive oil
salt and freshly ground black pepper

1 Combine the shallots, wine, half the oil, and the herbes de Provence in a shallow dish. Add the rabbit and turn to coat. Cover and marinate in the refrigerator for 2–3 hours.

2 Meanwhile, roast the tomatoes. Preheat the oven to 130°C (250°F/Gas ½). Toss the tomato slices with the oil and salt and pepper to taste. Arrange in one layer on an oiled rack set in a roasting tin. Roast for 2–2½ hours or until slightly shrivelled. Remove and set aside. Increase the oven temperature to 190°C (375°F/Gas 5).

3 Take the rabbit from the marinade (reserve it) and pat dry with kitchen paper. Season. Heat the remaining oil in a flameproof casserole and brown the rabbit pieces.

4 Sprinkle the rabbit with the flour and cook, turning, for 2–3 minutes. Pour in the marinade and stock. Cover the casserole and place in the oven to cook for 50–55 minutes or until the rabbit is very tender. Reheat the tomatoes in the oven for the last 10 minutes. Sprinkle with thyme, to serve.

Jointing a rabbit

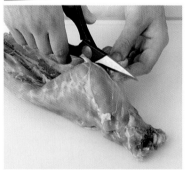

1 Cut through the ball and socket joint to free each hind leg. Cut off the forelegs close to the rib cage. Remove the last of the backbone.

2 Turn over onto the back and cut up through the breastbone, so the breast meat falls apart in 2 flaps. Turn over, tucking the flaps under.

3 Cut across the rabbit at the lower end of the rib cage, to leave 4 rib bones attached to the loin. Square off the flaps.

4 hrs 15 mins

preparation	marinating and baking tomatoes	cooking	baking
5 mins	3 hrs	15 mins	55 mins

Partridge with Roast Pears, Kohlrabi, and Walnuts

Sweet fruit, turnip-like kohlrabi, and nuts are perfect with game birds in this easy dish. Choose young kohlrabi as older ones may be woody.

Serves 4

Ingredients

4 sprigs of thyme
4 oven-ready partridges
85g (3oz) butter
salt and freshly ground
  black pepper
8 streaky bacon rashers,
  each cut into thirds
2 kohlrabi, each cut into
  eighths
200ml (7fl oz) chicken stock
2 onions, each cut into eighths
4 small firm pears, quartered
  and cored
30g (1oz) walnut halves
150ml (5fl oz) pear or
  apple cider
mashed potato, to serve

1 Push a sprig of thyme inside each bird. Secure the legs to the bodies using wooden cocktail sticks. Smear half the butter over the birds. Season lightly and lay the bacon over the breasts.

2 Preheat the oven to 200°C (400°F/Gas 6). Put the kohlrabi and stock in a saucepan, bring to the boil, and cook for 2 minutes. Drain, reserving the stock.

3 Melt the remaining butter in a large roasting tin. Add the kohlrabi, onions, and pears, and turn them over in the butter. Push to one side of the tin. Scatter the walnuts over the bottom of the tin and set the partridges on top. Roast for 45 minutes or until everything is golden and cooked through, turning the fruit and vegetables over once during cooking.

4 Lift the birds, fruit, vegetables, and nuts out of the tin onto warmed serving plates; keep warm. Add the cider and reserved stock to the tin. Boil over high heat, stirring and scraping up the browned bits, for 3 minutes until well reduced and slightly thickened. Taste the gravy for seasoning.

5 Remove the cocktail sticks from the birds and spoon the gravy over them. Serve hot, with mashed potato.

1 hr 5 mins

preparation	cooking	boiling
15 mins	45 mins	5 mins

Shepherd's Pie

For this economical one-dish meal you can use fresh minced lamb, or meat left over from Sunday lunch. Replace the wine with stock, if you prefer.

Serves 4–6

Ingredients
750g (1lb 10oz) minced lamb, finely chopped
2 tbsp sunflower oil
1 large onion, chopped
1 garlic clove, crushed
2 carrots, sliced
90ml (3fl oz) dry red wine
2 tbsp plain flour
250ml (8fl oz) lamb stock
1 tbsp Worcestershire sauce
2 tbsp chopped flat-leaf parsley
1 tbsp rosemary, finely crushed

For the potato and leek mash
900g (2lb) floury potatoes, such as King Edward, peeled
2 large leeks, halved lengthways and sliced across
60g (2oz) butter
150ml (5fl oz) milk, warmed
salt and freshly ground black pepper

1 To make the mash, cut the potatoes into large chunks and place in a large saucepan. Cover with water and bring to the boil, then simmer for 12 minutes. Add the leeks and cook for a further 5 minutes or until the potatoes are tender. Drain well. Return the potatoes and leeks to the pan and mash. Place over low heat and mix in the butter and milk. Season with salt and pepper to taste. Set aside.

2 Preheat the oven to 200°C (400°F/Gas 6). To make the filling, fry the minced lamb in a large frying pan over medium-high heat for 5 minutes or until broken up and lightly browned. Remove the meat from the pan and set aside.

3 Pour off the fat from the pan, then add the oil and heat it. Fry the onion and garlic, stirring, for 3–5 minutes or until softened. Return the lamb to the pan together with the carrots. Stir everything together.

4 Add the wine, increase the heat to high, and boil for 2–3 minutes to reduce the wine. Mix in the flour, then stir in the stock, Worcestershire sauce, parsley, and rosemary. Add salt and pepper to taste. Bring to the boil, stirring, then reduce the heat to low and simmer for 5 minutes.

5 Spoon the filling into a large baking dish. Top with the potato and leek mash, spreading it evenly. Set the dish on a baking tray and bake for 30 minutes or until the mash topping is golden. Remove the pie from the oven and leave to settle for 5 minutes before serving.

Using leftover cooked lamb
If you have lamb left over from a roast, you can use it for this pie instead of the minced lamb. It's already been cooked, so just cut it into very small pieces and add with the carrots in step 3. Use any gravy in place of some or all of the lamb stock.

1 hr 25 mins	preparation 15 mins	cooking 35 mins	baking 30 mins	standing 5 mins

Irish Stew

For this dish, the lamb is not browned before simmering long and slow, so the flavour of the stock is important. If possible, make it with lamb bones.

Serves 4–6

Ingredients

4 lamb neck fillets, cut into large chunks
1 litre (1¾ pints) lamb stock or beef stock
2 onions, thickly sliced
450g (1lb) carrots, thickly sliced
900g (2lb) floury potatoes, such as King Edward, peeled and cut into large chunks
large sprig of thyme
1 bay leaf
salt and freshly ground black pepper
chopped flat-leaf parsley, to garnish

1 Put the chunks of lamb in a large, heavy-based saucepan and cover with the stock. Bring to the boil, then reduce the heat and simmer gently for 40 minutes, skimming off any scum from the surface.

2 Add the onions, carrots, and potatoes together with the thyme and bay leaf. Bring back to the boil, then reduce the heat to low and cover the pan. Simmer gently for 25–30 minutes or until the lamb is very tender.

3 Remove and discard the bay leaf, then season with salt and pepper to taste. Sprinkle with parsley and serve hot.

Making meat stock
Combine meat bones, cracked into pieces, with aromatics such as onion, leek, carrot, celery, and a bouquet garni. Cover with water and simmer gently for 4–5 hours, skimming occasionally. Strain. Keep refrigerated.

2 hrs

preparation	cooking
20 mins	1 hr 40 mins

Lamb Shanks in Red Wine

It's worth doubling this recipe and freezing half for another time.
Thaw in the refrigerator overnight, then reheat on the hob.

Serves 6

Ingredients

6 lamb shanks, approx. 1.8kg
   (4lb) in total, excess fat and
   sinew removed
3 tbsp vegetable oil
30g (1oz) plain flour
750ml (1¼ pints) beef
   stock, plus more if needed
salt and freshly ground
   black pepper
30g (1oz) butter
1 celeriac, approx. 500g
   (1lb 2oz), trimmed and peeled,
   cut into 1cm (½in) cubes
250g (9oz) mushrooms,
   quartered
3 tbsp redcurrant jelly
bunch of watercress,
   to garnish (optional)

For the marinade

2 tsp black peppercorns
2 tsp juniper berries
4 shallots, roughly chopped
2 garlic cloves, peeled
2 onions, quartered
2 carrots, roughly sliced
1 bouquet garni, made with
   5–6 sprigs of flat-leaf parsley,
   2–3 sprigs of thyme,
   and 1 bay leaf
2 tbsp red wine vinegar
750ml (1¼ pints) dry red wine

1 For the marinade, coarsely crush the peppercorns and juniper berries, then tip them into a saucepan. Add the remaining marinade ingredients, bring to the boil, and simmer for 2 minutes. Pour into a large dish and cool. Add the lamb shanks, cover, and leave in the refrigerator for 1–2 days, turning occasionally.

2 Preheat the oven to 180°C (350°F/Gas 4). Remove the lamb shanks and pat dry with kitchen paper. Strain the marinade; reserve the vegetables and liquid separately.

3 Heat the oil in a flameproof casserole and brown the shanks all over. Remove. Add the marinade vegetables and cook, stirring frequently, for 5–7 minutes or until they start to brown. Sprinkle with the flour and cook, stirring, for 3–5 minutes or until lightly browned. Stir in the marinade liquid, scraping the bottom of the pot well.

4 Return the lamb with any juices and add the bouquet garni from the marinade, the stock, and some salt and pepper. Cover and transfer to the oven. Cook the shanks, turning them occasionally, for 2–2¼ hours or until tender.

5 Melt the butter in a frying pan, add the celeriac, and season. Cook, stirring occasionally, for 8–10 minutes or until tender. Transfer to a bowl. Add the mushrooms to the pan and cook for 3–5 minutes or until all the liquid has evaporated and they are tender. Add to the celeriac.

6 Transfer the lamb shanks to a plate and keep warm. Reserve some of the shallots and carrots, then press the sauce through a sieve into a large pan. Whisk in the redcurrant jelly with plenty of pepper. Bring back to the boil and simmer for 20–30 minutes or until reduced by half.

7 Add the mushrooms, celeriac, and reserved carrots and shallots. Check the seasoning. Return the lamb shanks to the sauce and reheat for 5–10 minutes. Serve hot.

52 hrs
15 mins

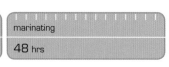

preparation	marinating	cooking	boiling	cooking
50 mins plus cooling	48 hrs	2 hrs 45 mins	30 mins	10 mins

Lamb and Apricot Tagine

Here lamb is simmered gently with warm spices and apricots. You can use other dried fruit – cranberries, sour cherries, or figs – instead.

Serves 6

Ingredients

2 tbsp olive oil
1 onion, chopped
600g (1lb 5oz) boneless lamb,
  cut into bite-sized chunks
½ tsp ground coriander
1 cinnamon stick
½ tsp ground ginger
6 cloves
½ tsp ground turmeric
salt and freshly ground
  black pepper
12 dried apricots
2 tbsp honey
chopped coriander, to garnish
couscous, cooked (see the
  technique below) to serve

1 Heat the oil in a large pan with a lid, add the onion and lamb, and cook until the lamb is browned all over. Cook the lamb in batches, if required.

2 Add the coriander, cinnamon stick, ginger, cloves, and turmeric, and stir to mix with the lamb and onion. Cook for 1–2 minutes, stirring. Pour in enough water to cover the lamb and add salt and pepper to taste.

3 Bring to a simmer, then cover the pan and cook gently for 1½ hours. Add the apricots and simmer for a further 30 minutes or until the lamb is very tender. Add more water if the tagine looks a bit dry.

4 Remove the lid and stir in the honey. Simmer, uncovered, for a further 10 minutes to reduce the liquid until it is sauce-like. Check the seasoning, then sprinkle with coriander and serve with couscous.

Preparing couscous

1 Put the couscous in a large bowl and pour over boiling water just to cover, stirring with a fork. Leave for about 5 minutes or until plump.

2 Add butter or oil and seasoning to the couscous, then stir and toss with a fork to fluff the grains and incorporate the butter or oil.

2 hrs 30 mins

preparation	cooking
10 mins	2 hrs 20 mins

Roast Rack of Lamb

A trimmed rack of lamb is worth the preparation. For easy carving, be sure the butcher has removed the chine bone (backbone).

Serves 4

Ingredients

1 rack of lamb with 8 cutlets, trimmed (see the technique below)

½ tbsp olive oil

few sprigs of rosemary, finely chopped

salt and freshly ground black pepper

150ml (5fl oz) hot vegetable stock

1 tsp redcurrant jelly

400g can flageolet beans, drained and rinsed

handful of mint, finely chopped

1 Preheat the oven to 200°C (400°F/Gas 6). Rub the lamb all over with the oil, sprinkle over the rosemary, and season well with salt and pepper. Set the rack, fat-side up, in a roasting tin and put into the oven to roast for 40 minutes, or longer for well-done meat.

2 Remove the lamb from the tin and place it on a carving board. Keep warm (covered with foil) while you prepare the beans. Set the roasting tin on the hob over medium-high heat, add the stock, and bring to the boil. Reduce to a simmer, then stir in the redcurrant jelly until melted. Add the flageolet beans and mix into the liquid, then simmer gently for 5 minutes. Remove from the heat and stir through the mint.

3 Slice the rack between the bones into 8 cutlets and serve with the beans and some minted new potatoes.

Trimming rack of lamb
Using a cleaver, trim off the ends of the bones in a straight line. Then with a sharp knife, score across the bones about 5cm (2in) from the ends. Cut out the meat and fat from between the bones, to the scored line. Finally, scrape all traces of skin and meat from the exposed bones.

55 mins

preparation	roasting		cooking
5 mins	40 mins		10 mins

Roast Rib of Beef

Rib of beef roasted on the bone is beautifully juicy. Be sure to take the joint out of the refrigerator 30–60 minutes before cooking.

Serves 4

Ingredients

1 beef rib joint (with 2 bones), approx. 2.25kg (5lb), chine bone removed
olive oil, for coating
salt and freshly ground black pepper
1–2 tbsp wholegrain mustard

1 Preheat the oven to 200°C (400°F/Gas 6). Set the joint in a roasting tin and prepare it for roasting (see step 1 below), then put it in the oven and roast for 15 minutes.

2 Reduce the oven temperature to 180°C (350°F/Gas 4) and continue roasting for a further 1 hour or until cooked to your taste. The most accurate way to test is with a meat thermometer (see step 2 below): at 65°C (130°F) the meat will be medium-rare and at 70°C (160°F) it will be medium.

3 Remove the joint from the oven and place it on a carving board. Cover loosely with foil and leave to rest in a warm place for about 20 minutes before slicing the meat from the bones. Traditional accompaniments are roast potatoes, Yorkshire pudding, creamed horseradish, and seasonal vegetables. Keep the beef bones for making stock.

Roasting beef

1 Set the joint in a roasting tin, bone side down. Brush all over with oil and season well, then rub the mustard over the fatty area.

2 At the end of the roasting time, insert a meat thermometer into the thickest part, away from the bones, to test for doneness.

1 hr 45 mins

preparation 10 mins

roasting 1 hr 15 mins

standing 20 mins

THE RECIPES MAINS MEAT

188

Beef Stroganoff

This classic Russian dish is quickly made. Take care not to overcook the strips of steak so they remain tender and juicy.

Serves 4

Ingredients

700g (1½lb) fillet steak, rump, or sirloin, trimmed
3 tbsp plain flour
1 tbsp paprika, plus extra for sprinkling
salt and freshly ground black pepper
50g (1¾oz) butter, or 4 tbsp olive oil
1 onion, thinly sliced
225g (8oz) chestnut mushrooms, sliced, or 30–60g (1–2oz) dried porcini mushrooms, rehydrated (see the technique below)
300ml (10fl oz) soured cream or crème fraîche, plus optional extra for serving
1 tbsp Dijon mustard
lemon juice

1 Thinly slice the steak into 5cm (2in) strips. Put the flour in a plastic bag and season with the paprika and some salt and pepper. Toss the beef strips in the flour to coat.

2 Heat half the butter or oil in a deep-sided frying pan, add the onion, and fry over low heat for 8–10 minutes or until soft and golden. Add the mushrooms and fry for a few minutes or until just soft.

3 Remove the onions and mushrooms with a slotted spoon and keep warm. Increase the heat and add the remaining butter or oil. When hot, fry the beef strips, in batches, for 3–4 minutes or until browned, stirring so they colour evenly.

4 Return all the beef to the pan together with the onions and mushrooms and season with salt and pepper to taste. Cook briskly, stirring, for 1 minute.

5 Lower the heat, then stir in the cream or crème fraîche and mustard. Cook gently for 1 minute; do not allow the sauce to come to the boil. Add lemon juice to taste, then divide among warmed plates. Top each serving with a spoonful of soured cream, if you like, and sprinkle with paprika. Serve hot.

Rehydrating mushrooms

To rehydrate dried mushrooms – either wild or cultivated – put them into a bowl and pour over hot water to cover. Leave to soak for at least 15 minutes, then remove from the liquid with a slotted spoon. If you plan to use the soaking liquid in your recipe, strain it through a coffee filter or muslin to remove any sand or grit.

40 mins

preparation
15 mins

cooking
25 mins

Steak and Mushroom Pie

The filling for this pie is easy to make – everything goes into the pot, with no initial browning – but it turns out to be rich and savoury.

Serves 4–6

Ingredients

35g (1¼oz) plain flour, plus
  extra for sprinkling
salt and freshly ground
  black pepper
1kg (2¼lb) braising steak,
  cut into 2.5cm (1in) cubes
900ml (1½pints) beef stock
  or water, plus more if needed
500g (1lb 2oz) mixed wild
  mushrooms, sliced, or
  75g (2½oz) dried wild
  mushrooms, rehydrated
  (see the technique on p191)
4 shallots, finely chopped
6 sprigs of flat-leaf parsley,
  finely chopped
425g (15oz) ready-made butter
  puff pastry, thawed if frozen
1 egg, beaten with ¼ tsp salt,
  to glaze

1 Preheat the oven to 180°C (350°F/Gas 4). Put the flour in a plastic bag and season with salt and pepper. Toss the steak cubes in the seasoned flour to coat, then tip into a flameproof casserole; discard leftover flour. Add the stock, mushrooms, and shallots and bring to the boil, stirring well.

2 Cover the casserole and transfer to the oven to cook for 2–2¼ hours or until the meat is tender. Stir occasionally, and top up with more stock or water if necessary.

3 Stir in the parsley and season with salt and pepper to taste. Spoon into a 2litre (3½pint) pie dish, with a pie funnel set in the centre. Leave to cool completely. Increase the oven heat to 220°C (425°F/Gas 7).

4 Lightly flour a work surface and roll out most of the pastry to a rough shape at least 2.5cm (1in) larger than the dish. Trim to neaten, then cut a strip from the edge of the pastry shape to fit the rim of the pie dish. Brush the rim with a little water, lay the strip of pastry on it, and press down to seal. Brush the strip with egg glaze.

5 Roll up the large piece of pastry around the rolling pin and drape it over the pie, without stretching. With your fingertips, press the pastry lid firmly to the strip of pastry on the rim of the dish to seal. Trim off any excess pastry to make a neat finish.

6 Brush the pastry lid with the egg glaze. Cut a hole in the centre of the lid, over the pie funnel, to allow steam to escape during baking. Cut shapes from the remaining pastry and the trimmings, and use to decorate the pie. Stick them on with egg glaze, then brush them with glaze.

7 Chill the pie for 15 minutes before placing it in the oven to bake for 25–35 minutes or until the pastry is golden brown. If it browns too quickly, cover it with foil. Serve hot.

4 hrs
45 mins

preparation	cooking		preparation	chilling	baking
1 hr 20 mins	2 hrs 25 mins		10 mins	15 mins	35 mins

Beef Wellington

This rich, luxurious dish is perfect for entertaining. If the pastry starts to become too brown during baking, cover loosely with a sheet of foil.

Serves 6

Ingredients

1 piece of beef fillet, approx. 1kg (2¼lb), cut from the thick end, trimmed of fat
salt and freshly ground black pepper
2 tbsp sunflower oil
500g (1lb 2oz) puff pastry, or use shop-bought butter puff pastry
beaten egg, for glazing

For the mushroom duxelles

45g (1½oz) unsalted butter
2 shallots, finely chopped
1 garlic clove, crushed
250g (9oz) mixed wild mushrooms, finely chopped
1 tbsp brandy or Madeira

To serve

new potatoes
green vegetables, such as asparagus
home-made or ready-made gravy

1 Preheat the oven to 220°C (425°F/Gas 7). Season the beef with salt and pepper. Heat the oil in a large frying pan and fry the beef until browned all over. Transfer to a roasting tin and roast for 10 minutes. Remove and leave to cool.

2 Make the duxelles (see the technique below). Roll out one-third of the pastry to a rectangle about 5cm (2in) larger than the beef. Place it on a baking sheet and prick all over with a fork. Bake for 12–15 minutes or until crisp. Cool.

3 Spread one-third of the duxelles over the centre of the pastry. Set the beef fillet on top and spread the remaining duxelles over the meat. Roll out the remaining pastry and drape over the beef. Brush the edges with egg glaze and press to seal. Brush egg glaze all over the pastry case. Cut a slit in the top.

4 Bake for 30 minutes for rare beef or 45 minutes for well done. Remove from the oven and leave to rest for about 10 minutes before slicing with a very sharp knife to serve with the vegetables, new potatoes, and gravy.

Making mushroom duxelles

1 Melt the butter in a frying pan and fry the shallots and garlic, stirring, for 2–3 minutes or until soft. Add the mushrooms.

2 Cook, stirring, for 4–5 minutes or until the juices have evaporated. Add the brandy or Madeira and bubble for 30 seconds. Cool before using.

| 1 hr 45 mins | frying 5 mins | roasting 10 mins | cooking 10 mins | blind baking 15 mins | preparation 10 mins | baking 45 mins | standing 10 mins |

Roast Leg of Pork

This recipe is easy to adapt for a cooked ham or gammon on the bone (bake for 1 hour only). The pork is also excellent cold.

Serves 8–10

Ingredients

1 leg of pork, from the bone end, approx. 4.5kg (10lb)
8 oranges
1 tbsp Dijon mustard
180g (6oz) dark soft brown sugar
approx. 20 cloves

For the sauce
4 tbsp Grand Marnier
½ tsp grated nutmeg
½ tsp ground cloves

1 Preheat the oven to 180°C (350°F/Gas 4). Wipe the pork with kitchen paper, then set it in a roasting tin. Squeeze the juice from 6 of the oranges. Pour some of the juice over the pork and roast for 3–3½ hours; pour more orange juice over the joint every 30 minutes to keep it moist.

2 To test if the pork is cooked, insert a metal skewer near the centre of the leg and leave it for 30 seconds; it should be warm to the touch when withdrawn. To test accurately, insert a meat thermometer, which should register 77°C (170°F). Remove the pork from the oven and discard the skin as shown below. Increase the oven temperature to 200°C (400°F/Gas 6).

3 Slice the remaining oranges, discarding any pips. Mix the mustard and sugar together and spread over the joint. Overlap the orange slices on top. Stud each slice with a clove. Roast for 30–45 minutes, basting every 10 minutes with the juices in the tin. Transfer the pork to a warmed serving platter, cover with foil, and keep warm.

4 Pour the Grand Marnier into the roasting tin. Bring to the boil, whisking to dissolve the juices. Stir in the nutmeg and cloves. Transfer to a warmed sauce boat. Lift the orange slices from the pork, then carve it. Serve the pork with the orange slices and sauce.

Removing the skin

Take the pork from the oven and allow it to cool slightly. Then cut through the skin around the bone end of the joint. Use the knife to peel the skin from the fat layer beneath, starting from the wider end of the joint.

4 hrs 40 mins

preparation	roasting
25 mins	4 hrs 15 mins

Roast Pork Belly with Caramelized Apples

Pork belly is a fatty cut, but the thick layer of fat keeps the meat moist during roasting. Score the skin well for great crackling.

Serves 4

Ingredients

1 pork belly joint, approx. 900g (2lb)
salt
3 onions, halved
sherry, white wine, cider, or beer, for the gravy
thyme sprigs, to garnish (optional)

For the marinade

6 garlic cloves, peeled
½ tsp salt
½ tsp fennel or dill seed
5 juniper berries
8 white or black peppercorns
1 tsp wholegrain mustard

For the apples

75g (2½oz) butter
4 dessert apples, peeled, sliced, and tossed in lemon juice
3 tbsp golden caster sugar
a little lemon juice, cider, cider vinegar, white wine, sparkling wine, ale, lager, stock, or water, for the sauce

1 Crush the first five marinade ingredients in a pestle and mortar to make a smooth paste, then add the mustard. Score the skin and underside of the pork belly and trim off excess fat and sinew. Rub the paste all over. Rub the skin side of the joint with salt. Leave to marinate for 30 minutes.

2 Preheat the oven to 240°C (475°F/Gas 9), or its highest setting. Wipe the liquid and any excess salt from the pork joint. Arrange the onions, cut-side down, in a roasting tin and set the pork on top, skin-side up. Pour 1cm (½in) water into the tin and place in the oven. Roast for 40–45 minutes or until the pork skin is crisp and bubbly.

3 Turn the oven temperature down to 150°C (300°F/Gas 2) and roast for a further 30–45 minutes or until the pork is cooked through. During roasting, top up the water in the tin if necessary. Remove the pork from the oven, transfer to a carving board, and leave to rest, uncovered.

4 Meanwhile, melt the butter in a large frying pan. Add the apples and sprinkle over the sugar. Cook until the slices are golden brown on both sides. Sprinkle with a good squeeze of lemon or other liquid and stir well to create a little sauce. Remove from the heat and keep warm.

5 Pour off any fat from the roasting tin, leaving the onions, cooked-on bits, and liquid. Add a good splash of sherry, white wine, cider, or beer and simmer, stirring to deglaze the tin, for 3–4 minutes. Strain the gravy into a jug.

6 Carve the pork into thick "fingers" and place on warmed plates. Add the caramelized apples and their sauce. Garnish with thyme, if you like, and serve with the gravy.

2 hrs 30 mins

preparation	marinating	roasting	cooking	to serve
10 mins	30 mins	1 hr 30 mins	10 mins	10 mins

Glazed Gammon

A joint of gammon makes a good Sunday lunch for the family. You can glaze and roast a ready-cooked gammon or ham joint in the same way.

Serves 4–6

Ingredients

1 boneless unsmoked gammon
    joint, approx. 1.8kg (4lb)
500ml (16fl oz) dry cider
2 bay leaves
3 tbsp orange marmalade
1 tbsp soft brown sugar
1.1kg (2½lb) new potatoes,
    large ones halved
1 tbsp olive oil
grated zest of 1 orange
salt and freshly ground
    black pepper
4 heads of chicory, trimmed
    and quartered lengthways

1 Place the gammon joint in a large pan, add the cider and bay leaves, and pour in enough hot water to immerse the joint in liquid. Put the lid on and bring to the boil, then reduce to a simmer and cook for 40 minutes.

2 Preheat the oven to 180°C (350°F/Gas 4). Remove the gammon from the pan (discard the cooking liquid) and carefully peel away the outer skin, leaving a layer of fat. Score the fat, then glaze (as shown below). Place the gammon in a roasting tin. Toss the potatoes with the oil, orange zest, and some salt and pepper, then add to the tin.

3 Place in the oven to roast for 40 minutes. Add the chicory to the tin and toss with the potatoes and the juices in the tin, then roast for a further 20 minutes.

4 Remove the gammon from the tin and leave to rest in a warm place for at least 15 minutes. Slice the gammon and serve with the potatoes and chicory.

Glazing gammon

1 Using a sharp knife, score the fat down to the meat in a diamond pattern. This will allow the glaze to penetrate and flavour the meat.

2 Warm the marmalade gently in a small pan to melt it, then spread evenly over the scored fat. Sprinkle over the brown sugar.

2 hrs 10 mins

preparation	cooking	roasting	standing
15 mins	40 mins	1 hr	15 mins

Toad in the Hole

Ideal comfort food, this dish is perfect as it is, but can easily be varied by adding sliced onions to the sausages or herbs to the batter.

Serves 4

Ingredients
125g (4½oz) plain flour
pinch of salt
2 eggs
300ml (10fl oz) milk
2 tbsp vegetable oil
8 Toulouse or other sausages
(see below)

1 To make the batter, put the flour into a bowl with the salt, make a well in the centre, and add the eggs with a little of the milk. Whisk together, gradually incorporating the flour. Add the remaining milk and whisk until smooth. Leave the batter to rest for at least 30 minutes.

2 Preheat the oven to 220°C (425°F/Gas 7). Pour the oil into a roasting tin or shallow baking dish large enough to hold the sausages in one layer, with plenty of space between and around them. Add the sausages and toss them in the oil. Place the tin in the oven and cook for 5–10 minutes or until the sausages are starting to brown.

3 Reduce the oven temperature to 200°C (400°F/Gas 6). Carefully pour the batter around the sausages, then return the tin to the oven and cook for a further 30 minutes or until the batter is risen, golden, and crisp. Serve hot.

Choosing your sausages
Fresh pork sausages are traditional for this dish, although you can use beef or venison, if you prefer. Toulouse pork sausages have a coarser texture than others such as Cumberland. The choice is up to you, but remember that the higher the meat content, the better the flavour of the sausage.

1 hr 30 mins

preparation	resting	baking
20 mins	30 mins	40 mins

Liver and Bacon with Onions

Quick to cook, tender calves' liver is delicious with salty bacon in a buttery vermouth sauce. Take care not to overcook the liver.

Serves 4

Ingredients

350g (12oz) calves' liver
200g (7oz) sweet-cured, thin-cut, smoked streaky bacon rashers
1 tbsp olive oil
25g (scant 1oz) unsalted butter
4 shallots, thinly sliced
120ml (4fl oz) vermouth
1 tsp Dijon mustard
dash of mushroom ketchup or Worcestershire sauce (optional)
salt and freshly ground black pepper

To serve

mashed potatoes
green vegetable, such as French beans

1 Cut the liver and the bacon rashers into strips about 6cm (2½in) long and 1.5cm (¾in) wide. Set aside.

2 Heat half the oil with half the butter in a frying pan over medium heat. Add the shallots and fry, stirring frequently, for 5 minutes or until soft and golden. Remove from the pan with a slotted spoon and reserve.

3 Add the remaining oil and butter to the pan and increase the heat to high. When the fat is hot, add the liver and bacon and stir-fry for 3–4 minutes or until the liver is well browned but still slightly pink inside.

4 Return the shallots to the pan. Pour in the vermouth and let it bubble for 1–2 minutes, stirring and scraping any bits stuck to the bottom of the pan.

5 Reduce the heat to medium and stir in the mustard and the mushroom ketchup (if using). Season with salt and pepper to taste and serve at once with mashed potatoes and a green vegetable, such as French beans.

Frying with butter

Butter is excellent for quick frying methods, giving a golden brown colour and good flavour. However, the milk solids in butter will turn brown when it gets very hot; if it gets too hot these will burn and blacken. If you want to use butter for frying at very high heat, clarify it first by heating gently, to remove the milk solids.

20 mins

preparation
10 mins

cooking
10 mins

Szechuan Spare Ribs

Spare ribs need slow cooking. These are first browned in chilli-flavoured oil, then simmered until tender, and finally coated in a delectable sauce.

Serves 6

Ingredients

4 tbsp dark soy sauce
4 tbsp cider vinegar
3 tbsp honey
1 tbsp toasted sesame oil
1 tsp chilli paste
4 tbsp dry sherry
4 tbsp vegetable oil
1 dried red chilli
1.4kg (3lb) meaty pork
  spare ribs

1 In a small bowl, whisk together the soy sauce, cider vinegar, honey, sesame oil, chilli paste, and sherry. Cover tightly with cling film and set the sauce mixture aside.

2 Heat the vegetable oil in a wok, add the chilli, and cook for 1 minute or until dark brown. Add 3–4 spare ribs and stir over high heat for 2–3 minutes or until browned on all sides. Transfer to a plate. Brown the remaining ribs in the same way, working in small batches.

3 Pour off all but 2 tbsp oil from the wok. Return the ribs to the wok, pour in enough water to cover, and bring to the boil. Reduce the heat and cover the wok. Leave to simmer for about 1 hour, stirring occasionally. The ribs are cooked when the meat shrinks slightly on the bone and feels tender to the tip of a knife.

4 Remove the chilli and discard. Pour the sauce mixture into the wok and stir well to mix. Simmer uncovered, stirring occasionally, for 25–30 minutes or until the liquid has reduced to a thick brown sauce and the ribs are glazed with the sauce. If the sauce isn't thick enough, remove the ribs and reduce the sauce further by boiling fast. Serve the ribs on a warmed platter, coated with the sauce.

On the barbecue
If you want to give the ribs a smoky flavour, you can finish them on the barbecue. Make a charcoal fire and allow it to burn down to medium heat. Place the glazed ribs on the barbecue grid and cook for 3–5 minutes, turning and brushing them with the sauce.

1 hr 50 mins

preparation
20 mins

cooking
1 hr 30 mins

Pork Pies

These little pies are great picnic food. "Hot water" pastry must be used warm, as soon as it is made, because it will harden as it cools.

Makes 12

Ingredients

200g (7oz) pork belly, trimmed of fat and skin, diced
200g (7oz) pork shoulder, trimmed and diced
50g (1¾oz) unsmoked back or streaky bacon, trimmed and diced
10 sage leaves, finely chopped
¼ tsp grated nutmeg
¼ tsp ground allspice
salt and freshly ground black pepper

For the hot water pastry

400g (14oz) plain flour, plus extra for sprinkling
½ tsp salt
150g (5½oz) lard or beef dripping, diced
1 egg, beaten, for glazing

1 Preheat the oven to 200°C (400°F/Gas 6). Put the pork belly, shoulder, bacon, sage, spices, and some seasoning into a food processor. Process until the meat is quite finely chopped, but not mushy. Set aside.

2 To make the hot water pastry, put the flour and salt in a bowl and make a well in the centre. Measure 150ml (5fl oz) boiling water, add the lard, and stir until the fat has melted. Pour the mixture into the well in the flour and start mixing with a wooden spoon. Then use your hands to bring it all together to make a soft dough. Cut off a quarter of the dough, wrap it in a clean tea towel, and keep warm.

3 Working quickly, turn out the rest of the dough onto a well-floured work surface and roll out to 5mm (¼in) thick. Cut out 12 circles big enough to line the holes in a muffin tray; the pastry should hang over the edges slightly. Pack the pork filling into the pastry cases. Brush a little beaten egg around the top edge of each.

4 Roll out the reserved dough. Cut out 12 lids to fit the pastry cases. Set them in place and press the edges to seal. Brush the lids with beaten egg. Use a chopstick or similar implement to make a hole in the centre of each lid, or make two slits, to allow the steam to escape during baking.

5 Bake the pies for 30 minutes, then reduce the oven temperature to 160°C (325°F/Gas 3). Bake for a further 30 minutes or until golden brown. Remove from the oven and leave to cool in the muffin tray for 10 minutes before turning out. The pies can be eaten hot or cold.

1 hr 50 mins

preparation	baking	cooling	chilling (optional)
40 mins	1 hr	10 mins	overnight

Macaroni Cheese

Here's an interesting take on the old favourite, using penne with garlicky mushrooms. Gruyère or Emmental cheese can replace the Cheddar.

Serves 6

Ingredients
15g (½oz) butter, plus extra
   for greasing
3 shallots, finely chopped
3 garlic cloves, finely chopped
125g (4½oz) mixed wild
   mushrooms, sliced
125g (4½oz) chestnut or
   button mushrooms, sliced
salt and freshly ground
   black pepper
375g (13oz) penne pasta

For the topping and sauce
2 slices of white bread,
   crusts removed
small bunch of chives, snipped
250g (9oz) mature Cheddar
   cheese, grated
1 litre (1¾ pints) milk
6 black peppercorns
1 slice of onion
1 bay leaf
30g (1oz) butter
2 tbsp plain flour
pinch of grated nutmeg

1 Melt the butter in a sauté pan, add the shallots, and stir for 1 minute until soft. Add the garlic, mushrooms, and some salt and pepper. Cook, stirring, for 3–5 minutes or until all the liquid has evaporated and the mushrooms are tender. Remove from the heat and set aside.

2 To make the topping, blitz the bread in a food processor or blender to form coarse crumbs. Combine with about a quarter of the chives and 30g (1oz) of the cheese. Set aside.

3 Heat the milk in a saucepan with the peppercorns, onion slice, and bay leaf until bubbles appear around the edge. Remove from the heat and leave to infuse for 10 minutes.

4 Melt the butter in another saucepan and whisk in the flour. Remove from the heat and strain in two-thirds of the warm milk. Return to the heat and whisk until the sauce boils. Add the grated nutmeg and season well, then simmer for 2 minutes. Remove from the heat, add the remaining cheese and milk, and stir until smooth. Check the seasoning.

5 Preheat the oven to 180°C (350°F/Gas 4). Fill a large pan with water, bring to the boil, and add 1 tbsp salt. Add the pasta and simmer for 5–7 minutes (or according to the packet instructions) until al dente. Drain. Butter a 2 litre (3½ pint) baking dish. Mix the pasta with the sauce, mushrooms, and remaining chives. Spoon into the dish and sprinkle over the topping. Bake for 25–30 minutes or until bubbling and golden.

⚠ Rescue it!

If you add the grated cheese to the sauce while it is on the heat, or reheat the sauce after the cheese has been added, the cheese might get too hot and become stringy or leak melted fat. If this happens, try stirring in a squeeze of lemon juice or a spoonful of white wine.

1 hr
5 mins

preparation
35 mins

cooking
30 mins

Cheese and Courgette Soufflés

A soufflé base can be prepared well ahead. Warm it gently and fold in the stiffly whisked egg whites just before baking.

Serves 6

Ingredients

60g (2oz) unsalted butter, plus extra for greasing
2 shallots, finely chopped
500g (1lb 2oz) courgettes, coarsely grated
salt and freshly ground black pepper
20g (¾oz) plain flour
175ml (6fl oz) hot milk
120ml (4fl oz) double cream
pinch of grated nutmeg
4 eggs, separated, plus 2 egg whites
90g (3oz) Cheddar cheese, coarsely grated

1 Preheat the oven to 190°C (375°F/Gas 5). Grease six 350ml (12fl oz) ramekins with butter. Melt half the butter in a frying pan and cook the shallots for about 2 minutes or until soft. Add the courgettes, season, and cook, stirring, for 3–5 minutes or until just tender. Drain in a sieve.

2 Melt the remaining butter in a medium saucepan, add the flour, and cook, whisking, for 30–60 seconds or until the mixture starts to foam. Remove from the heat and slowly whisk in the hot milk. Return to the heat and bring to the boil, still whisking. When the sauce thickens, whisk in the cream. Season with the nutmeg and some salt and pepper. Simmer for 2 minutes. Remove from the heat and whisk in the egg yolks. Stir in the Cheddar, shallots, and courgettes.

3 Whisk the egg whites with a pinch of salt until stiff peaks form. Stir about a quarter into the warm base, then gently fold this into the remaining whites. Spoon into the prepared dishes and bake for 10–15 minutes or until puffed and brown. Serve immediately.

Separating eggs

1 Crack the shell, then hold the egg over a bowl, insert your fingers into the break, and gently pry the two halves apart.

2 Gently shift the yolk back and forth between the shell halves, keeping the yolk intact and allowing the white to fall into the bowl.

1 hr 5 mins

preparation
35 mins

cooking
30 mins

Feta Filo Pie

Crisp pastry encases a delicious blend of spinach, feta, and pine nuts.
Filo dries out easily, becoming brittle, so keep it covered while you work.

Serves 6

Ingredients

900g (2lb) fresh spinach leaves,
  washed and shaken dry
100g (3½oz) unsalted butter
2 red onions, finely chopped
1 tsp ground cumin
1 tsp ground coriander
1 tsp ground cinnamon
60g (2oz) dried apricots, chopped
60g (2oz) pine nuts, toasted
6 sheets filo pastry, 40 x 30cm
  (16 x 12in), thawed if frozen
sea salt and freshly ground
  black pepper
300g (10oz) feta cheese,
  crumbled

1 Pack the spinach into a large saucepan, cover, and cook over medium heat, turning occasionally, for 8–10 minutes or until just wilted. Drain well. When cool, squeeze handfuls to remove excess water. Chop finely and set aside.

2 Melt 25g (scant 1oz) of the butter in a small frying pan and gently fry the onions with the spices, stirring occasionally, for 7–8 minutes or until softened. Stir in the apricots and pine nuts, then set aside to cool slightly.

3 Preheat the oven to 200°C (400°F/Gas 6). Line a 20cm (8in) springform cake tin with filo (as below). Stir the spinach into the onion mixture and season to taste. Spread half in the pastry case, sprinkle over the feta, and add the remaining spinach mixture. Piece by piece, fold the pastry over the spinach, buttering each piece as you go. Brush the top with any remaining butter. Set the tin on a baking tray.

4 Bake for 35–40 minutes or until crisp and golden. Cool for 10 minutes, then turn out and cut into wedges.

Lining the tin with filo

1 Melt the remaining butter. Brush over the bottom and sides of the tin, line the bottom with baking parchment, and butter the paper.

2 Drape a sheet of filo in the tin, leaving the ends hanging over the edge. Butter the pastry. Layer in 5 more sheets, buttering each.

1 hr 20 mins

preparation	baking	cooling
30 mins	40 mins	10 mins

Courgette, Broad Bean, and Pea Quiches

Little pastry cases can be baked blind without a paper lining and beans to weigh them, as long as you prick them well with a fork.

Serves 6

Ingredients

200g (7oz) plain flour, plus extra
  for dusting
100g (3½oz) unsalted butter,
  cut into pieces, plus extra
  for greasing
1 egg yolk
40g (1¼oz) Parmesan cheese,
  grated
salt and freshly ground
  black pepper
milk, if needed

For the filling

675g (1½lb) fresh young
  broad beans, shelled,
  or 225g (8oz) frozen
  broad beans
400g (14oz) fresh peas, shelled,
  or 125g (4½oz) frozen peas
200g (7oz) courgettes, cut into
  1cm (½in) cubes
6 egg yolks
150ml (5fl oz) double cream
1 tbsp chopped mint
pinch of grated nutmeg

1 Preheat the oven to 180°C (350°F/Gas 4). Put the flour into a food processor and with the motor running, drop the pieces of butter, one by one, through the feed tube. As soon as all the butter has been mixed into the flour, add the egg yolk, Parmesan, and some salt and pepper. Blitz briefly to mix. If necessary, add a bit of milk to bring the ingredients together to make a pastry dough. Wrap in cling film and chill in the refrigerator for at least 30 minutes or until needed.

2 Bring a saucepan of water to the boil. Add the fresh broad beans and blanch for 3 minutes. Drain and rinse under cold, running water, then pop the beans out of their skins. Fill the saucepan with water again, bring to the boil, and blanch the fresh peas for 2–3 minutes; drain. (If using frozen broad beans and peas, cook them according to the packet instructions.) Set aside.

3 Grease six mini tart tins, 10cm (4in) in diameter and 4cm (2in) deep, with butter, then dust with flour. Roll out the pastry on a lightly floured surface, cut out rounds, and use to line the tins, pressing well into the corners and the flutes. Trim the pastry level with the top of the tin. Chill in the refrigerator for 10 minutes.

4 Pick the pastry cases all over with a fork, then set them on a baking tray. Bake "blind" for 8 minutes (see p272) or until the pastry is set and starting to brown. Allow to cool, then fill with the broad beans, peas, and courgettes.

5 Mix together the egg yolks and cream. Add the chopped mint, nutmeg, and some salt and pepper. Pour the mixture into the pastry cases, filling right up to the top. Bake for about 25 minutes or until the filling is just set. Leave to stand for 5 minutes before serving.

 1 hr 33 mins

	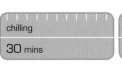		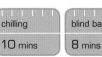		

preparation	chilling	boiling	chilling	blind baking	baking	standing
10 mins	30 mins	5 mins	10 mins	8 mins	25 mins	5 mins

Spanish Omelette

If you have an ovenproof frying pan, you can slide it under a hot grill to brown the top rather than turning the omelette over.

Serves 4

Ingredients

115g (4oz) frozen peas
6 tbsp olive oil
350g (12oz) floury potatoes,
  such as King Edward, peeled
  and cut into 2cm (¾in) cubes
2 small red onions, finely chopped
2 peppers (1 red and 1 green),
  deseeded and diced
30g (1oz) chorizo, diced
6 eggs
salt and freshly ground
  black pepper

1 Cook the peas in a pan of boiling water according to the packet directions. Drain and set aside.

2 Heat 4 tbsp of the oil in a large non-stick frying pan over medium heat. Add the potatoes, onions, and peppers and cook, stirring often, for 10 minutes. Add the chorizo and continue cooking, stirring well, for 5–10 minutes or until the potatoes are tender.

3 Lightly beat the eggs in a large bowl. Season with salt and pepper. Use a slotted spoon to transfer the potato mixture to the eggs. Add the peas and gently stir to mix.

4 Pour off the oil from the pan and wipe with kitchen paper to remove any crisp bits stuck on the bottom. Add the remaining oil to the pan and heat. Pour in the egg mixture, reduce the heat to low, and smooth the surface. Leave to cook for 10–15 minutes or until the omelette is beginning to set and the base is golden brown.

5 Carefully slide the omelette onto a plate. Place a second plate, upside down, on top and turn them over together, then slide the tortilla back into the pan. Cook for a further 5 minutes or until the other side is golden brown.

6 Leave the omelette to settle for at least 5 minutes before serving, warm or cold, cut in wedges.

1 hr 5 mins

preparation	cooking
20 mins	45 mins

Chilli and Tofu Stir-fry

Keep the heat under the wok high so the tofu and all the vegetables fry quickly, and stir and toss them constantly so they cook evenly.

Serves 4

Ingredients

2 tbsp sunflower oil
85g (3oz) unsalted cashew nuts
300g (10oz) firm tofu, diced
1 red onion, thinly sliced
2 carrots, thinly sliced
1 red pepper, deseeded and
  chopped
1 celery stick, chopped
4 chestnut mushrooms, sliced
175g (6oz) bean sprouts
2 tsp chilli sauce
2 tbsp light soy sauce
1 tsp cornflour
175ml (6fl oz) vegetable stock
basmati or sticky rice, to serve

1 Heat the oil in a wok and add the cashews. Stir-fry for 30 seconds or until lightly browned. Remove the cashews from the wok with a slotted spoon and set aside.

2 Add the tofu to the wok and stir-fry until golden brown. Remove and set aside. Stir-fry the onion and carrots for 5 minutes, then add the red pepper, celery, and mushrooms and stir-fry for a further 3–4 minutes. Finally, add the bean sprouts and stir-fry for 2 minutes.

3 Return the cashews and tofu to the wok and drizzle in the chilli sauce. In a small bowl, mix the soy sauce with the cornflour, then pour into the wok together with the stock. Toss over the heat for 2–3 minutes or until the sauce is bubbling. Serve immediately, with basmati or sticky rice.

Stir-frying
To ensure that all the elements of a stir-fry will be ready at the same time, cut the ingredients into pieces about the same size, and add those that need the longest cooking time to the wok or pan first. For example, carrots need longer than peppers.

25 mins

preparation
10 mins

cooking
15 mins

Spaghetti Bolognese

When browning the minced meat for the sauce, use a brisk heat and stir frequently with a wooden spoon or spatula to break up any lumps.

Serves 4

Ingredients
450g (1lb) spaghetti
grated Parmesan cheese,
   to serve

For the sauce
30g (1oz) butter
2 tbsp olive oil
100g (3½oz) pancetta cubes
1 small onion, finely chopped
1 celery stick, finely chopped
1 carrot, finely chopped
2 garlic cloves, crushed
200g (7oz) lean minced pork
200g (7oz) lean minced beef
100ml (3½fl oz) beef stock, plus
   extra if needed
2 tbsp tomato purée
400g can chopped tomatoes
salt and freshly ground
   black pepper
75ml (2½fl oz) milk, warmed

1 Melt the butter with the olive oil in a deep, heavy-based saucepan and fry the pancetta for 1–2 minutes. Add the onion, celery, carrot, and garlic and continue to fry, stirring occasionally, for 10 minutes or until softened but not browned.

2 Add the pork and beef and cook, stirring frequently, for 10 minutes or until it is crumbly and evenly coloured. Stir in the stock, tomato purée, and tomatoes. Season with salt and pepper to taste.

3 Bring to a simmer, then reduce the heat to very low, cover the pan, and cook gently for 1½ hours. Stir occasionally to prevent sticking, and add more stock if needed. Stir the milk into the sauce and simmer, covered, for a further 30 minutes. When the sauce has finished cooking, check the seasoning.

4 Bring a large pan of water to a rolling boil. Add a generous seasoning of salt and then the spaghetti, bending the strands as they soften to fit in the pan. Stir once, then cook for 8–10 minutes (or according to the instructions on the packet) until al dente. Drain well.

5 Divide among heated soup plates, forming the spaghetti into a nest if you like, and spoon the sauce into the centre. Serve with freshly grated Parmesan cheese.

Cooking dried spaghetti
Dried spaghetti is cooked until "al dente", which means it should offer a slight resistance when you bite it. The instructions on the packet are a good guide – start the timing when the water comes back to the boil and test pasta texture near the end of the suggested time.

3 hrs

preparation	frying	cooking		boiling
15 mins	15 mins	2 hrs 15 mins		15 mins

Crab Ravioli

You can use a machine to stretch and roll out pasta dough, but it is satisfying to do it by hand with a rolling pin. You just need patience.

Serves 4

Ingredients

200g (7oz) Italian "00" flour
pinch of salt
2 eggs, beaten, plus extra
    beaten egg for brushing
1 tbsp olive oil, plus extra
    for greasing
melted butter or olive oil,
    for drizzling

For the filling

175g (6oz) white crabmeat
1 red onion, finely chopped
1 spring onion, finely chopped
1 red chilli, or to taste,
    deseeded and finely chopped
salt and freshly ground
    black pepper

1 Sift the flour and salt onto a work surface, make a well in the centre, and pour the eggs and oil into it. Using your fingertips, draw the flour into the eggs, gradually incorporating all the flour to form a sticky dough. Knead for 10 minutes or until the dough is smooth and elastic. Wrap in oiled cling film and leave to rest for 30 minutes.

2 To make the filling, place all the ingredients in a bowl and mix together until thoroughly combined. Taste to check the seasoning, adding more salt and pepper if needed.

3 Divide the pasta dough in half and roll each piece with a pasta machine (or using a rolling pin) to a rectangular sheet about 3mm (⅛in) thick. Lay one sheet on the work surface; keep the other sheet covered with a tea towel to prevent it from drying out.

4 Place teaspoonfuls of the filling in rows of small mounds on the sheet of pasta, spacing the mounds 4cm (1½in) apart. Brush a little beaten egg around the mounds, then place the second sheet of pasta on top. Press the pasta down around the mounds with your fingertips to seal, pushing out any trapped air as you go.

5 Cut between the mounds using a pasta wheel or sharp knife to divide the stuffed pasta into squares. Place on a floured tea towel and leave to dry for 1 hour.

6 Bring a large pan of salted water to the boil. Add the ravioli, in batches, and cook for 4–5 minutes or until they float to the surface. Remove with a slotted spoon. When all are cooked, serve them hot, drizzled with melted butter or olive oil and sprinkled with pepper.

| 1 hr | preparation 15 mins | resting 30 mins | cooking 15 mins |

Cannelloni

When pouring over the béchamel sauce, don't leave any pasta uncovered or it won't soften and cook evenly in the oven.

Serves 4

Ingredients

450g (1lb) spinach, washed
   and shaken dry
250g (9oz) ricotta cheese
1 egg, beaten
60g (2oz) Parmesan cheese,
   grated
pinch of grated nutmeg
16 dried cannelloni tubes
olive oil for greasing
1 quantity béchamel sauce
   (see Building Blocks, p50)

For the Napoli sauce

1 tbsp extra virgin olive oil
1 small red onion, finely chopped
1 celery stick, finely chopped
2 garlic cloves, crushed
400g can chopped tomatoes
75ml (2½fl oz) vegetable stock
handful of basil leaves, torn
salt and freshly ground
   black pepper

1 First make the Napoli sauce. Heat the oil in a saucepan and cook the onion, stirring occasionally, for 5–6 minutes or until beginning to soften. Add the celery and garlic and cook for 2 minutes, then stir in the tomatoes and stock. Bring to the boil, then simmer for 15 minutes or until the sauce has reduced a little. Stir in the basil and season with salt and pepper to taste.

2 While the sauce is simmering, put the spinach into a large pan, cover, and cook gently, shaking the pan occasionally, until the spinach has wilted. Drain well in a colander, pressing out as much liquid as possible, then chop roughly. Put the ricotta in a bowl and mix in the beaten egg and half the Parmesan. Add the spinach and season with the nutmeg and some salt and pepper.

3 Preheat the oven to 190°C (375°F/Gas 5). Spoon or pipe the filling into the cannelloni tubes and arrange them in one layer in a lightly oiled baking dish. Pour the béchamel sauce over the cannelloni to cover them completely, then spoon the Napoli sauce evenly on top. Sprinkle over the remaining Parmesan. Bake for 35 minutes or until golden and bubbling. Serve hot.

Preparing spinach

Spinach tends to trap a lot of soil, so the leaves need thorough washing. Immerse the spinach in several changes of cold water to clean it, then drain in a colander and pat dry in a tea towel or with kitchen paper. Fold large leaves in half and pull off the central rib and stalk. The spinach is now ready to eat raw or to cook.

1 hr

preparation	cooking
25 mins	35 mins

Pasta with Rocket Pesto

Pesto is traditionally made with basil, but rocket is a good substitute or addition, giving the pesto a fresh peppery flavour.

Serves 4

Ingredients

500g (1lb 2oz) tagliatelle
  or pappardelle
grated Parmesan cheese,
  to serve

For the rocket pesto

50g (1¾oz) pine nuts
50g (1¾oz) rocket leaves
10g (¼oz) basil leaves
  (optional)
30g (1oz) Parmesan cheese,
  grated
1–2 garlic cloves, crushed
100ml (3½fl oz) extra virgin
  olive oil
salt and freshly ground
  black pepper

1 First, toast the pine nuts for the pesto. Put the nuts in a small frying pan and gently toast over low heat for 2–3 minutes, stirring frequently, until golden brown. Cool.

2 Make the rocket pesto (as shown below). This quantity may be more than you need. If so, keep the leftover pesto in an airtight container in the refrigerator for up to 5 days or in the freezer for up to 2 weeks.

3 Bring a large pot of water to the boil. Add a generous seasoning of salt, then drop in the pasta and stir to separate the strands. When the water returns to the boil, cook for 8–10 minutes or the time suggested on the packet, until al dente. Drain well and toss with as much pesto as you like. Serve immediately, with extra Parmesan for sprinkling.

Making pesto

1 Put the pine nuts, rocket and basil leaves (if using), Parmesan, garlic, and 2–3 tbsp oil into a food processor. Blitz to a thick paste.

2 With the motor running on a low speed, slowly add the rest of the oil through the feed tube. Season with salt and pepper to taste.

23 mins

preparation
10 mins

cooking
13 mins

Lasagne

You can use fresh or dried lasagne sheets. Dried sheets don't need to be pre-cooked, but a rinse with water first ensures they will soften.

Serves 8

Ingredients
6 tbsp olive oil
3 large onions, finely chopped
675g (1½lb) lean minced beef
3–6 garlic cloves, chopped
3 tbsp tomato purée
3 x 400g cans chopped
   tomatoes
2 tsp dried oregano
3 bay leaves
2 tbsp pesto
salt and freshly ground
   black pepper
50g (1¾oz) butter
3 heaped tbsp plain flour
1 litre (1¾pints) hot milk
300g (10oz) Cheddar cheese,
   grated
450g (1lb) lasagne sheets

1 Heat the olive oil in a large, heavy-based saucepan over medium heat, add the onions, and cook, stirring occasionally, for 5 minutes or until starting to soften. Add the beef and cook, stirring constantly, for 5 minutes or until broken up and no longer pink. Add the garlic and cook for 1 minute, then stir in the tomato purée, tomatoes, oregano, and bay leaves. Bring to the boil, then reduce the heat and simmer for 20 minutes. Stir in 1 tbsp pesto and season well with salt and pepper. Remove from the heat and set aside.

2 Melt the butter in a saucepan over low heat, whisk in the flour, and cook until the mixture starts to foam. Remove from the heat and slowly whisk in the hot milk. Return to the heat and bring to the boil, still whisking. Reduce the heat and simmer for 2 minutes or until thickened. Remove from the heat and stir in the Cheddar cheese, then season with salt and pepper to taste.

3 Preheat the oven to 180°C (350°F/Gas 4). Pour a 1cm (½in) layer of the beef sauce over the bottom of a large baking dish. Cover with a layer of lasagne sheets. Add another 1cm (½in) layer of beef sauce, followed by a small amount of the cheese sauce. Top with a layer of lasagne sheets. Repeat the layering until all the meat sauce and lasagne sheets have been used up, finishing with an even 5mm (¼in) layer of cheese sauce on top.

4 Drizzle the remaining pesto over the cheese sauce. Place in the oven and bake for 35–40 minutes or until golden brown and bubbling. Remove from the oven and leave the lasagne to settle for 10 minutes before serving.

1 hr 30 mins	cooking	preparation	baking
	45 mins	5 mins plus cooling	40 mins plus resting

Risotto Primavera

A risotto is simple to make. Just keep it bubbling merrily and stir as often as you can to achieve the desired creamy texture.

Serves 4

Ingredients

2 tbsp olive oil
50g (1¾oz) butter
1 onion, finely chopped
salt and freshly ground
    black pepper
3 garlic cloves, finely chopped
300g (10oz) risotto rice, such
    as arborio or carnaroli
250ml (8fl oz) white wine
900ml (1½ pints) hot vegetable
    or chicken stock
125g (4½oz) shelled fresh or
    frozen broad beans
bunch of asparagus spears,
    trimmed and cut into
    bite-sized pieces
2 small courgettes, diced
30g (1oz) Parmesan cheese,
    grated, plus extra for serving

1 Heat half the oil and butter in a large, heavy-based pan over medium heat. Add the onion and cook, stirring occasionally, for 3–4 minutes or until soft. Season with salt and pepper, then add the garlic and cook for 1 minute.

2 Add the rice to the pan and make the risotto (see the technique below). Meanwhile, drop the broad beans into a large pan of boiling salted water and cook for 3–4 minutes or until just tender; drain well. If using fresh broad beans, slip them out of their skins and blanch for 3 minutes, as shown on p218. Set aside.

3 Heat the remaining oil in a frying pan over medium heat, add the asparagus and courgettes, and cook, stirring, for about 5 minutes or until just tender.

4 Add all the vegetables to the risotto with the remaining butter and stir in gently. Then stir in the Parmesan and check the seasoning. Serve with some extra Parmesan.

Cooking risotto rice

1 Stir the rice so all the grains are coated with fat. Increase the heat, add the wine, and allow to bubble for 1–2 minutes, stirring.

2 Add the hot stock, a ladleful at a time, and cook briskly, stirring well; wait for each ladleful to be absorbed before adding the next.

3 When all the stock has been added, the risotto will be creamy and the rice al dente. Total cooking time will be 30–40 minutes.

1 hr
15 mins

preparation	cooking
15 mins	1 hr

Paella

This is named after the wide, shallow pan in which it is traditionally cooked. The ingredients should form a relatively shallow layer in the pan.

Serves 8–10

Ingredients

2 large pinches of saffron
   threads
500g (1lb 2oz) raw, unpeeled
   king or tiger prawns
1kg (2¼lb) mussels
750g (1lb 10oz) skinless,
   boneless chicken thighs,
   cut into small chunks
salt and freshly ground
   black pepper
4 tbsp olive oil
250g (9oz) chorizo, cut
   into 1cm (½in) slices
2 large onions, finely chopped
2 red peppers, sliced
750g (1lb 10oz) paella or other
   short-grain rice
3 garlic cloves, finely chopped
2 x 400g cans chopped
   tomatoes
375g (13oz) French beans,
   cut into 1cm (½in) slices
1–2 tbsp chopped parsley,
   to garnish

1 Put 3–4 tbsp boiling water in a small bowl and sprinkle over the saffron threads. Leave to soak for 15 minutes.

2 Meanwhile, peel the prawns, leaving the end tail section intact. If the intestinal vein is dark, remove it (devein, see p145). Scrub the mussels well and remove the beards (see p142). Discard any mussels that have broken shells, or that do not close when tapped on the side of the kitchen sink.

3 Season the chicken pieces. Heat the oil in a 30–35cm (12–14in) paella pan, or other wide frying or sauté pan, and sauté the chicken, turning, for 10–12 minutes or until browned. Transfer to a plate. Add the chorizo to the pan and sauté for 1–2 minutes on each side or until browned. Transfer to the plate using a slotted spoon.

4 Add the onions and red pepper to the pan and cook, stirring occasionally, for 5–7 minutes or until softened. Stir in the rice and stir well for 2–3 minutes to coat all the grains with the flavoured oil.

5 Pour in 1.5 litres (2¾ pints) water and add the garlic, the saffron with its soaking liquid, and plenty of salt and pepper. Stir well. Push the chicken pieces down into the rice. Scatter the chorizo slices over, then add the tomatoes, French beans, prawns, and mussels.

6 Bring to the boil, then simmer, uncovered, for 25–30 minutes or until all the liquid has been absorbed and the rice is tender but still a bit firm. Do not stir during this time or the rice will become sticky. If the rice isn't cooked at the end of this time, add a little more water and simmer for a few more minutes.

7 Remove from the heat. Discard any mussels that have not opened, then cover the pan with a tea towel and leave the paella to settle for 5 minutes. Sprinkle with chopped parsley and serve.

1 hr
45 mins

preparation

1 hr

cooking

45 mins

Aubergine Massaman Curry

Checking the seasoning at the end of cooking is very important: taste and adjust the flavour with sugar or more fish sauce.

Serves 4–6

Ingredients

2 red chillies, deseeded

1 lemongrass stalk, tough outer leaves removed

5cm (2in) piece of fresh root ginger, roughly chopped

5 cardamom pods, crushed and seeds removed

1 tbsp sunflower oil

1 onion, finely chopped

salt and freshly ground black pepper

600ml (1 pint) hot vegetable stock

400ml can coconut milk

1 cinnamon stick, broken

splash of dark soy sauce

splash of fish sauce (nam pla)

4 potatoes, peeled and cut into bite-sized pieces

6 baby aubergines, halved lengthways, or 2 large aubergines, roughly chopped

400g (14oz) basmati rice, rinsed and drained

85g (3oz) roasted unsalted peanuts, roughly chopped

1 tbsp palm sugar or demerara sugar (optional)

lime wedges, to serve

1 Put the chillies, lemongrass, ginger, and cardamom seeds in a food processor with a drop of the sunflower oil. Blitz together to make a paste.

2 Heat the remaining oil in a large, heavy-based pan over medium heat, add the onion, and cook for 3–4 minutes or until soft. Add the paste with some seasoning and cook for a few more minutes. Stir in the stock and coconut milk and bring to the boil. Add the cinnamon stick, soy sauce, and fish sauce, then simmer gently for 20 minutes. Stir in the potatoes and aubergines and cook for a further 20 minutes.

3 Meanwhile, put the rice in a saucepan and add 600ml (1 pint) water and some salt. Bring to the boil, then cover and simmer for 10 minutes. Remove from the heat and leave, still covered, for 10 minutes. Fluff up with a fork.

4 Stir half the peanuts and the sugar, if using, into the curry. Ladle into warmed bowls and sprinkle with the remaining peanuts. Serve with the rice and lime wedges.

Deseeding chillies

1 Cut the chilli lengthways in half. Using the tip of your knife, scrape out the seeds and remove the membrane and stem.

2 To finely chop, flatten each half and cut lengthways into strips. Hold the strips together and cut across to make small equal-sized pieces.

1 hr 15 mins

preparation
15 mins

cooking
1 hr

Puy Lentils with Goat's Cheese

Small, grey-green Puy lentils are ideal for warm or cool salads because of the way they keep their shape and texture when cooked.

Serves 4

Ingredients

350g (12oz) Puy lentils, rinsed
1 carrot, diced
1 shallot or small onion, finely chopped
2 sprigs of thyme
1 bay leaf
175g (6oz) black olives, pitted and chopped
85g (3oz) goat's cheese, any rind removed, crumbled
2 tbsp extra virgin olive oil
salt and freshly ground black pepper
salad leaves, to serve (optional)

1 Place the lentils, carrot, shallot, thyme, and bay leaf in a saucepan with 1.2 litres (2 pints) of water. Bring to the boil, then simmer gently for 15–20 minutes or until the lentils are tender.

2 Drain the lentils well. Transfer to a serving bowl and remove the bay leaf and thyme sprigs. Add the olives, goat's cheese, and olive oil and stir together. Season with salt and pepper to taste. If you like, add a handful of salad leaves and toss through the lentils. Serve warm.

Cooking lentils

Because of their shape and thin shell, lentils cook more quickly than other pulses, and they do not need to be soaked before cooking. While most whole lentils tend to keep their shape after cooking, those that are split or very small will eventually break down and become mushy if cooked for an extended time.

30 mins

preparation
10 mins

cooking
20 mins

SALADS AND SIDES

Just because it's on the side doesn't mean it can be sidelined. Create bright, fresh-tasting salads and wonderfully cooked side dishes that will improve your cooking expertise.

Caesar Salad

Toss the salad ingredients with a piquant, tangy dressing. Success here depends on crisp lettuce and the best quality Parmesan cheese.

Serves 6–8

Ingredients

1 cos (romaine) lettuce, approx.
   1kg (2¼lb), torn into pieces
1 very fresh egg
125g (4½oz) Parmesan cheese,
   grated

For the garlic croûtons

½ day-old baguette
4 tbsp olive oil
3 garlic cloves, peeled

For the dressing

6 canned anchovy fillets
3 garlic cloves, finely chopped
1 tbsp Dijon mustard
juice of 1 lemon
freshly ground black pepper
175ml (6fl oz) olive oil

1 First make the garlic croûtons. Cut the baguette into 1cm (½ in) slices and then into cubes. Heat the oil in a large frying pan, add the garlic and bread cubes, and fry, stirring constantly, for 2–3 minutes or until golden. Tip the croûtons onto kitchen paper to drain off any excess oil. Discard the garlic.

2 Make the dressing in a large serving bowl as shown below. To assemble the salad, add the lettuce to the dressing and toss until well coated. Crack the egg into a small bowl and beat it with a fork, then add it to the dressed leaves and toss together thoroughly.

3 Add half the croûtons and two-thirds of the Parmesan and toss again. Taste a piece of lettuce for seasoning, adding salt only if necessary (the cheese and anchovies are already salty). Serve the salad from the bowl and the remaining Parmesan and croûtons separately.

Making the dressing

1 Crush the anchovy fillets with the back of a table fork. Mix in the garlic, mustard, lemon juice, and pepper to taste.

2 Gradually add the oil, whisking constantly, so the dressing thickens and emulsifies. When the oil has been incorporated, taste for seasoning.

28 mins

preparation	cooking
25 mins	3 mins

Tomato, Red Onion, and Mozzarella Salad

For a salad as simple as this, the quality of its ingredients is important: ripe, flavourful tomatoes, fresh greens, and sweet mozzarella.

Serves 4

Ingredients

8 ripe plum tomatoes, sliced
6 cherry tomatoes, halved
1 small red onion, sliced
handful of basil leaves, torn
extra virgin olive oil,
   for drizzling
salt and freshly ground
   black pepper
2 handfuls of wild rocket leaves
balsamic vinegar, for drizzling
2 balls of mozzarella cheese,
   torn up roughly

1 Put the tomatoes, red onion, and half of the basil leaves in a bowl. Drizzle over some olive oil and season with salt and pepper to taste. Gently mix together with your fingers to coat the tomatoes with oil.

2 Arrange the rocket leaves on a serving platter and drizzle over a little olive oil and some balsamic vinegar. Season with salt and pepper. Spoon the tomato and basil mixture evenly over the rocket, then add the pieces of mozzarella. Scatter the remaining basil leaves on top and drizzle with a little more olive oil and balsamic vinegar. Serve immediately.

Choosing olive oil
Olive oil is available in a wide range of flavours, from delicate, fruity oils to strong oils that can be quite peppery and bitter. "Extra virgin" oil is considered to be the best. Buy in small quantities and keep in a cool, dark place (not the refrigerator).

10 mins

preparation
10 mins

Salade Niçoise

Preparing and dressing the ingredients separately keeps flavours distinct in this salad. Take care not to overcook the tuna or it will dry out.

Serves 6

Ingredients

1kg (2¼lb) potatoes, peeled
1kg (2¼lb) fresh tuna steaks,
    cut into 2.5cm (1in) cubes
375g (13oz) French beans
6 eggs, hard-boiled and
    quartered
500g (1lb 2oz) tomatoes,
    skinned and quartered
10 canned anchovy fillets
125g (4½oz) black olives

For the herb vinaigrette

120ml (4fl oz) red wine vinegar
2 tsp Dijon mustard
3 garlic cloves, finely chopped
salt and freshly ground
    black pepper
375ml (13fl oz) olive oil
7–10 sprigs of thyme
bunch of chervil

1 To make the vinaigrette, whisk the vinegar with the mustard, garlic, and salt and pepper to taste in a bowl. Slowly whisk in the olive oil. Chop the herbs, add to the bowl, and whisk well.

2 Cook the potatoes in boiling salted water until just tender. Drain, cut into chunks, and put them in a large bowl. Add 75ml (2½fl oz) of the vinaigrette, stir, and cool.

3 Put the tuna cubes in a shallow, non-metallic dish and pour over 75ml (2½fl oz) of the vinaigrette. Cover and marinate in the refrigerator, turning occasionally, for 1 hour.

4 Cook the beans in boiling salted water for 5–7 minutes or until just tender, then drain. Put the beans in a bowl, add 3 tbsp of the vinaigrette, and toss to coat. Set aside.

5 Preheat the grill. Grill the tuna cubes, turning and basting with the marinade, for about 4 minutes or until lightly browned. Arrange all the ingredients on a large platter. Drizzle over the remaining dressing and serve.

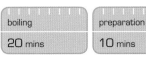

1 hr 50 mins	boiling 20 mins	preparation 10 mins	marinating 1 hr	boiling 10 mins	preparation 5 mins	grilling 5 mins

Coleslaw

This version of an old favourite is pepped up with caraway seeds, soured cream, and mustard powder. Vary the flavourings to suit your taste.

Serves 8–10

Ingredients

500g (1lb 2oz) carrots,
   coarsely grated
1 white cabbage, approx.
   1.35kg (3lb)
1 onion, finely diced

For the soured cream dressing

2 tbsp caster sugar
250ml (8fl oz) soured cream
175ml (6fl oz) cider vinegar
2 tsp mustard powder
2 tsp caraway seeds
salt and freshly ground
   black pepper
250ml (8fl oz) mayonnaise

1 Put the carrots into a bowl of iced water and leave aside for about 30 minutes; the carrot strips will crisp up. Drain them very well, then wrap in a clean tea towel and shake to remove all the excess water.

2 While the carrots are crisping, prepare and quarter the cabbage (as shown below). Cut out and discard the core from each quarter. Shred the leaves using a knife or a mandolin (see p160), discarding any thick ribs. Alternatively, shred the cabbage in a food processor, using the slicing blade.

3 To make the dressing, put the sugar, soured cream, and cider vinegar in a bowl and stir in the mustard powder, caraway seeds, and salt and pepper to taste. Add the mayonnaise and whisk to combine. Taste for seasoning.

4 Combine the onion, carrots, and cabbage in a bowl and pour the dressing over. Stir to coat all the vegetables evenly. Cover and chill for at least 4 hours so the flavours mellow. Give the coleslaw another good stir before serving.

Preparing cabbage

Use a very large chef's knife or a cleaver on tough items like cabbage. First, cut the cabbage in half: plunge the knife down the middle and use your other hand, fingers outstretched, to push the blade through if necessary. Then place each half flat-side down and cut into quarters, applying pressure if needed.

4 hrs 20 mins

preparation	chilling
20 mins	4 hrs

Tabbouleh

A Middle Eastern mezze (appetizer) selection often includes salads such as tabbouleh and cacik with pitta. An easy way to serve a large group.

Serves 6–8

Ingredients

200g (7oz) bulghur wheat
500g (1lb 2oz) tomatoes, peeled,
    deseeded, and chopped
3 spring onions, chopped
bunch of parsley, leaves picked
    and chopped
juice of 3 lemons
125ml (4fl oz) olive oil
a generous 1½ bunches of mint,
    leaves picked and chopped
salt and freshly ground
    black pepper
6–8 pitta breads

For the cacik

2 small cucumbers, deseeded
    and diced
½ bunch of mint, leaves picked
    and chopped
3 garlic cloves, finely chopped
½ tsp ground coriander
¼ tsp ground cumin
500ml (16fl oz) plain yoghurt

1 Put the bulghur wheat in a large bowl and pour over enough cold water to cover generously. Leave to soak for 30 minutes, then drain in a sieve. Remove any remaining water by squeezing handfuls.

2 In a large bowl, combine the bulghur, tomatoes, spring onions, parsley, lemon juice, olive oil, mint, and plenty of salt and pepper. Mix together, then taste for seasoning. Cover and chill for at least 2 hours.

3 Meanwhile, make the cacik (see the technique below). When ready to serve, take the tabbouleh and cacik from the refrigerator and allow to come to room temperature. Warm the pitta breads in a low oven or under the grill for 3–5 minutes, then cut into strips. Serve with the two salads.

Making cacik

Put the cucumber in a colander, sprinkle with salt, and stir to mix. Leave to drain for 15–20 minutes, then rinse under cold running water. Now, put the cucumbers in a bowl, add the rest of the cacik ingredients, and stir well. Taste for seasoning. Cover and chill for at least 2 hours.

Roast Baby Leeks with Sun-dried Tomato Dressing

Baby leeks are delicious simply roasted and tossed with a piquant dressing. Asparagus can be prepared this way too.

Serves 4

Ingredients

2 sun-dried tomato halves
   in oil
extra virgin olive oil
red wine vinegar
a few black and green olives,
   finely chopped
handful of basil, chopped
salt and freshly ground
   black pepper
10 baby leeks

1 Preheat the oven to 200°C (400°F/Gas 6). Finely chop the sun-dried tomatoes. Mix with a little of the tomato oil, a splash of olive oil, a splash of red wine vinegar, a few finely chopped black and green olives, and the chopped basil. Season with salt and pepper to taste. Set aside.

2 Blanch the baby leeks in a saucepan of boiling water for 2 minutes. Drain well, then toss them with a little olive oil in a roasting tin. Roast the leeks for 10 minutes or until golden and tender. Spoon the tomato dressing over to serve.

Preparing baby leeks
While mature leeks need to be trimmed to remove coarse outer leaves and all of the root end, baby leeks are almost completely edible. Just trim off the tips of the green to neaten. They are tender enough to eat raw, thinly sliced, in a salad.

15 mins

preparation
5 mins

cooking
10 mins

Roast Potatoes

Tender, fluffy potatoes with a crisp, golden exterior are ideal. Try goose fat instead of oil or add herbs such as rosemary, for a change.

Serves 4

Ingredients

900g (2lb) floury potatoes,
   such as Maris Piper, peeled
   and quartered
flaked sea salt
1 tbsp plain flour
4 tbsp olive oil

1 Preheat the oven to 220°C (425°F/Gas 7). Put the potatoes in a saucepan of salted water and bring to the boil, then par-boil over medium heat for about 10 minutes until the potatoes are nearly cooked (test with a sharp knife). Drain well, then return to the pan.

2 Lay a folded tea towel over the pan and set it aside for 5 minutes so the potatoes can dry out (the towel will absorb the steam). Add the flour to the potatoes, put the lid on the pan, and shake it up and down a few times to coat the potatoes with flour and give them rough edges.

3 Spoon the oil into a large roasting tin and warm in the oven until the oil is really hot. Remove from the oven and carefully add the potatoes one by one, turning each in the hot oil. Season with sea salt. Return to the oven and roast for 30–40 minutes or until the potatoes are golden and crisp. Turn them halfway through cooking. Serve hot.

Par-boiling

Root vegetables such as potatoes and parsnips are often par-boiled (partly boiled) before roasting. This initial cooking in boiling water softens them, ensuring that when roasted they will be completely cooked by the time they are golden and crisp on the outside.

1 hr
5 mins

preparation

25 mins

cooking

40 mins

Gratin Dauphinois

Simmering potatoes in milk and then in cream keeps them sweet and ensures they will be perfectly tender when baked.

Serves 6–8

Ingredients

750g (1lb 10oz) floury potatoes, such as Maris Piper or King Edward, peeled
600ml (1 pint) milk
grated nutmeg
salt and freshly ground black pepper
300ml (10fl oz) double cream
1 garlic clove, halved
melted butter, for greasing
45g (1½oz) Gruyère cheese, coarsely grated

1 With a mandolin or a large sharp knife, cut the potatoes into 3mm (⅛in) slices. Set aside, covered with a damp tea towel (do not soak them in water; this would remove the starch that gives the gratin its creamy consistency).

2 Bring the milk almost to the boil in a saucepan. Season it with a little grated nutmeg, salt, and pepper, then add the potatoes. Reduce the heat and cook gently, stirring occasionally, for 10–15 minutes or until almost tender.

3 Drain the potatoes in a colander, discarding the milk (or save it for another use, such as soup, if you like). Return the potatoes to the saucepan and pour in the cream. Cook gently, stirring occasionally, for 10–15 minutes or until very tender. Taste for seasoning. Preheat the oven to 190°C (375°F/Gas 5).

4 Rub the cut sides of the garlic clove over the bottom and sides of a 1.5 litre (2¾ pint) baking dish, then brush with melted butter. Layer the potatoes and cream mixture in the dish. Sprinkle the cheese evenly over the top. Bake for 20–25 minutes or until golden brown. Test with a small knife; the blade should feel hot when withdrawn. Serve hot.

Using a mandolin

The adjustable blade of a mandolin enables you to cut uniform wafer-thin slices or shreds. To protect your fingers, hold the vegetable in the carrier while you slide it up and down across the very sharp blade.

1 hr 5 mins

preparation	cooking in milk	cooking in cream	baking
10 mins	15 mins	15 mins	25 mins

Green Beans with Toasted Hazelnuts

After boiling, "refreshing" green vegetables with cold water stops them cooking further and retains their bright colour and flavour.

Serves 4

Ingredients
250g (9oz) fine green
   beans, trimmed
salt
25g (scant 1oz) butter
75g (2½oz) shelled hazelnuts,
   toasted (see the technique
   below) and roughly chopped

1 Put the beans in a saucepan of boiling salted water, and boil for 5–6 minutes or until they are tender but still have a bit of firmness to them. Drain in a colander, then refresh under cold running water.

2 Give the beans a good shake in the colander, then transfer to a serving dish. Top with the butter and toasted hazelnuts. Serve hot, with roast chicken or lamb.

Toasting shelled hazelnuts
Browning nuts enriches their flavour and makes them more crunchy. Spread them out on a baking tray and toast in a preheated 180°C (350°F/Gas 4) oven for 7–12 minutes, shaking the tray frequently to prevent burning. If you want to remove their papery brown skins, wrap the nuts in a cloth and rub off the skins.

10 mins

preparation	cooking
5 mins	5 mins

Ratatouille

This popular Mediterranean dish is delicious hot or cold. Be patient – the long, gentle cooking is what makes the vegetables meltingly tender.

Serves 4

Ingredients

4 tbsp olive oil
1 onion, chopped
1 garlic clove, chopped
1 courgette, sliced
1 small aubergine, approx.
  225g (8oz), cut into
  2.5cm (1in) cubes
1 red pepper, cored, deseeded,
  and cut into 2.5cm (1in) pieces
150ml (5fl oz) vegetable stock
400g can chopped tomatoes
2 tsp chopped oregano, plus
  2–3 sprigs to garnish
salt and freshly ground
  black pepper

1 Heat the oil in a large flameproof casserole over medium heat. Add the onion and cook for about 5 minutes or until soft and translucent. Stir in the garlic, courgette, aubergine, and red pepper, and cook for a further 5 minutes, stirring.

2 Add the stock, tomatoes with their juice, and the chopped oregano to the casserole and bring to the boil. Reduce the heat to low, partially cover the pot, and continue cooking until the vegetables are tender, stirring occasionally.

3 Season with salt and pepper to taste. Spoon the ratatouille into a serving bowl and serve immediately, garnished with oregano sprigs, or leave to cool and serve cold (keep in a covered container in the refrigerator).

Preparing peppers

Place the pepper on its side and cut off both ends. Stand it on one of the cut ends and slice it in half. Remove the core and seeds. Open each section and lay it flat. Using the knife in a sideways motion, cut away the remaining pale, fleshy ribs. Cut the peppers into smaller sections, following the natural divisions of the pepper. Then chop or slice as directed in the recipe.

55 mins

preparation
15 mins

cooking
40 mins

DESSERTS

Desserts are an art and offer the possibility to practise a wide range of techniques – from preparing excellent caramel to accomplishing flawless créme pâtissière.

Oaty Blackberry and Apple Crumble

This crumble topping can be used with other fruit, such as peaches or nectarines, plums, or mixed berries. A proper custard is essential with it.

Serves 6–8

Ingredients

1kg (2¼lb) apples, peeled, cored, and thickly sliced
350g (12oz) blackberries
200g (7oz) dark muscovado sugar
125g (4½oz) plain flour
125g (4½oz) unsalted butter, diced
125g (4½oz) porridge oats

For the custard

3 egg yolks
2 tbsp caster sugar
½ teaspoon cornflour
150ml (5fl oz) milk
150ml (5fl oz) double cream
2–3 strips of thinly pared lemon zest

1 Preheat the oven to 180°C (350°F/Gas 4). Put the fruit in a shallow 2.25 litre (4 pint) baking dish. Sprinkle about 3 tbsp of the muscovado sugar over the fruit. Cover with foil and bake for 15 minutes to soften the fruit.

2 Meanwhile, put the flour in a mixing bowl and rub in the butter until the mixture resembles breadcrumbs, as shown below. Add the remaining sugar and the oats; toss to mix. Remove the fruit from the oven and give it a quick stir. Spread the crumble mixture evenly over the top. Return to the oven and bake for 30 minutes or until the topping is golden and the fruit juices are bubbling up at the sides.

3 To make the custard, whisk together the egg yolks, caster sugar, cornflour, and 3 tbsp milk. Bring the remaining milk, cream, and lemon zest to simmering point in a saucepan. Remove from the heat and leave to infuse for 10 minutes, then strain into the egg yolks, whisking constantly. Pour the mixture back into the saucepan and cook over low heat, stirring, for 6–8 minutes or until the custard thickens enough to coat the back of the spoon. Pour the custard into a jug and serve with the crumble.

Making crumble

A crumble topping is really pastry without the liquid to bind it. So, just as when making pastry, handle the mixture as lightly as possible when rubbing the butter into the flour. If using a food processor, take care not to overwork the mixture.

1 hr 10 mins

baking	preparation	baking	preparing custard
15 mins	5 mins	30 mins	20 mins

Lemon Sponge Pudding

Fold a pleat into the centre of the greaseproof paper and foil used to cover the basin, to allow for expansion of the pudding as it steams.

Serves 4–6

Ingredients

grated zest and juice
  of 2 lemons
juice of ½ large orange
60g (2oz) light soft
  brown sugar
115g (4oz) unsalted
  butter, softened (see p275),
  plus extra for greasing
60g (2oz) caster sugar
1 tbsp golden syrup
2 eggs, beaten
175g (6oz) self-raising
  flour, sifted
custard or cream,
  to serve

1 Grease a 1 litre (1¾ pint) pudding basin. Stir together half the lemon juice, the orange juice, and the brown sugar in a bowl. Pour this into the pudding basin.

2 Put the butter, caster sugar, golden syrup, and lemon zest in a mixing bowl and beat together until creamy and pale. Gradually add the eggs, beating as you go and adding a little of the flour to prevent any curdling. Then fold in the remaining flour until it is thoroughly combined. Stir through the remaining lemon juice.

3 Pour the mixture into the pudding basin and cover (see the technique below). Set the basin in a large heavy-based pan and pour in enough boiling water to come halfway up the side of the basin. Cover with the lid and simmer gently for about 1½ hours, topping up with more boiling water when needed. Carefully lift the basin out of the pan and remove the string, foil, and paper. Turn the pudding out onto a rimmed plate. Serve piping hot with custard or cream.

Covering the basin

1 Lay a piece of pleated, buttered greaseproof paper over the basin. Tie with string under the rim and make a loop for a handle.

2 Cover with pleated foil, moulding the foil tightly under the rim of the basin. Place the basin in a pan that is deep enough to hold it.

2 hrs 10 mins

preparation 40 mins

cooking 1 hr 30 mins

Apricot Frangipane Tart

To prevent the tart case from shrinking during baking, take care not to stretch the pastry when you drape it over the tin and ease it in.

Serves 10

Ingredients
250g (9oz) shortcrust pastry
plain flour, for dusting
crème fraîche, to serve

For the filling
200g (7oz) unsalted butter,
    softened (see p275)
200g (7oz) caster sugar
1 tsp vanilla essence
5 egg yolks
200g (7oz) ground almonds
4–5 ripe apricots, halved
    and stoned

1 Preheat the oven to 180°C (350°F/Gas 4). Roll out the pastry on a lightly floured surface to a 35cm (14in) circle about 3mm (⅛in) thick. Roll up around the rolling pin, then unroll over a 25cm (10in) round, loose-bottomed tart tin. Gently ease the pastry over the bottom, into the corners, and up the side of the tin to line evenly. Trim the edge level with the rim of the tin, then bake the pastry case "blind" until fully baked (see the technique below). Set aside.

2 To make the filling, beat the butter with the sugar in a large bowl using a hand-held electric mixer until pale and creamy. Mix in the vanilla essence. Add the egg yolks, one at a time, and beat gently until incorporated. Gradually stir in the ground almonds.

3 Pour the filling into the pastry case and spread evenly. Arrange the apricots on top, cut-side down, on top, pressing them in slightly so they fit snugly. Bake for 25–35 minutes or until the filling is set and golden. Leave to cool, and serve at room temperature with crème fraîche.

Baking pastry "blind"

1 Prick the bottom of the pastry case all over with a fork. Cut a circle of baking parchment to fit and snip the edge all round.

2 Place the parchment circle in the pastry case to line it, then fill with an even layer of baking beans. Bake for 15–20 minutes.

3 Remove the paper and beans. For a fully baked pastry case, return to the oven and bake for 5–8 minutes or until golden.

1 hr 25 mins

preparation	baking blind		preparation	baking
10 mins	30 mins		10 mins	35 mins

Whisky and Cream Bread and Butter Pudding

This comforting favourite is turned into an adult treat with whisky and fruity buns. You could also use roughly broken up panettone.

Serves 4

Ingredients

50g (1¾oz) unsalted butter, softened
50g (1¾oz) sultanas
2 tbsp whisky
4 richly fruited hot cross buns
3 eggs
2 egg yolks
300ml (10fl oz) whole milk
150ml (5fl oz) double cream
2 tbsp demerara sugar

1 Grease a 1.5 litre (2¾pint) baking dish with 10g (¼oz) of the softened butter. Place the sultanas in a small bowl with the whisky and leave to soak for 30 minutes.

2 Slice the buns horizontally in half and butter the cut sides with the remaining soft butter. In a large jug, make a custard mixture by beating together the eggs, egg yolks, milk, and double cream with a balloon whisk until well blended. Set aside.

3 Arrange four halves of buttered hot cross buns, butter-side up, over the bottom of the baking dish. Sprinkle over the soaked sultanas with the whisky. Top with the remaining halves of buttered hot cross buns, butter-side up again.

4 Pour over the custard mixture. Use a fish slice to press the hot cross buns down into the custard. Leave aside for about 20 minutes so some of the custard is soaked up. Meanwhile, preheat the oven to 160°C (325°F/Gas 3).

5 When ready to bake, scatter the demerara sugar over the surface and set the dish on a baking tray. Bake for 40 minutes or until golden on top and slightly risen; check to be sure the middle is lightly set and not runny. Remove from the oven and leave to settle for 10 minutes before serving.

Softening butter
For "softened" butter (at room temperature) take it out of the refrigerator about an hour before you are going to use it. If you've forgotten to do this, you can slice and then soften it in the microwave in 10-second bursts, but take care not to melt it.

1 hr 40 mins

soaking and preparation	resting	baking	resting
30 mins	20 mins	40 mins	10 mins

Rice Pudding

You could rinse and dry the vanilla pod, then bury it in a container of caster sugar. As you use the scented vanilla sugar, top up with fresh sugar.

Serves 4

Ingredients

85g (3oz) caster sugar
600ml (1 pint) milk
1 vanilla pod, slit open
200g (7oz) basmati rice
110ml (3¾fl oz) double cream
4 tbsp soft light brown sugar

1 Preheat the grill to high. Combine the caster sugar, milk, and vanilla pod in a saucepan and bring just to the boil. Add the rice and stir, then reduce the heat and simmer gently for 8–10 minutes.

2 Stir in the cream and simmer for a further 4–5 minutes or until the rice is tender. Remove the vanilla pod.

3 Divide the rice pudding among four heatproof serving bowls. Sprinkle 1 tbsp brown sugar evenly over the surface of each. Set the bowls on a baking sheet.

4 Slide the bowls under the hot grill and grill until the sugar is bubbling and caramelized. (Alternatively, use a blowtorch to glaze the rice pudding.) Serve immediately.

Using other types of rice

In a pudding made with a long-grain rice such as basmati, the grains of rice tend to keep their shape. Short- and medium-grain rice, such as pudding rice and risotto rice, make puddings with a creamier texture because the rice grains cling together.

25 mins

cooking
20 mins

grilling
5 mins

Pears Baked in Marsala

Make this ahead to serve with sweetened whipped cream. Using cold cream and chilling the bowl and whisk will make cream whip faster.

Serves 4–6

Ingredients

6–8 ripe pears, peeled
100g (3½oz) caster sugar
250ml (8fl oz) dry Marsala
1 tsp pure vanilla extract
1 cinnamon stick
250ml (8fl oz) double or
    whipping cream
2 tbsp icing sugar

1 Preheat the oven to 150°C (300°F/Gas 2). Place the pears in a baking dish, cut-side up, and sprinkle with the caster sugar, Marsala, and vanilla. Pour in 250ml (8fl oz) water and add the cinnamon stick.

2 Bake for 30–50 minutes, depending on ripeness, or until the pears are tender. Baste the pears occasionally with the Marsala liquid in the dish.

3 Meanwhile, in a medium bowl whip the cream until soft peaks form (see the technique below). Sift in the icing sugar and continue whipping until thick again. Serve the pears warm or chilled, in their syrup, with the whipped cream.

Whipping cream

1 To avoid splatters, start to whip slowly with a whisk or hand-held electric mixer. When the cream begins to thicken, increase speed.

2 At soft-peak stage, lifting the whisk makes peaks with tips that flop over. For stiff peaks, continue whipping until tips stand upright.

1 hr

preparation
10 mins

baking
50 mins

plus whipping cream

American Blueberry Pancakes

Dropping the blueberries on top of the half-cooked pancakes prevents the berry juice from leaking out into the pan and burning.

Makes 30 pancakes

Ingredients

30g (1oz) unsalted butter, plus extra for frying and to serve
200g (7oz) self-raising flour
1 tsp baking powder
40g (1¼oz) caster sugar
250ml (8fl oz) milk
2 large eggs, beaten
1 tsp pure vanilla extract
150g (5½oz) blueberries
maple syrup, to serve

1 Melt the butter in a small saucepan; set aside to cool. Sift the flour and baking powder into a bowl. Stir in the sugar. Make a well in the centre.

2 In a jug, lightly beat together the milk, eggs, and vanilla extract until well blended. Gradually pour into the well in the flour, whisking to mix the egg mixture with the flour to make a smooth batter. Whisk in the melted butter.

3 Fry the pancakes (see the technique below). After turning, continue to cook for 1–2 minutes or until golden brown on both sides. Remove the pancakes from the pan, place them on a plate, and keep warm in a low oven.

4 Wipe out the frying pan with kitchen paper, then add more butter and fry the next batch of pancakes. Watch that the butter doesn't get too hot. When they are all cooked, serve warm with butter and maple syrup.

Frying pancakes

1 Melt a knob of butter in a large, non-stick frying pan over medium heat. Pour 1 tbsp of the batter into the pan to form a round pancake.

2 Continue to add spoonfuls of batter, leaving space for them to spread. As they begin to cook, sprinkle with a few blueberries.

3 They are ready to turn over when small bubbles appear and pop, leaving small holes. Turn them over carefully with a palette knife.

30 mins

preparation
10 mins

cooking
20 mins

Classic Crème Caramel

This is a delicious dessert infused with the taste of vanilla. For a stronger flavour, split the pod open and retain the tiny black seeds in the custard.

Serves 6

Ingredients

600ml (1 pint) whole milk
1 vanilla pod
225g (8oz) golden
  caster sugar
2 whole eggs
4 egg yolks

1 Preheat the oven to 150°C (300°F/Gas 2). Pour the milk into a heavy-based saucepan, add the vanilla pod, and bring almost to the boil. Remove from the heat, cover the pan, and leave to infuse for 20 minutes.

2 Put half of the sugar into another heavy-based saucepan and pour in 75ml (2½fl oz) cold water. Use to make the caramel (see the technique below). Pour the caramel into six 150ml (5fl oz) ramekins. Set aside.

3 Put the remaining sugar in a large jug with the eggs and egg yolks and whisk until the sugar has dissolved. Discard the vanilla pod, then pour the milk into the egg mixture. Whisk to mix. Strain into the ramekins, dividing the mixture evenly.

4 Set the ramekins in a roasting tin and pour boiling water into the tin to come two-thirds of the way up the sides of the ramekins. Bake for 1 hour. Remove the tin from the oven and leave the ramekins in the hot water for 30 minutes, then remove and cool. Chill overnight. Turn out to serve.

Making caramel

1 Bring to the boil, swirling the liquid in the pan occasionally to ensure the sugar dissolves. Use a wet pastry brush to remove sugar syrup from the side of the pan.

2 Boil for about 15 minutes, without stirring, until the caramel is a dark golden colour. Stop the cooking by plunging the base of the pan into a large bowl of iced water.

THE RECIPES DESSERTS PUDDINGS

14 hrs 20 mins	preparation	baking	setting	chilling
	50 mins	1 hr	30 mins	overnight

Peach Tarte Tatin

For this summery variation of a French classic, choose ripe but firm peaches that will hold their shape. Mango slices would also work well.

Serves 6

Ingredients

3 egg yolks
½ tsp pure vanilla extract
215g (7½oz) plain flour,
  plus extra for dusting
60g (2oz) caster sugar
¼ tsp salt
90g (3oz) unsalted butter,
  diced

For the filling

200g (7oz) caster sugar
1kg (2¼lb) peaches

1 In a small bowl, mix the egg yolks with the vanilla. In a large bowl, stir together the flour, sugar, and salt. Add the butter and rub in with your fingertips until the mixture resembles breadcrumbs. Add the egg mix and bring together to a dough. Knead briefly until smooth. Chill for 30 minutes.

2 For the filling, put the sugar in a saucepan and heat gently until melted, occasionally swirling the sugar in the pan. Bring to the boil and cook, without stirring, until the caramel starts to turn golden around the edge (it might crystallize if you stir it). Lower the heat and continue cooking, swirling the syrup in the pan once or twice so it colours evenly, until it is golden.

3 Remove from the heat and immediately plunge the base of the pan into a bowl of iced water, to stop the cooking. Pour the caramel into a 23–25cm (9–10in) tatin dish and quickly tilt the dish so the bottom is coated with a thin, even layer. Leave to cool.

4 Immerse the peaches in a pan of boiling water for about 10 seconds, then transfer to a bowl of cold water. Cut them in half, remove the stones, and peel off the skin. Then cut the peach halves lengthways in half. Tightly pack the peach wedges, rounded-side down, on top of the caramel in neat concentric circles.

5 On a lightly floured work surface, roll out the dough to a 28cm (11in) round. Wrap it around the rolling pin and unroll to drape over the dish. Tuck the edge of the dough down inside the rim of the dish, around the peaches. Chill for 15 minutes. Preheat the oven to 200°C (400°F/Gas 6).

6 Bake for 30–35 minutes. Allow the tart to cool for at least 30 minutes. To unmould, set an upturned rimmed serving plate on top of the baking dish. Holding the dish and plate firmly together, turn them over, then remove the baking dish. Serve the tart cut into wedges.

1 hr 35 mins

preparation	chilling and filling	rolling	chilling	baking
10 mins	30 mins	5 mins	15 mins	35 mins

Chocolate Fondant

Chocolate must be melted gently because it may scorch. An alternative method is to microwave it, stopping frequently to check progress.

Serves 4

Ingredients

125g (4½oz) unsalted butter, diced, plus extra for greasing

150g (5½oz) caster sugar, plus 4 tsp for coating the ramekins

125g (4½oz) dark chocolate, chopped

3 large eggs

35g (1¼oz) plain flour

icing sugar, for dusting

1 Preheat the oven to 200°C (400°F/Gas 6). Lightly butter four 100ml (3½fl oz) ramekins, or other individual baking dishes no bigger than 150ml (5fl oz) each. Put 1 tsp caster sugar into each ramekin, and tilt and rotate to coat the bottom and sides evenly.

2 Place the butter and chocolate in a heatproof bowl and set it over a pan of barely simmering water to melt as shown below. Set aside.

3 Beat the remaining sugar with the eggs, then mix in the flour. Fold the melted chocolate into the egg mixture. Spoon into the ramekins. Bake for 10–12 minutes or until risen. Dust with icing sugar and serve immediately.

Melting chocolate
Put the chopped chocolate in a heatproof bowl set over a pan of steaming hot water; the base of the bowl must not touch the water. Allow the chocolate to soften and remove the bowl from the pan of water. Stir the chocolate with a wooden spoon until smooth.

22 mins

preparation
10 mins

baking
12 mins

Summer Pudding

Make when summer berries are juicy and sweetly flavourful. Reserve some of their juice to baste any white patches on the turned-out pudding.

Serves 6

Ingredients

12 slices white bread,
    crusts removed
125g (4½oz) blackcurrants
125g (4½oz) redcurrants
150g (5½oz) caster sugar
250g (9oz) mixed berries,
    such as strawberries,
    raspberries, mulberries,
    blueberries, and cherries
bunch of redcurrants,
    to decorate (optional)
mint sprigs, to decorate

1 Line a 900ml (1½ pint) pudding basin with bread slices, beginning with a circle cut to fit the base, then overlapping slices evenly around the side. There should be enough bread left for the top.

2 Put the currants in a heavy-based pan with the sugar and cook until soft and the juices have run. Stir in the berries and cook for 1 minute or until just softening.

3 Spoon some of the fruit juices over the bread in the basin, then fill the basin with the fruit. Make sure the fruit is packed in well. Cover the fruit with the remaining slices of bread, cutting them neatly to fit.

4 Set the basin in a dish to catch any overspill of juice, then cover with cling film. Place a small plate on top of the bread lid and set a weight (such as cans of food) on the plate. Chill overnight.

5 Turn the pudding out onto a serving plate. Decorate with a small bunch of redcurrants, if using, and mint sprigs.

12 hrs 25 mins

preparation	cooking		preparation	chilling
5 mins	10 mins		10 mins	overnight

Lemon and Lime Tart

Here, chocolate pastry encases a creamy citrus filling. Be sure the dough is evenly mixed so there are no dark streaks to spoil the appearance.

Serves 6

Ingredients
125g (4½oz) plain flour
75g (2½oz) icing sugar
25g (scant 1oz) cocoa powder
pinch of salt
75g (2½oz) unsalted butter,
  chilled and diced
3 eggs
125g (4½oz) golden caster
  sugar
200ml (7fl oz) double cream
grated zest and juice of
  1 lemon and 1 lime

1 Sift the flour, icing sugar, cocoa powder, and salt into a mixing bowl. Add the butter and rub together with your fingertips until the mixture resembles fine breadcrumbs. Add 1–2 tbsp iced water to bind, then gather the mixture into a dough. Knead briefly to mix. Chill for 30 minutes.

2 Preheat the oven to 200°C (400°F/Gas 6). Roll out the pastry dough on a lightly floured surface and use to line a 20cm (8in) round loose-bottomed tart tin. Line the pastry case with baking parchment, then fill with ceramic baking beans. Bake "blind" for 15 minutes (see p272). Lift out the beans and paper. Set the tart case aside. Turn the oven down to 160°C (325°F/Gas 3).

3 Put the eggs and caster sugar in a mixing bowl and beat with a hand-held electric mixer until pale and creamy. Add the cream and the lemon and lime zests and juice and stir to combine. Pour the mixture into the tart case and smooth the top. Bake for 30–35 minutes or until the filling is set. Allow to cool to room temperature before unmoulding to serve.

Zesting citrus
To remove the zest (the coloured outer part of citrus peel), use the fine holes on a grater, running the fruit diagonally across the surface rather than vertically; or try a special citrus zester, which takes thread-like strips.

1 hr 35 mins

preparation	chilling	blind baking	baking
15 mins	30 mins	15 mins	35 mins

Custard Tart

This is a great tart to bake around Christmas time. The crust is made from amaretti biscuits, but other crisp biscuits can also be used.

Serves 8

Ingredients

125g (4½oz) unsalted butter, melted, plus extra for greasing
250g (9oz) amaretti biscuits, crushed to fine crumbs

For the filling

500ml (16fl oz) whole milk
1 vanilla pod, split lengthways
50g (1¾oz) caster sugar
2 tbsp cornflour
4 egg yolks
125ml (4½fl oz) double cream, whipped to soft peaks
7g (¼oz) powdered gelatine
60ml (2fl oz) dark rum, or more to taste
pinch of grated nutmeg

1 Preheat the oven to 180°C (350°F/Gas 4). Butter a 23cm (9in) springform tin. Mix the butter with the biscuits and press over the bottom and 2.5cm (1in) up the side of the tin. Chill until firm, then bake for 10–15 minutes or until set and lightly browned. Leave to cool.

2 Put the milk and vanilla pod in a heavy-based saucepan. Bring just to the boil, then remove from the heat, cover, and leave to infuse for 10–15 minutes. Remove the vanilla pod, then prepare the custard (see the technique below). Cover to prevent a skin from forming. Cool until tepid.

3 Dissolve the gelatine in the rum, then stir into the tepid custard. Set the bowl in a larger bowl of iced water and stir gently until starting to thicken. Remove and whisk briskly to lighten the custard. Gently fold in the whipped cream.

4 Pour the filling into the biscuit crust and smooth with a palette knife. Chill for 2–3 hours or until set. Run a knife around the tart to loosen it, then remove the side of the tin. Sprinkle nutmeg over the tart and serve in wedges.

Making custard for a tart

1 Set aside a quarter of the milk. Add the sugar to the remaining milk in the saucepan and stir until it has dissolved.

2 Whisk the cornflour with the yolks. Whisk in the sweetened milk until smooth. Pour back into the pan and cook, stirring constantly.

3 When thick enough to coat the back of the spoon, remove from the heat and stir in the reserved milk. Strain into a cold bowl.

3 hrs 45 mins

preparation	blind baking	cooking	chilling
10 mins plus chilling	15 mins	20 mins	3 hrs

Strawberry Fool

Here, a sweet berry purée is layered with a simple fool. For a very smooth purée, press it through a nylon sieve to remove the strawberry seeds.

Serves 4

Ingredients

500g (1lb 2oz) strawberries, hulled, plus extra to decorate
icing sugar, to taste
600ml (1 pint) double cream, mascarpone, or fromage frais

1 Make the strawberry purée and then the strawberry cream (see the technique below). Taste the strawberry cream (fool) and add a little more icing sugar, if it is not sweet enough.

2 Spoon some of the remaining strawberry purée into four individual glass dishes. Add a layer of strawberry fool to each. Continue layering until both mixtures have been used up. Garnish each glass with one or two beautiful strawberries and serve.

Making a fruit fool

1 Put the strawberries in a food processor and blitz until puréed. Sift in a little icing sugar to taste (depending on how sweet you like it).

2 Whip the cream using a hand-held electric mixer or balloon whisk until soft peaks form when the whisk is lifted from the bowl.

3 Add half of the strawberry purée to the whipped cream and fold in gently with a large metal spoon until evenly combined.

20 mins

preparation
20 mins

Vanilla Ice Cream

Nothing beats home-made ice cream. After making with a machine or by hand, leave to "ripen" in the freezer for at least 4 hours before serving.

Serves 4

Ingredients

300ml (10fl oz) whole milk
1 vanilla pod
3 egg yolks
85g (3oz) caster sugar
300ml (10fl oz) double cream
raspberries, to serve (optional)

1 Put the milk in a heavy-based saucepan. Split the vanilla pod lengthways and scrape out the seeds into the milk; add the pod too. Bring the milk almost to the boil. Remove from the heat, cover, and leave to infuse for 30 minutes.

2 Beat the egg yolks with the sugar in a large bowl. Stir in the infused milk, then strain back into the pan. Cook over low heat, stirring constantly with a wooden spoon, until the custard thickens slightly – just enough to coat the back of the spoon. Do not allow the custard to boil, or it will curdle. Pour the custard into a clean bowl and let it cool completely. Whisk the cream into the cooled custard, then chill well (preferably overnight).

3 To freeze the ice cream by hand, pour the mixture into a freezerproof container and freeze for at least 3–4 hours, then whisk thoroughly (or blitz in a food processor) to break up any ice crystals. Freeze for a further 2 hours and repeat the whisking process, then keep in the freezer until needed.

4 You could freeze using an ice-cream machine, as shown below. About 20–30 minutes before serving, remove the ice cream from the freezer so it can soften slightly for scooping.

Using an ice-cream machine
Pour the mixture into the chilled bowl of the machine and churn according to the manufacturer's instructions. Freezing should take 20–30 minutes. Transfer to a freezerproof container and keep in the freezer until needed.

7 hrs
25 mins

preparation	cooling	preparation	cooking	chilling	
10 mins	30 mins	5 mins	10 mins plus cooling	6 hrs	plus thawing

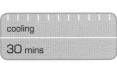

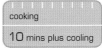

Orange Sorbet

The faster the freezing process, the smoother the sorbet will be,
so be sure the orange mixture is very cold before folding in the egg white.

Serves 4

Ingredients
2 large oranges
125g (4½oz) caster sugar
1 tbsp orange-flower water
1 egg white

1 Using a vegetable peeler, pare the zest from the oranges in long strips, taking care not to include the pith. Put the sugar and 300ml (10fl oz) water in a pan and heat gently until the sugar has dissolved. Add the orange zest and simmer gently for 10 minutes. Remove from the heat and allow the syrup to cool.

2 Cut the oranges in half and squeeze out the juice. Add to the syrup. Stir in the orange-flower water. Strain into a bowl, cover, and chill. In another very clean bowl, whisk the egg white to soft peaks, then fold into the orange mixture.

3 If you do not have an ice-cream machine, pour the orange mixture into a freezerproof container and freeze for at least 4 hours or until almost frozen solid. Mash the mixture with a fork to break up any ice crystals, then freeze again until solid.

4 If using an ice-cream machine, pour the mixture into the bowl and churn according to the manufacturer's instructions. Then transfer the sorbet to a freezerproof container and keep in the freezer until ready to use.

5 Remove the sorbet from the freezer 15–30 minutes before serving to allow it to soften slightly for scooping.

Adding Campari
For a grown-up sorbet, add 75ml (2½fl oz) Campari after you have strained the mixture. This alcoholic sorbet can be kept in the freezer for up to a month; if you freeze it for any longer, the alcohol taste will become too strong.

4 hrs 55 mins

preparation	freezing	to serve
25 mins	4 hrs	30 mins

Profiteroles with Ice Cream

The choux puffs can be made up to 3 days in advance; keep them in an airtight container. Assemble the profiteroles just before serving.

Makes 30–35

Ingredients
75g (2½oz) unsalted butter, diced, plus extra for greasing
1 tsp salt
100g (3½oz) plain flour, sifted
5 eggs
750ml (1¼pints) good-quality chocolate ice cream, softened

For the chocolate sauce
375g (13oz) dark chocolate, chopped
250ml (8fl oz) double cream
2 tbsp Cognac (optional)

1 Preheat the oven to 200°C (400°F/Gas 6). Brush a baking sheet with butter. Prepare the choux pastry (see the technique below). Fit a piping bag with a plain nozzle and add the dough. Pipe the dough in 2.5cm (1in) mounds on the baking sheet, spaced well apart. You may need to bake in batches.

2 Beat the remaining egg with the remaining salt and brush this glaze over the profiteroles. Press down lightly on each mound with the back of a fork in a criss-cross pattern.

3 Bake for 25–30 minutes or until firm and brown. Transfer to a wire rack. With a sharp knife, make a slit in each profiterole to release steam. Leave to cool.

4 Put the chocolate in a medium heavy-based saucepan with the cream. Heat gently, stirring with a wooden spoon, until the chocolate has melted and the mixture is smooth and thick. If using Cognac, stir it in. Keep the sauce warm.

5 Fill each profiterole with a small ball of ice cream. Pile in a shallow dish, pour over the warm chocolate sauce, and serve immediately.

Making choux pastry

1 Put the butter into a saucepan with 175ml (6fl oz) water and ½ tsp salt. Heat until melted. Bring just to the boil. Add the flour all at once.

2 Beat vigorously until the dough is smooth. Return to low heat and beat to dry out the dough, then remove the pan from the heat.

3 Add 4 of the eggs, one at a time, beating the dough thoroughly after each addition until shiny and soft. You may not need all the eggs.

1 hr 15 mins

preparation	baking	preparation
30 mins	30 mins plus cooling	15 mins

Chocolate Mousse with Hazelnuts

You can substitute almost any spirit or liqueur for the whisky – rum, brandy, or Grand Marnier taste particularly good with chocolate.

Serves 6

Ingredients

60g (2oz) hazelnuts
250g (9oz) dark chocolate, broken into large chunks
15g (½oz) unsalted butter, diced
3 eggs, separated
2 tbsp whisky
50g (1¾oz) caster sugar

For the whisky cream
125ml (4fl oz) double cream
1 tbsp caster sugar
2 tsp whisky

1 Preheat the oven to 180°C (350°F/Gas 4). Spread the nuts on a baking sheet and bake until lightly browned. Rub in a rough towel while hot, to remove the skins. Grind in a food processor, reserving a few whole nuts to decorate.

2 Make the chocolate mix (see the technique below). Turn off the heat, mix in the ground hazelnuts and whisky. Leave to cool until tepid. Meanwhile, put 60ml (2fl oz) water in a small pan, add the sugar, and heat until dissolved. Boil, without stirring, until the sugar syrup reaches 120°C (248°F) on a sugar thermometer, or a teaspoon of it will form a firm, pliable ball.

3 Whisk the egg whites until stiff. Gradually whisk in the sugar syrup until the meringue is cool and stiff. Stir a quarter into the tepid chocolate mix, then gently fold in the remaining meringue. Spoon into glasses and chill for 1 hour.

4 To make the whiskey cream, whip the cream until soft peaks form. Add the sugar and whisky and whip again until thick. Top each mousse with the reserved hazelnuts and serve with the cream.

Making the chocolate mix

Put the chocolate in a heavy-based saucepan and add 65ml (2¼fl oz) water. Heat gently, stirring, for 3–5 minutes or until melted and very smooth. Remove from the heat and stir in the butter. Return to low heat and whisk in the egg yolks, one by one, whisking for 4 minutes to ensure the yolks are cooked.

1 hr 40 mins

preparation	boiling	preparation	chilling
25 mins	10 mins	5 mins	1 hr

Cold Lemon Soufflé

The foil collar around the dish should stand well above the rim so the finished dessert will have the appearance of a risen baked soufflé.

Serves 8

Ingredients
250ml (8fl oz) double cream
10g (¼oz) powdered gelatine
4 eggs, separated, plus
  2 egg whites
grated zest of 3 large lemons
  and pared strips of zest
  from 1 large lemon, plus
  juice of all 4 lemons (approx.
  150ml/5fl oz)
250g (9oz) caster sugar,
  plus 2 tbsp for candying
  the lemon zest

1 Cut a piece of foil 5cm (2in) longer than the circumference of a 1 litre (1¾pint) soufflé dish. Fold the foil lengthways in half, then wrap it around the dish. Secure with tape.

2 Whip the cream until soft peaks form; chill. Dissolve the gelatine in 75ml (2½fl oz) water.

3 Put the egg yolks, grated lemon zest, lemon juice, and two-thirds of the sugar in a pan. Cook, stirring, just until the mixture boils. Pour into a large bowl and beat with a hand-held electric mixer for 5–7 minutes or until thick enough to leave a "ribbon" trail when the whisk is lifted. Stir in the gelatine.

4 Heat the remaining sugar with 120ml (4fl oz) water until dissolved. Boil, without stirring, until the syrup reaches 120°C (248°F) on a sugar thermometer, or a teaspoon of it will form a firm, pliable ball. Whisk the 6 egg whites in a large bowl until stiff peaks form. Gradually whisk in the hot syrup and continue whisking until the meringue is cool and stiff.

5 Set the bowl of lemon mixture in a larger bowl of iced water and stir gently until starting to thicken. Remove from the iced water. Gently fold in the chilled whipped cream, then fold in the meringue in two batches. Pour the soufflé mixture into the prepared dish; it should come up at least 5cm (2in) above the rim, but below the edge of the foil collar. Chill for at least 2 hours or until set.

6 Cut the pared lemon zest into very fine strips. Drop into a pan of boiling water and simmer for 2 minutes; drain. In the same pan, heat the 2 tbsp sugar with 2 tbsp water until dissolved. Add the zest and simmer for 8–10 minutes or until the moisture has evaporated. Remove with a fork, gently separate, and set on baking parchment to cool.

7 About 30 minutes before serving, remove the soufflé from the refrigerator. Sprinkle with the candied lemon zest, then very carefully remove the foil collar.

3 hrs
25 mins

preparation	chilling	preparation	resting
40 mins	2 hrs	15 mins	30 mins

Classic Pavlova

Named after a Russian ballerina, pavlova should resemble a tutu,
so if necessary, lower the heat to keep the meringue snowy white.

Makes 6 slices

Ingredients

6 egg whites, at room
　temperature
pinch of salt
350g (12oz) caster sugar
2 tsp cornflour
1 tsp vinegar
300ml (10fl oz) double cream
mango, melon, and passion fruit,
　to decorate

1 Preheat the oven to 180°C (350°F/Gas 4). Line a baking sheet with greaseproof paper. Put the egg whites into a large, spotlessly clean bowl with the salt, then make the meringue mixture (see the technique below).

2 Spoon the meringue onto the baking sheet and spread to form a 20cm (8in) circle. Flatten slightly to make a dip in the middle. Bake for 5 minutes, then reduce the oven to 140°C (275°F/Gas 1) and bake for a further 1¼ hours or until the outside of the meringue feels crisp to a light touch. Allow it to cool completely before transferring to a serving plate.

3 Whip the cream until soft peaks will form. Spoon it onto the meringue base. Decorate with the fruit and serve.

Making meringue mixture

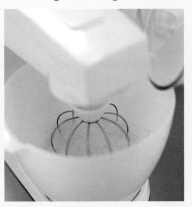

1 Whisk the egg whites until stiff, then start whisking in the sugar, 1 tbsp at a time, whisking well after each addition.

2 Continue whisking until the meringue is stiff and glossy. Add the cornflour and vinegar and whisk them in thoroughly.

1 hr
35 mins

preparation	baking	garnish
10 mins	1 hr 20 mins	5 mins

Lemon Meringue Pie

To unmould the pie, set the tin centrally on a can of food; the side of the tin will drop down, leaving the pie on the tin base. Slide onto a plate.

Makes 8 slices

Ingredients

400g (14oz) ready-made
  shortcrust pastry
6 eggs, separated
3 tbsp cornflour
3 tbsp plain flour
400g (14oz) caster sugar
1 tbsp grated lemon zest
juice of 3 lemons
45g (1½oz) unsalted butter,
  diced, plus extra for greasing
½ tsp cream of tartar
½ tsp pure vanilla extract

1 Preheat the oven to 200°C (400°F/Gas 6). Lightly grease a 23cm (9in) loose-bottomed flan tin. Roll out the pastry on a lightly floured surface and use to line the tin.

2 Line the pastry case with greaseproof paper, then fill with baking beans. Place on a baking sheet and bake "blind" for 15–20 minutes or until the pastry looks pale golden. Lift out the paper and beans, return to the oven, and bake for 5–8 minutes or until the pastry is golden and dry. Transfer to a wire rack to cool. Reduce the oven to 180°C (350°F/Gas 4).

3 Lightly beat the egg yolks in a bowl. Mix the cornflour, flour, and 225g (8oz) of the sugar in a pan with 360ml (12fl oz) water. Heat gently, stirring, until the sugar has dissolved. Increase the heat slightly and cook, stirring, for 3–5 minutes or until starting to thicken.

4 Beat several spoonfuls of the hot mixture into the egg yolks. Pour this mixture into the pan and slowly bring to the boil, stirring constantly. Boil for 3 minutes, then stir in the lemon zest and juice and butter. Continue boiling for a further 2 minutes or until the mixture is thick and glossy, stirring constantly and scraping down the side of the pan as necessary. Remove from the heat; cover to keep warm.

5 Whisk the egg whites in a large, clean bowl until foamy. Sprinkle over the cream of tartar and whisk in. Continue whisking, adding the remaining sugar 1 tbsp at a time. Add the vanilla extract with the last spoonful of sugar, whisking until the meringue is thick and glossy.

6 Pour the lemon filling into the pastry case, then top with the meringue, spreading it so it completely covers the filling right up to the pastry edge. Set the tin on a baking sheet. Bake for 12–15 minutes or until the meringue is lightly golden. Transfer the pie to a wire rack and leave to cool completely before serving.

1 hr
20 mins

preparation	baking blind		preparation	baking	
10 mins	30 mins	plus cooling	25 mins	15 mins	plus cooling

Strawberry Tart

This is a very rich pastry. If it starts to crumble when rolling out, bring it together with your hands, or roll out between sheets of cling film.

Serves 6–8

Ingredients

150g (5½oz) plain flour,
  plus extra for dusting
100g (3½oz) unsalted butter,
  chilled and diced
50g (1¾oz) caster sugar
1 egg yolk
½ tsp pure vanilla extract
6 tbsp redcurrant jelly,
  for glazing
300g (10oz) strawberries,
  washed and thickly sliced

For the crème pâtissière

400ml (14fl oz) whole milk
100g (3½oz) caster sugar
50g (1¾oz) cornflour
2 eggs
1 tsp pure vanilla extract

1 Combine the flour and butter in a bowl and rub in until the mixture resembles fine breadcrumbs. Stir in the sugar. Lightly beat the egg yolk with the vanilla, add to the crumb mixture, and bring together to form a dough; add a little water if dry. Wrap in cling film and chill for 1 hour.

2 Preheat the oven to 180°C (350°F/Gas 4). Roll out the pastry dough to 3mm (⅛in) thick and use to line a 23cm (9in) round loose-bottomed tart tin, leaving about 2cm (¾in) hanging over the side. Prick the base of the pastry case with a fork, then line with baking parchment. Fill with baking beans.

3 Set the tart tin on a baking sheet and bake "blind" for 20 minutes. Lift out the paper and beans, then bake for a further 5–8 minutes. Trim off the overhanging pastry. Melt the jelly with 1 tbsp water and brush a little over the base of the pastry case. Cool.

4 Make the crème pâtissière (see the technique below). Pour into a bowl, cover, and cool completely, then spread it in the pastry case. Top with the strawberries. Brush them with the warmed jelly glaze. Leave to set before serving.

Making crème pâtissière

1 Bring the milk to the boil in a heavy-based saucepan. Beat the remaining ingredients in a bowl. Pour the hot milk into the egg mixture, whisking all the time.

2 Return the mixture to the pan and bring to the boil over medium heat, whisking constantly. When it thickens, lower the heat and cook for 2–3 minutes, stirring well.

2 hrs 10 mins

preparation	chilling		preparation	baking blind		boiling and whisking	garnish
10 mins	1 hr		10 mins	30 mins plus cooling		15 mins plus cooling	5 mins

Fragrant Blackcurrant and Rosemary Cheesecake

Rosemary is a strongly flavoured herb, so be sure to chop it
very finely and to stir it evenly through the biscuit crumb mixture.

Serves 8–10

Ingredients

200g (7oz) digestive biscuits,
 crushed

1 tbsp chopped rosemary, plus
 a sprig to decorate (optional)

85g (3oz) unsalted butter,
 melted, plus extra for greasing

675g (1½lb) cream cheese,
 softened

225g (8oz) caster sugar

2 eggs

1 tsp pure vanilla extract

For the topping

225g (8oz) blackcurrants

granulated sugar, to taste

1 tsp arrowroot

1 In a large bowl, mix the crushed biscuits with the chopped rosemary and stir in the melted butter. Press the mixture onto the bottom and about 2.5cm (1in) up the side of a buttered 20cm (8in) springform tin. Preheat the oven to 150°C (300°F/Gas 2).

2 Beat the cream cheese until light and fluffy. Add the sugar, eggs, and vanilla extract and beat just until smoothly blended. Spoon into the biscuit crust and level the surface. Bake for 1–1¼ hours or until set. Turn off the oven and leave until cold, then chill.

3 Lightly poach the blackcurrants in 4 tbsp water until the juices run. Sweeten to taste. Blend the arrowroot with 1 tsp water and stir in. Cook, stirring, until thickened and the juices are clear. Leave to cool.

4 Remove the cheesecake from the tin and place on a serving plate. Spoon the blackcurrant topping over so that the fruit trickles down the sides a little. Lay a sprig of rosemary alongside, if you like.

⚠ Rescue it!

If cracks appear in the cheesecake, they can be easily hidden by the topping. To prevent cracks appearing, don't beat too much air into the filling mixture – this will make it rise during baking and then fall, creating cracks. It also helps if the cheesecake is left to cool for a while in the turned-off oven, with the door ajar.

1 hr 40 mins	preparation	baking	cooking	to serve
	15 mins	1 hour 15 mins plus chilling	5 mins plus cooling	5 mins

BREAD AND BAKING

Take uncertainty out of baking with the help of this collection of bread, cake, biscuit, and bun recipes. Follow clear and detailed instructions that will increase your baking confidence.

Wholemeal Bread

Sunflower seeds add crunch to this hearty bread. For a breakfast loaf, you can use finely crushed bran cereal flakes in place of the wheat bran.

Makes 2 loaves

Ingredients

2½ tsp dried yeast, or
   15g (½oz) fresh yeast
425ml (14½fl oz) buttermilk
75g (2½oz) sunflower seeds,
   toasted and coarsely chopped
45g (1½oz) rolled oats
45g (1½oz) wheat bran
75g (2½oz) polenta, plus extra
   for the baking sheet
45g (1½oz) soft light brown
   sugar
1 tbsp salt
250g (9oz) strong wholemeal
   flour
250g (9oz) strong white flour,
   plus more if needed
melted butter, for greasing
1 egg white, beaten until frothy,
   to glaze

1 Sprinkle or crumble the yeast over 4 tbsp lukewarm water and set aside for 2 minutes. Stir gently, then leave for 2–3 minutes more until completely dissolved. Heat the buttermilk in a saucepan until just tepid.

2 Put the sunflower seeds, rolled oats, wheat bran, polenta, brown sugar, and salt in a large bowl. Add the dissolved yeast and buttermilk and mix with your hand. Stir in the wholemeal flour with half of the white flour and mix again. Add the remaining white flour, 60g (2oz) at a time, mixing well. Keep adding flour until the dough pulls away from the side of the bowl in a ball, and is soft and slightly sticky.

3 Turn the dough out onto a floured work surface. Sprinkle the dough and your hands with flour, then knead for 8–10 minutes or until very smooth and elastic. If the dough sticks while kneading, sprinkle the work surface with a little flour.

4 Wash the large bowl and brush it with melted butter. Put the ball of dough in the bowl and flip it so the surface is lightly buttered. Cover with a damp tea towel and leave to rise in a warm place for 1½–2 hours or until doubled in size.

5 Sprinkle two baking sheets with polenta. Knock back the dough to deflate it, then divide in half. Flour your hands and pat one piece of dough into a rough 38 x 10cm (15 x 4in) rectangle, leaving the corners rounded. Fold the rectangle in half and gently press the halves together. Transfer to one of the baking sheets. Repeat to shape the remaining dough.

6 Cover with a dry tea towel and leave to rise in a warm place for about 1 hour. Meanwhile, preheat the oven to 190°C (375°F/Gas 5). Brush the loaves with the egg glaze.

7 Bake the loaves for 40–45 minutes or until well browned. To test if they are ready, turn them over and tap the base with your knuckles: the bread should sound hollow and the sides should feel crisp. Cool on a wire rack.

4 hrs
15 mins

preparation	proving		resting	proving		baking
25 mins	2 hrs		5 mins	1 hr		45 mins

Sourdough Bread

A "starter" has to be made ahead of time. Despite this, the bread is easy to make and the leftover starter can be used to bake more loaves.

Makes 1 large loaf

Ingredients
225g (8oz) strong white flour, plus extra for dusting
7g (¼oz) sachet fast-action dried yeast

For the dough
675g (1½lb) strong white flour
7g (¼oz) sachet fast-action dried yeast
1 tbsp caster sugar
1 tsp salt
1 tbsp fennel seeds
oil for greasing

1 To make the starter, mix together the flour and dried yeast in a large bowl. Using a wooden spoon, gradually stir in 600ml (1 pint) tepid water to make a smooth batter. Cover with a damp cloth and leave for 2 days, stirring daily and dampening the cloth when necessary to keep it moist.

2 For the dough, mix the flour, yeast, sugar, salt, and fennel seeds together in a large bowl. Make a hollow well in the middle. Stir the starter dough, which will have separated, then measure 150ml (5fl oz) and add to the dough mix with 360ml (12fl oz) tepid water. Mix to a soft pliable dough, adding a further 1–2 tbsp water if the dough is too dry.

3 Knead the dough on a lightly floured surface for about 10 minutes or until smooth and elastic. Shape into a ball and place in an oiled bowl. Cover loosely and leave in a warm place to rise for 1 hour or until doubled in size.

4 Grease a large baking tray with oil. Knock back the dough to deflate it. Shape into a flattish round and place on the baking tray. Cover with a damp cloth and leave to rise for 1 hour or until doubled in size.

5 Preheat the oven to 220°C (425°F/Gas 7). Lightly dust the loaf with flour, then use a sharp knife to slash the top in a crisscross pattern. Bake for 15 minutes, then reduce the oven to 190°C (375°F/Gas 5) and bake for a further 20–25 minutes. Transfer to a wire rack and leave to cool.

Testing "doneness"
When baked, the sourdough bread will be a lovely golden colour. To check that it is thoroughly cooked, turn the loaf over and tap the base – the loaf should sound hollow, not dense.

3 hrs

preparation	proving		kneading	proving		baking
15 mins	1 hr		5 mins	1 hr		40 mins

THE RECIPES BREAD AND BAKING BREAD

319

Soda Bread with Pumpkin

This quickly made bread doesn't require any kneading. Adding grated pumpkin to the dough ensures that the loaf will keep moist for days.

Makes 1 loaf

Ingredients

300g (10oz) plain flour,
  plus extra for dusting
100g (3½oz) wholemeal
  self-raising flour
1 tsp bicarbonate of soda
½ tsp fine salt
125g (4½oz) pumpkin or
  butternut squash, peeled,
  deseeded, and roughly grated
30g (1oz) pumpkin seeds
300ml (10fl oz) buttermilk

1 Preheat the oven to 220°C (425°F/Gas 7). Mix the flours with the bicarbonate of soda and salt in a large bowl. Add the grated pumpkin and seeds and stir well to combine so that no clumps remain. Make a well in the centre and pour in the buttermilk. Stir together to form a dough (see the technique below).

2 Place the shaped loaf on a baking sheet lined with baking parchment. Use a sharp knife to slash a cross into the top (this helps the bread to rise during baking).

3 Bake for 30 minutes, then reduce the oven temperature to 200°C (400°F/Gas 6) and bake for a further 20 minutes or until crusty and browned. The bread should sound hollow when tapped on the base.

4 Transfer to a wire rack and allow to cool for at least 20 minutes before serving. The bread can be kept, well wrapped, for up to 3 days.

Working the dough

1 With your hands, quickly draw the flour into the liquid to make a soft, slightly sticky dough. Do not overwork the dough.

2 Add a little more buttermilk if it seems dry. Bring the mixture together into a ball, then turn out onto a lightly floured surface.

3 Knead the dough for 1–2 minutes or until smooth and evenly blended. Shape the dough into a round loaf 15cm (6in) in diameter.

1 hr
30 mins

preparation	baking	cooling
20 mins	50 mins	20 mins

Hot Cross Buns

These delicious treats are too good to keep just for Easter. Knead in the dried fruit evenly so that each spicy bun will be full of sweet fruit.

Makes 10–12

Ingredients
200ml (7fl oz) milk
50g (1¾oz) unsalted butter
1 tsp pure vanilla extract
2 tsp dried yeast
100g (3½oz) caster sugar
500g (1lb 2oz) strong white
   flour, sifted, plus extra
   for dusting
1 tsp salt
2 tsp mixed spice
1 tsp ground cinnamon
1 egg, beaten, plus extra
   beaten egg for glazing
150g (5½oz) mixed dried
   fruit such as raisins,
   sultanas, and mixed peel
vegetable oil, for greasing

For the paste
3 tbsp plain flour
3 tbsp caster sugar

1 Heat the milk, butter, and vanilla extract in a pan until the butter has just melted. Cool until tepid. Whisk in the dried yeast and 1 tbsp of sugar. Leave for 10 minutes or until frothy.

2 Put the remaining sugar, the flour, salt, and spices into a bowl. Mix in the egg. Add the milk mixture and form a dough. Knead on a floured surface for 10 minutes or until smooth and elastic. Press the dough out into a rectangle, scatter over the dried fruit, and knead briefly to combine.

3 Shape into a ball, place in an oiled bowl, and cover with cling film. Leave to rise in a warm place for 1–2 hours or until doubled in size. Knock back to deflate, then divide into 10–12 pieces and roll into balls. Place them on baking sheets lined with baking parchment. Cover with cling film and leave to rise for 1–2 hours or until doubled in size.

4 Preheat the oven to 220°C (425°F/Gas 7). Brush the buns with beaten egg to glaze. To make the paste, mix the flour and sugar with enough water to make a spreadable consistency. Put the paste into a piping bag and pipe a cross on top of each bun, as directed below. Bake for 15–20 minutes or until risen and golden brown. Transfer to a wire rack and allow to cool for at least 15 minutes before serving.

Piping the crosses
You can use a piping bag fitted with a fine nozzle, or a small disposable piping bag with the tip cut off. The paste should be thin enough to be piped, but not runny. Pipe a straight line across the centre of the top, then pipe a second line at right angles to this.

5 hrs
10 mins

preparation	proving	kneading	proving	baking	cooling
30 mins	2 hrs	5 mins	2 hrs	20 mins	15 mins

Brioche Nanterre

Baked in a loaf tin, a buttery brioche is ideal for slicing. When fully cooked, the turned-out loaf should sound hollow when tapped on the base.

Makes 1 loaf

Ingredients
2½ tsp dried yeast
2 tbsp caster sugar
375g (13oz) strong white
   bread flour, plus extra
   for dusting
1½ tsp salt
5 eggs, beaten
vegetable oil, for greasing
175g (6oz) unsalted butter,
   cut into cubes and softened
beaten egg, for glazing

1 Whisk the yeast with 1 tsp sugar and 2 tbsp warm water. Set aside for 10 minutes. Meanwhile, line a 900g (2lb) loaf tin with baking parchment.

2 Sift the flour, salt, and remaining sugar into a large bowl. Make a well in the centre and pour in the eggs and the yeast mixture. Bring together into a sticky dough. Turn out onto a floured work surface and knead for 10 minutes or until elastic but still a bit sticky. Put the dough in an oiled bowl, cover with cling film, and leave in a warm place for 2–3 hours.

3 Tip the dough onto a floured work surface and knock back gently to deflate. Work in the butter (see the technique below). Divide the dough into eight pieces and shape each into a ball. Fit them into the prepared tin in one layer. Cover with cling film and a tea towel and leave at room temperature for 2–3 hours or until the dough has doubled in size.

4 Towards the end of the rising time, preheat the oven to 200°C (400°F/Gas 6). Brush the top of the loaf with beaten egg, then bake for about 30 minutes or until risen and golden brown. Leave to cool for a few minutes, then turn out onto a wire rack to cool.

Making brioche dough

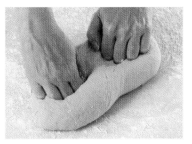

1 Shape the dough into a flattened ball and scatter one-third of the cubed butter over the surface.

2 Fold the dough over the butter to enclose it, then knead gently for 5 minutes to mix in the butter.

3 Repeat, adding the remaining butter in two batches. Knead until no streaks of butter can be seen.

7 hrs 5 mins

preparation	proving	kneading	proving	baking
20 mins	3 hrs	15 mins	3 hrs	30 mins

Blinis

Serve these buckwheat-based pancakes while they are still warm,
or wrap in foil and then reheat in a moderate oven for about 10 minutes.

Makes 48 blinis

Ingredients

½ tsp dried yeast
200ml (7fl oz) milk, heated
   until tepid
100g (3½oz) soured cream
100g (3½oz) buckwheat flour
100g (3½oz) strong
   white flour
½ tsp salt
2 eggs, separated
50g (1¾oz) unsalted butter,
   melted and cooled, plus
   extra for frying
soured cream, smoked salmon,
   freshly ground black pepper,
   and chives, to serve (optional)

1 Add the yeast to the tepid milk and whisk until dissolved. Whisk in the soured cream. In a large bowl, mix together the two flours and the salt, then make a well in the centre and gradually pour in the yeast mixture, whisking constantly. Whisk in the egg yolks, then add the butter and whisk to make a smooth batter. Cover the bowl with cling film and leave in a warm place for at least 2 hours or until bubbles have appeared all over the surface.

2 In a clean bowl, whisk the egg whites until they form soft peaks. Fold into the batter, then fry the blinis (see the technique below). Cook each batch for 1–2 minutes or until bubbles start to appear on the surface. When the bubbles begin to pop, turn and cook for another minute on the other side.

3 Transfer the blinis to a warmed plate and cover with a clean tea towel. Continue to fry the blinis, adding more butter as needed, until all the batter is used up. To serve as delicious canapés, top with soured cream and smoked salmon, season with pepper, and garnish with snipped chives.

Frying blinis

1 Gently fold the egg whites into the batter with a spatula until well combined, with no lumps of egg white. Transfer the batter to a jug.

2 Heat a knob of butter in a large, non-stick frying pan over medium heat. Add spoonfuls of batter to make 6cm (2½in) rounds.

| 2 hrs 45 mins | preparation 20 mins | resting 2 hrs | cooking 15 mins | reheating 10 mins |

Scones

Take care not to overmix the dough because this can make the scones heavy. Don't be tempted to make the dough smooth – leave it rough.

Makes 8–10 scones

Ingredients

60g (2oz) unsalted butter, plus extra for greasing
250g (9oz) strong white flour
2 tsp baking powder
½ tsp salt
2 tbsp caster sugar
175ml (6fl oz) buttermilk, plus extra if needed
jam, butter, and clotted cream, to serve (optional)

1 Preheat the oven to 220°C (425°F/Gas 7). Brush a baking sheet with melted butter. Sift the flour, baking powder, and salt into a medium bowl. Stir in the sugar. Add the butter and cut it into small pieces using two round-bladed knives, tossing the butter pieces to coat with flour.

2 Rub the mixture with your fingertips until it resembles fine breadcrumbs, lifting to aerate it. Work quickly so the warmth of your hands does not melt the butter. Gradually pour in the buttermilk, tossing to mix with the crumbly mix. Stir just until the crumbs hold together, then gather into a ball of dough. Add a little more buttermilk if the crumbs seem dry.

3 Turn the dough out onto a floured surface and knead lightly for 3–5 seconds. Pat out to a round 1cm (½in) thick. Cut out rounds with a 7cm (2¾in) pastry cutter. Gather the trimmings, pat out, and cut more rounds.

4 Arrange the scones 5cm (2in) apart on the baking sheet. Bake for 12–15 minutes or until lightly browned. Serve freshly baked with jam, butter, and clotted cream, if desired.

Using buttermilk
Buttermilk adds a subtle tangy flavour and makes the lightest, most tender scones. If you cannot find buttermilk in the supermarket, you can substitute your own "soured" milk made by mixing ½ tsp bicarbonate of soda with 175ml (6fl oz) milk.

35 mins

preparation
20 mins

baking
15 mins

Banana, Cranberry, and Walnut Loaf

Use this recipe as a template and substitute other fruits and nuts – dried blueberries or cherries; hazelnuts, pecan nuts, or almonds.

Makes 2 loaves

Ingredients

115g (4oz) unsalted butter, softened
175g (6oz) caster sugar
2 large eggs, beaten
1 tsp milk
300g (10oz) plain flour
½ tsp salt
1 tsp bicarbonate of soda
1 tsp mixed spice
3 bananas, mashed
85g (3oz) dried cranberries
60g (2oz) walnuts, roughly chopped

1 Preheat the oven to 160°C (325°F/Gas 3). Grease two 450g (1lb) loaf tins or one 900g (2lb) tin, then line with baking parchment.

2 In a large bowl, beat the butter and sugar together with a handheld electric mixer until pale and creamy. Beat in the eggs and milk. Stir in the flour, salt, bicarbonate of soda, and spice, mixing well. Finally, mix in the bananas, cranberries, and walnuts.

3 Spoon into the tins, dividing evenly if using two tins. Bake in the middle of the oven, allowing 45–50 minutes for the smaller loaves and 1–1¼ hours for the large loaf. To test if the loaf is cooked, insert a skewer into the centre; if it comes out clean, the loaf is ready.

4 Remove from the oven and leave to cool in the tins for about 10 minutes, then turn out onto a wire rack to cool completely. Keep in an airtight tin.

Shelling nuts
As a general rule, unshelled nuts will keep twice as long as shelled. For walnuts, use a nutcracker, pressing gently on the unseamed centre of the nut and rotating it a few times.

1 hr 20 mins

preparation	cooking	cooling
20 mins	50 mins	10 mins

Fruit Cake

This light cake is a quick and easy alternative to a classic rich fruit cake. To add punch, you can soak the dried fruit in alcohol first.

Serves 8–12

Ingredients

175g (6oz) unsalted butter, softened

175g (6oz) light soft brown sugar

3 large eggs

250g (9oz) self-raising flour, sifted

2–3 tbsp milk

300g (10oz) mixed dried fruit such as sultanas, raisins, glacé cherries, and mixed peel

1 Preheat the oven to 180°C (350°F/Gas 4). Line a 20cm (8in) deep round cake tin with baking parchment.

2 In a bowl, beat the butter and sugar together with a hand-held electric mixer until pale and creamy. Beat in the eggs, one at a time, adding a little of the flour after each one. Fold in the remaining flour and the milk. Add the dried fruit and fold in until well combined.

3 Spoon the mixture into the tin and level the top. Bake for 1½–1¾ hours or until firm to the touch and a skewer inserted into the middle of the cake comes out clean. Leave to cool in the tin, then turn out and peel off the lining paper. Store the cake in an airtight tin.

Soaking dried fruit

If you soak dried fruit in alcohol – rum, whisky, brandy, or whatever you fancy – or in fruit juice, it will plump up and gain extra flavour. To prevent the moist fruit from sinking to the bottom of the cake, toss it with a little of the flour, separating the pieces as you toss.

2 hrs 10 mins

preparation 25 mins

baking 1 hr 45 mins

Gingerbread Biscuits

These fragrant biscuits are quick and easy to make. For successful baking, use heavy-duty baking sheets that won't buckle in the oven.

Makes 45 biscuits

Ingredients

250g (9oz) plain flour, plus extra for sprinkling
2 tsp baking powder
175g (6oz) caster sugar
a few drops of pure vanilla extract
½ tsp mixed spice
2 tsp ground ginger
100g (3½oz) clear honey
1 egg, separated
4 tsp milk
125g (4½oz) unsalted butter, softened
125g (4½oz) ground almonds
chopped hazelnuts or almonds, to decorate

1 Preheat the oven to 180°C (350°F/Gas 4). Line two baking sheets with greaseproof paper.

2 Sift the flour and baking powder into a bowl. Add the sugar, vanilla extract, mixed spice, ginger, honey, egg yolk, milk, butter, and ground almonds. Using a wooden spoon or hand-held electric mixer, beat together to form a soft dough. Shape into a ball.

3 Roll out the dough thinly on a lightly floured surface to a thickness of 5mm (¼in). Cut out the biscuits using shaped cutters and place on the baking sheets, spaced slightly apart to allow for spreading.

4 Beat the egg white and brush over the biscuits, then sprinkle over the chopped nuts. Bake for 8–10 minutes or until light golden brown. Remove from the oven and allow to cool on the baking sheets for 5 minutes, then transfer to a wire rack and leave to cool completely.

Chopping nuts
Nuts can be chopped using a large, sharp knife, or in a food processor, quickly pulsing on and off to avoid chopping too finely and ending up with ground nuts or nut butter.

45 mins

preparation		baking	cooling
30 mins		10 mins	5 mins

Macaroons

These almond meringue biscuits (not to be confused with classic French macarons) can be baked on rice paper, which can be eaten too.

Makes 24 macaroons

Ingredients

2 egg whites
225g (8oz) caster sugar
125g (4½oz) ground almonds
30g (1oz) rice flour
a few drops of almond extract
24 blanched almonds

1 Preheat the oven to 180°C (350°F/Gas 4). Put the egg whites in a spotlessly clean mixing bowl. Using an electric mixer, beat them until stiff. Gradually whisk in the sugar, 1 tbsp at a time, to make a thick, glossy meringue. Use a large metal spoon or spatula to gently, but thoroughly, fold in the ground almonds, rice flour, and almond extract.

2 Line two baking sheets with edible rice paper or baking parchment. Use two teaspoons to scoop and shape the mixture on the baking sheets, as shown below, then bake in the oven.

3 Transfer the macaroons to a wire rack to cool completely. If you baked them on edible rice paper, cut or tear the paper neatly around the edge of the macaroons. Or lift the macaroons carefully off the baking parchment.

Shaping and baking macaroons

1 Place small spoonfuls of the mixture, spaced well apart, on a paper-lined baking sheet. Clean and dry the spoons between scoops.

2 Continue scooping and shaping the macaroons on the other baking sheet, then gently set an almond in the centre of each macaroon.

3 Bake the macaroons in the centre of the oven for 12–15 minutes or until light golden and just firm to a gentle touch.

25 mins

preparation
10 mins

baking
15 mins

Chocolate Cake

For the best flavour, use chocolate with about 70 per cent cocoa solids.
If you prefer, you can melt it in the microwave, stirring it frequently.

Serves 12

Ingredients

200g (7oz) dark chocolate,
  broken into pieces
310g (11oz) unsalted butter,
  softened, plus extra for
  greasing
225g (8oz) light muscovado
  sugar
3 eggs, separated
100g (3½oz) self-raising flour
½ tsp bicarbonate of soda
60g (2oz) cocoa powder
60g (2oz) ground almonds
4 tbsp milk
120ml (4fl oz) double cream
200g (7oz) icing sugar, sifted

1 Preheat the oven to 180°C (350°F/Gas 4). Butter two 20cm (8in) round cake tins and line with baking parchment. Melt 60g (2oz) of the chocolate in a heatproof bowl set over a pan of simmering water; the base of the bowl should not touch the water. Set aside to cool slightly.

2 In a large bowl, cream together 225g (8oz) of the butter with the muscovado sugar using a hand-held electric mixer until light and fluffy. Add the egg yolks and cooled melted chocolate and beat in. Sift the flour, bicarbonate of soda, and cocoa into the bowl. Add the ground almonds and milk and gently fold everything together until well mixed.

3 Whisk the egg whites in a clean bowl to form stiff peaks. Stir a large spoonful into the chocolate mix, then gently fold in the remainder. Divide the mixture between the prepared tins. Bake for 25–30 minutes or until the sponges bounce back when lightly pressed in the centre. Set the tins on a wire rack and leave to cool.

4 For the icing, combine the remaining chocolate with the cream in a large heatproof bowl set over a pan of gently simmering water. Stir occasionally until the chocolate has melted and the mixture is smooth. Remove and cool. In a separate bowl, beat the remaining butter with the icing sugar until fluffy. Add the chocolate mixture and beat until smooth.

5 Turn out the sponges. Sandwich them together with a third of the icing, then spread the remaining icing over the top and sides of the cake.

Ensuring cakes retain moisture
While the cakes are cooling in the tins on a wire rack, cover them with a damp tea towel – this will keep them beautifully moist. Allow them to get completely cold before turning out and icing.

1 hr

| preparation | baking | icing |
| 20 mins | 30 mins | 10 mins |

Sachertorte

To achieve a shiny, smooth finish on this beautiful cake, spread the chocolate glaze while it is still warm; if it cools too much it will thicken.

Serves 6–8

Ingredients

250g (9oz) unsalted butter, softened
250g (9oz) caster sugar
250g (9oz) dark chocolate, melted
½ tsp pure vanilla extract
5 eggs, separated
250g (9oz) plain flour
6–8 tbsp apricot glaze or sieved apricot jam, heated until runny

For the chocolate glaze

300ml (10fl oz) whipping cream
200g (7oz) dark chocolate, chopped
a few drops of pure vanilla extract

1 Preheat the oven to 180°C (350°F/Gas 4). Line a 23cm (9in) round deep cake tin with baking parchment. Beat together the butter and sugar until light and fluffy, then beat in the chocolate and vanilla extract. Beat in the egg yolks, one at a time, then fold in the flour.

2 Whisk the egg whites until stiff. Mix a little of the egg whites into the chocolate mixture to lighten it slightly, then carefully fold in the remaining egg whites. Pour the mixture into the cake tin and level the surface. Bake for 45–60 minutes or until the cake feels just firm to the touch in the centre and a skewer inserted into it comes out clean. Set the tin on a wire rack. Cool, then unmould the cake.

3 For the glaze, pour the cream into a small saucepan and bring to the boil. Put the chopped chocolate in a bowl, then pour in the hot cream and stir until the chocolate melts. Add the vanilla extract. Cool slightly, stirring occasionally, until the mixture has a coating consistency.

4 Slice the cake in half horizontally. Sandwich the two halves together again with a thin layer of apricot glaze. Spread the remainder over the top and sides of the cake. Reserve 3 tbsp of the chocolate glaze; spread the rest over the cake, as shown below. Leave in a cool place until the glaze has set. Beat the reserved glaze, warming it gently if it is too thick, then use it to pipe "Sacher" on top of the cake.

Spreading the glaze

Pour the chocolate glaze over the cake and spread quickly over the top and sides with a large palette knife. If the glaze has cooled too much to spread evenly, gently heat it again.

1 hr 40 mins

preparation
25 mins

baking
1 hr
plus cooling

glazing
15 mins

Shortbread

A combination of plain flour and cornflour gives shortbread its crisp texture. Be sure to use good-quality butter for the essential rich flavour.

Makes 8 slices

Ingredients
100g (3½oz) unsalted butter, softened, plus extra for greasing
50g (1¾oz) caster sugar, plus extra for dusting
100g (3½oz) plain flour
50g (1¾oz) cornflour

1 Lightly grease a 18cm (7in) round cake tin. In a bowl, beat the butter using a hand-held electric mixer until creamy. Add the sugar and beat into the butter until the mixture is pale and fluffy.

2 Sift the flour and cornflour into the bowl and work everything together with your hands until thoroughly combined to make a stiff dough. Transfer the dough to the tin and press it out evenly. Smooth the surface and prick all over with a fork. Mark into eight wedges. Cover and chill for at least 1 hour or until firm.

3 Preheat the oven to 160°C (325°F/Gas 3). Bake the shortbread for about 40 minutes or until pale golden and firm to the touch. While the shortbread is still warm, score the wedges again, then dust the surface with a little caster sugar and leave to cool completely in the tin. When cold, cut into the wedges or break carefully.

Making round biscuits
Rather than baking in a tin, shape the dough into a log, wrap in cling film, and chill until firm. Use a large sharp knife to cut the log across into rounds. Lay these on a greased baking sheet and bake for about 20 minutes. Sprinkle with sugar and cool slightly before transferring to a wire rack.

1 hr 55 mins

preparation 15 mins

chilling 1 hr

baking 40 mins

Swiss Roll

There is a clever trick to help you when rolling up a light sponge – follow these simple steps and you'll be able to do it perfectly.

Serves 8–10

Ingredients

3 large eggs
100g (3½oz) caster sugar, plus extra for dusting
pinch of salt
75g (2½oz) self-raising flour
1 tsp pure vanilla extract
6 tbsp raspberry jam (or any other type of jam, or chocolate-hazelnut spread), for the filling

1 Preheat the oven to 200°C (400°F/Gas 6). Line the bottom of a 32.5 x 23cm (13 x 9in) Swiss roll tin with baking parchment. Set a large heatproof bowl over a pan of simmering water; the base of the bowl should not touch the water. Put the eggs, sugar, and salt in the bowl and whisk for 5 minutes or until pale and very thick.

2 Remove the bowl from the pan and set it on a work surface. Whisk for 1–2 minutes or until cool. Sift in the flour, add the vanilla extract, and gently fold in, keeping the volume you've whisked in. Pour into the tin and gently smooth out evenly. Bake for 12–15 minutes or until firm and springy.

3 Sprinkle a sheet of baking parchment evenly with caster sugar. Carefully turn out the sponge onto the sugared paper so it lies upside down. Leave to cool for 5 minutes, then carefully peel the lining paper from the sponge.

4 If the jam is too thick to spread, warm it gently in a small pan. Spread the jam over the top of the sponge, then roll up, as shown below. Sprinkle with sugar before serving.

Rolling up a sponge

1 Make an indentation with the back of a knife along one short side, 2cm (¾in) from the edge.

2 Starting at the indented edge, gently but firmly roll up the sponge, using the parchment to help roll.

3 Wrap the parchment around the sponge to keep it tightly rolled and in shape. Leave to cool completely.

40 mins

preparation	baking	filling and rolling
20 mins	15 mins	5 mins plus cooling

Carrot Cake

A moist, juicy texture is key for this stunning carrot cake.
Crisp walnuts contrast with the sweet frosting.

Serves 8–10

Ingredients

100g (3½oz) walnuts
225ml (7½fl oz) sunflower oil,
   plus extra for greasing
3 large eggs
225g (8oz) soft light brown
   sugar
1 tsp pure vanilla extract
200g (7oz) carrots, finely grated
100g (3½oz) sultanas
200g (7oz) self-raising flour
75g (2½oz) wholemeal
   self-raising flour
pinch of salt
1 tsp ground cinnamon, plus
   extra if desired
1 tsp ground ginger
¼ tsp grated nutmeg
finely grated zest of 1 orange

For the frosting

50g (1¾oz) unsalted butter,
   softened
100g (3½oz) cream cheese,
   softened
200g (7oz) icing sugar
½ tsp pure vanilla extract
2 oranges

1 Preheat the oven to 180°C (350°F/Gas 4). Oil a 23cm (9in) springform cake tin and line with baking parchment. Spread the walnuts in a small tin and toast in the oven for about 5 minutes or until browned. Rub them in a clean tea towel to remove the papery skins, if you like, then chop the walnuts coarsely. Set aside.

2 Combine the oil, eggs, sugar, and vanilla extract in a large bowl. Using a hand-held electric mixer, beat together until thick and lighter in colour. Squeeze the grated carrots thoroughly in a clean tea towel to remove excess liquid. Gently fold the carrots into the cake mixture with the walnuts and sultanas.

3 Sift the two flours into the bowl, then tip in any bran left in the sieve. Add the salt, spices, and grated orange zest. Fold everything together to combine thoroughly and evenly.

4 Pour the cake mixture into the tin and smooth the surface. Bake for 45 minutes or until a skewer inserted into the centre of the cake comes out clean. Set the tin on a wire rack and leave to cool before unmoulding the cake.

5 To make the frosting, combine the butter, cream cheese, icing sugar, and vanilla in a bowl. Grate in the zest of 1 orange. Using a hand-held electric mixer, beat together until smooth, pale, and fluffy. Spread the frosting over the cake with a palette knife, swirling attractively.

6 Use a citrus zester to take thread-like strips of zest from the remaining orange. Sprinkle these over the top of the cake, then sprinkle with a little extra cinnamon, if you like.

1 hr 20 mins

preparation	baking	icing
25 mins	45 mins	10 mins

Chocolate Brownies

To cut these moist and squidgy brownies into neat squares, keep dipping the knife in boiling water and wiping it dry between cuts.

Makes 24

Ingredients

100g (3½oz) hazelnuts
175g (6oz) unsalted butter, diced
300g (10oz) dark chocolate, broken into pieces
300g (10oz) caster sugar
4 large eggs, beaten
200g (7oz) plain flour
25g (scant 1oz) cocoa powder, plus extra for dusting

1 Preheat the oven to 200°C (400°F/Gas 6). Scatter the hazelnuts over a baking sheet, then toast in the oven for 5 minutes or until browned. Tip into a clean tea towel and rub to remove the skins. Chop the nuts roughly – some big chunks and some small. Set aside.

2 Line the bottom and sides of a 23 x 30cm (9 x 12in) brownie tin, or similar tin, with baking parchment, leaving excess parchment to rise above the rim. Put the butter and chocolate in a heatproof bowl set over a pan of simmering water and gently melt them, stirring until smooth. Remove and leave to cool.

3 Add the sugar to the chocolate mix and stir well. Add the eggs a little at a time, mixing well between additions. Sift the flour and cocoa powder into the bowl and fold in until the mixture is smooth and no patches of flour can be seen. Stir in the chopped nuts to distribute them evenly.

4 Pour into the prepared tin and spread evenly right into the corners. Bake for 12–15 minutes (see the technique below). Remove from the oven and set the tin on a wire rack to cool.

5 When the brownie cake is cold, turn it out of the tin, using the edges of the parchment to get a good grip. Cut into equal pieces using a long, sharp knife. Sift cocoa powder over the brownies before serving.

Testing brownies for "doneness"
If brownies are thoroughly baked, they will tend to be dry and crumbly. For a moister result, bake until just firm to the touch on top; they will still be soft underneath. A skewer inserted in the centre of the cake should come out coated with a little batter.

40 mins

preparation
25 mins   plus cooling

baking
15 mins   plus cooling

Chocolate Chip Cookies

If you're baking more than one sheet of cookies at a time, rotate and swap the sheets halfway through, for even browning.

Makes 45 cookies

Ingredients

125g (4½oz) unsalted butter, softened
125g (4½oz) light soft brown sugar
3 tbsp golden syrup
1 egg
225g (8oz) self-raising flour
150g (5½oz) milk, dark, or white chocolate chips

1 Preheat the oven to 180°C (350°F/Gas 4). Line several baking sheets with greaseproof paper.

2 Cream together the butter and sugar with a hand-held electric mixer until light and fluffy. Beat in the golden syrup and egg. Mix in the flour to make a soft dough.

3 Drop small mounds of the cookie dough on the prepared baking sheets, allowing plenty of room for spreading.

4 Press the mounds down with your fingers or a spoon to flatten into discs. Decorate each cookie with chocolate chips, pressing them into the dough. Bake for 15–20 minutes or until golden around the edges. Allow to cool and firm up on the baking sheets for a few minutes, then transfer to a wire rack to cool completely.

Sizing of cookies

You can make the cookies any size you like. For a large cookie, use a piece of dough about the size of a pingpong ball; for a small cookie, use a walnut-sized piece. Another idea is to scoop up the dough using an ice-cream scoop. Make all the cookies the same size and shape so they will bake evenly.

35 mins

preparation
15 mins

baking
20 mins

plus cooling

MAKE IT YOUR OWN

· ·

Now you're ready to experiment.
Trust your instincts, and fall in love
with flavour, food, and the great joy
of cooking. Focus on the seasons, and
with some helpful tips and tricks from
John Torode and Gregg Wallace, prepare
to dazzle and delight in the kitchen.

Spring

March to early June

Spring is the season of new beginnings. With the milder weather comes the birth of young green shoots and a new world of ingredients at your fingertips. Enjoy cooking with colourful, versatile, and fresh-tasting spring vegetables. Choose flavours to pair with seasonal tender lamb and delicate fish.

Here are the perfect cooking opportunities to celebrate the rich spring offerings:

The Easter roast (p358)
Roasted leg of lamb Leg of lamb studded with rosemary sprigs and roasted with shallots and garlic

The Mother's Day lunch (p364)
Sautéed trout on wilted spinach Whole trout served with anchovy, toasted pumpkin seed, and asparagus sauce on wilted garlic spinach

Gregg's Seasonal Recommendations

Spring cabbages are usually known as collard or spring greens, and have none of the coarseness of winter ones. Loose-leaved, fragrant, and nutty, steam them with asparagus and toss with butter. Fresh asparagus has superb flavour matches – find them on pp366–7.

What's in season?

At their best

Crisp textures and delicate flavours will stand out when cooking with vegetables of the season. Serve alongside tender lamb or baked fish.

fruit and vegetables

asparagus
broccoli
  calabrese, purple-sprouting
cabbage
cauliflower
celeriac
chicory
cooking apples
dandelion greens
garlic (young green shoots)
green-topped carrots
hop shoots
Jersey royal potatoes
kale
laver
leeks
lettuce
  Little gem, oakleaf, Lollo
  Rosso, round, curly
nettles
pears
pea shoots
radishes
rhubarb
sea kale
sorrel
spinach
spring onions
swede
turnips (young)
watercress
wild garlic
wild mushrooms
  morels, St George's

meat, poultry, and game

guinea fowl
lamb
rabbit
wild boar
wood pigeon

fish and seafood

abalone
clams
crab
crayfish
halibut
langoustines
lobster
mullet
  grey, red
mussels
oysters
prawns
rainbow trout
razor clams
scallops
sea bass
sea bream
shrimps
sole
trout
turbot
whelks
wild salmon

Make it your own...

Easter lunch

All the focus of the table will be on this impressive Easter show-stopper, bursting with aroma and flavour. To make this roast lamb recipe your own, make use of the delicious alternative flavour pairings over the page.

Serves 6–8
Ingredients

1.8kg (4lb) leg of lamb
two sprigs of fresh
    rosemary
1 tbsp olive oil
salt and freshly ground
    black pepper
3–4 whole bulbs of
    garlic, washed
6–8 whole echalion
    shallots, washed
For the gravy
150ml (5fl oz) red wine
450ml (15fl oz)
    vegetable stock
1 tbsp redcurrant jelly

The main event
Roasted leg of lamb

1 Tender meat Preheat the oven to 190ºC (375ºF/Gas 5). Place the lamb on a board and stud with rosemary, as shown below. Place the lamb in a roasting tin, drizzle over the oil, and season well. Scatter the whole garlic and shallots around the leg of lamb. Roast for 1 hour 40 mins for pink, and 2 hours for cooked through.

2 Sweet shallots and creamy garlic Check the meat after 1 hour and baste. If the garlic and shallots look like they are tender and ready, then set aside. They can be added back to the roasting tin for the final 10 minutes to warm through. When ready, remove the lamb to a carving board, cover with foil, and rest for 10 minutes.

3 Rich gravy Spoon off any excess fat from the juices in the roasting tin. Place the roasting tin on the heat and add the wine, stock, and redcurrant jelly. Stir well to scrape all the sediment from the base of the pan. Bring to the boil, reduce heat to medium, and simmer for 10 minutes, stirring occasionally. Pour in the meat juices from the rested lamb. Adjust the seasoning to taste. Pour, through a sieve if necessary, into a gravy boat. Serve the lamb with the roasted garlic, whole roasted shallots, and the gravy.

Studded leg of lamb

Fragrant rosemary Before placing the lamb onto the roasting tin, stud with rosemary. Break the rosemary into small sprigs. Use a small sharp knife to make incisions in the lamb and poke a sprig of rosemary into each hole.

John's Serving Suggestions

To serve the shallots, split and pop them out. Halve the garlic and squeeze it from the skin, using it as a condiment. Baby carrots go wonderfully with lamb, and mint sauce is a must! See pp362–3 for dishes to complete your Easter table.

Fragrant rosemary

Sweet shallots

Creamy garlic

Tender meat

5 ways with...
Lamb

Lamb, paired with rosemary and garlic, is a fantastic main dish. There are many more spring pairings that can bring out the best flavours in tender lamb – here are five to get you started.

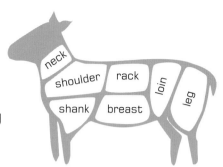

neck
shoulder
rack
loin
leg
shank
breast

Cooking cuts of lamb

As a general rule, prime cuts are best for roasting, spit roasting, and quick cooking methods such as frying or grilling; and tough, sinewy cuts respond best to long and slow braising or stewing.

Roasting – best end (rack); breast; leg; loin; rump; saddle; shoulder

Baking – fillet (eye of loin); best end cutlets; noisettes; medallions; shoulder; minced lamb

Braising & stewing – chump; leg; neck; shank; shoulder

Boiling & steaming – middle neck; scrag; shoulder

Frying – best end cutlets; chump chops; fillet (eye of loin); leg steaks; loin chops; saddle (butterfly) chops

Grilling – best end cutlets; butterflied leg; chump chops; fillet (eye of loin); leg steaks; loin chops; saddle chops

Spit roasting – leg (tunnel boned)

1 Harissa + honey

Lamb and harissa are a traditional North African flavour combination.

Mixed with honey, the **heat** of the harissa softens and the **sweet** and spicy pairing boldly complements the flavour of the lamb.

Mix honey and harissa to make a **glaze** or a sauce for lamb steaks, shanks, or shoulders. Alternatively, incorporate the flavours in a stew or tagine, or highlight them independently with honey-glazed lamb kofta served with yoghurt **sauce**.

2 Sorrel + watercress

Tart, **lemony** sorrel, paired with the **peppery** spice of watercress, adds a light, earthy **freshness** to the delicate flavour of lamb without overpowering it.

The sorrel and watercress can be **wilted** and blended to make a sauce, or finely chopped and mixed with breadcrumbs and herbs to make a **stuffing** for roast lamb. Alternatively, top a sorrel and watercress salad with grilled, **seasoned** lamb chops.

John's Advice on Choosing Lamb

Lamb should be pink or red in colour. Any meat that is darker coloured will be hogget or mutton and stronger in flavour. All lamb should have just a thin coating of white fat. Choose lamb with moderate marbling that will keep it moist when cooking.

3 Red wine + mushrooms

The flavour pairing of lamb, red wine, and mushrooms is **earthy**, rustic, and **hearty** – and the perfect antidote to potentially cold, damp weather in early spring.

Blend the flavours in a stew or pie or **showcase** the ingredients in a dish such as mushroom-crusted lamb cutlets and red wine sauce.

4 Rhubarb + coriander

Lamb with rhubarb is a classic Persian pairing, traditionally found in lamb khoresh, or lamb and rhubarb stew. The **tartness** of the rhubarb can be tempered with sugar and enhanced by the **delicate** flavour of the lamb, leading to a **complex** sweet and sour taste. Fresh herbs such as parsley and mint often **enhance** this dish, but as these herbs aren't in season until summer, fresh coriander is an excellent choice.

To experience these flavours another way, try topping rack of lamb with rhubarb **compote** and fresh coriander or with rhubarb and coriander chutney.

5 Yoghurt + spring onion

Lamb with yoghurt sauce has worldwide appeal. It is often found in dishes native to Greece, India, Morocco, and across the Middle East, and is best served with fresh herbs and crisp spring onions. The resulting combination of flavours is **bright**, **clean**, and perfect for spring.

Sample this flavour pairing in lamb burgers with **yoghurt sauce** and spring onions, in dahi gosht – a North Indian curry, or prepare a leg of lamb in a yoghurt and spring onion **marinade**.

The Easter table

Delicate vegetables and herbs create a spread of delicious spring-time fare

John's Presentation Tips
Keep the presentation relaxed and allow the bright spring colours to shine. Lightly crushing the potatoes will allow the buttery pepper flavours to go beyond the skin and into the potatoes – delicious!

Roasted baby carrots with lemon and cumin seeds
Trim and scrape 300g (10oz) young bunched carrots, leaving a little of the green stem in place. Place them in cold water to prevent them browning while you prepare the rest of the meal. Drain the carrots and place them in a roasting tin along with 2 tsp cumin seeds, $1/2$ tsp sugar, grated zest and juice of a small lemon, and 2 tbsp olive oil. Toss to coat. Roast at 190°C (375°F/Gas 5) for 30–35 minutes or until caramelized in places and just tender.
You could also try Roast baby leeks with sun-dried tomato dressing pp256–7

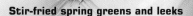

Stir-fried spring greens and leeks
Trim and wash 2 small leeks and diagonally slice into 2cm (3/4in) thick pieces. Finely shred 500g (1lb 2oz) spring greens. Heat 1 tsp vegetable oil in a large frying pan or wok, add 4 tbsp pine nuts, and stir-fry until golden. Remove from the heat and drain on kitchen paper. Add 2 tbsp more oil to the pan, add the leeks, and stir-fry over medium heat until they are softening – about 3 minutes. Add the greens, salt and pepper, and 4 tbsp water. Stir-fry for 3 minutes until the greens are tender. Top with the pine nuts and season well. Serve.
See Chilli and tofu stir-fry, pp224–5

Crushed new potatoes with watercress
Place 1kg (2¼lb) charlotte new potatoes
in a large pan, cover with salted water, and
bring to the boil. Boil for 15–20 minutes
or until tender. Drain and return to the pan.
Add 100g (3½oz) washed and chopped
watercress, 50g (1¾oz) butter, freshly
ground black pepper, and a good grating of
nutmeg. Cover the pan and shake well to coat
in the butter and watercress, which will wilt.
Use a large spoon to press the potatoes
lightly, so that they just burst and can soak
up the butter and watercress flavour.
You could also try Roast potatoes, pp258–9

Fresh mint sauce
Tear the leaves off a
50g (1¾oz) bunch of fresh
mint and finely chop. Place
in a bowl, stir in 3 tbsp
caster sugar, and leave to
infuse for 5 minutes – the
sugar helps draw the
flavours out of the mint.
Add 4 tbsp white wine
vinegar and 3 tbsp water.
Mix well.
**You could also try
Espagnole sauce pp62–5**

" Strange to see how a good
dinner and feasting
reconciles everybody. "
SAMUEL PEPYS

Make it your own...

Mother's Day lunch

Treat Mum on her day off with this beautiful dish that combines light, delicately flavoured spring ingredients – it's sure to appeal to all at the table. Find flavour pairings for fragrant asparagus over the page.

Serves 4
Ingredients

2 tbsp pumpkin seeds
115g (4oz) thin
    asparagus spears,
    trimmed
1 tbsp olive oil
20–30g (³⁄₄–1oz)
    plain flour
salt and freshly ground
    black pepper
4 trout, about 300g
    (10oz) each, cleaned,
    trimmed, rinsed, and
    patted dry
140g (5oz) butter
400g (14oz) fresh
    spinach, well washed
    and drained
2 green garlic cloves,
    finely chopped
50g can anchovies
    in olive oil
2 tbsp chopped
    flat-leaf parsley
juice of 1 lemon
lemon wedges and new
    potatoes, to serve

The main event
Sautéed trout on wilted spinach

1 Crunchy seeds Heat a non-stick frying pan. Add the pumpkin seeds and toss for a few minutes until lightly toasted. Tip out onto a plate immediately and set aside.

2 Charred asparagus Heat a griddle pan. Toss the asparagus in the olive oil and griddle each side for about 2 minutes until tender. Remove from the pan, cut into short lengths, and set aside.

3 Buttery pan-fried trout Put the flour on a large plate and season. Coat each trout on all sides with the flour. Lift out and gently shake to remove any excess. Heat 30g (1oz) of the butter in a large frying pan, until foaming. Add 2 trout, and brown over a medium heat for 3–4 minutes. Carefully turn and cook for 5 minutes more, until cooked through. Transfer to a plate and keep warm while you cook the remaining fish in a further 30g (1oz) of the butter. Remove the trout and keep warm with the rest of the fish.

4 Wilted spinach Meanwhile, shake excess water from the spinach. Place in a large hot pan with the green garlic and a grinding of pepper. Toss until just wilted but not soggy, about 2–3 minutes. Drain in a colander and place it over the pan. Cover and keep warm.

5 Tangy sauce Tip the anchovies and their oil into a small bowl and snip with scissors until finely chopped. Add the remaining butter to the pan with the chopped anchovies and their oil and cook, stirring until the anchovies "melt" into the butter. Stir in the parsley and sharpen with lemon juice. Add the toasted seeds and asparagus and heat through quickly. Season with a good grinding of pepper.

6 Press the spinach well against the sides of the colander to remove all excess moisture. Pile onto plates and top with the trout. Spoon the sauce over the trout. Garnish with lemon wedges and serve with new potatoes.

John's Mother's Day Lunch
Bream, seabass, or mackerel would also be delicious here. Roasting whole keeps them sweet and succulent. Stuff with strong flavours such as fennel, or finely shaved olives and capers, and the flavours will penetrate the fish from the inside.

Buttery
pan-fried trout

Charred
asparagus

Wilted
spinach

Tangy sauce

5 ways with...
Asparagus

The first shoots of asparagus in early spring are known as "thinnings", and have delicate stems. They are delicious matched with the elegant flavours of spring-time ingredients.

Cooking asparagus

Steam
1 Tie asparagus in a bundle.
2 Stand upright in 5cm (2in) of boiling water in a tall pot.
3 Cover and steam for 5–8 minutes.

Simmer
1 Lay asparagus flat in a large frying pan with about 2.5cm (1in) of water.
2 Simmer for up to 5 minutes.

Blanch
1 Steam or simmer as directed above.
2 Submerge the spears in ice-cold water immediately after cooking.

Stir-fry
1 Cut the spears diagonally into 2.5–5cm (1–2in) pieces.
2 Toss in a teaspoon of olive oil over a high heat for about 3 minutes.

Roast
1 Arrange on a baking sheet covered in parchment paper or a light coating of olive oil.
2 Bake at 230°C (445°F/Gas 8) for about 12–15 minutes.

Grill
1 Arrange spears under a pre-heated grill or on a griddle coated lightly in olive oil.
2 Cook for 3–6 minutes until tender, turning over halfway.

1 Salmon + garlic

A classic and **healthy** spring meal with salmon, asparagus, and garlic can be enjoyed any number of ways. Garlic adds a **complexity** to the slightly sweet, **delicate** flavours of salmon and asparagus. Showcase the ingredients with a simple grilled recipe or incorporate lemon and dill for a more **complex** taste.

Allow the salmon and asparagus to stand out – perhaps by serving salmon over a bed of asparagus – and incorporate the garlic with other flavours in a sauce or aïoli. These ingredients also **shine** in quiches and savoury tarts.

2 Parmesan + mushrooms

The **earthiness** of mushrooms combined with the bright tang of Parmesan cheese creates a perfect **enhancement** for the fresh taste of asparagus.

There are infinite ways to enjoy this **delicious** combination, including on pizzas, or in salads, tarts, quiches, and risottos. Why not try roasting the two spring vegetables together with a clove of garlic, adding a grating of Parmesan cheese before serving?

Gregg's Advice on Choosing Asparagus

Green and purple asparagus have the most pronounced flavour, while white is milder and sweeter. Choose fresh, sprightly spears with a clean-looking cut end. They should be firm to the touch, likely to crack if bent, and the growing tips should be tightly closed.

3 Chicory + balsamic

The distinctive, **savoury** flavour of asparagus pairs well with the **delicate**, slightly bitter flavour of fresh chicory. A splash of sharp balsamic vinegar brings **brightness** and a kick to the asparagus and savoury chicory without overpowering them, adding **depth** and complexity.

For a light spring salad, try tossing roasted asparagus and fresh baby chicory leaves in tangy balsamic vinegar. To make this salad really shine, add goat's cheese or sliced almonds.

4 Potatoes + mustard

The fresh taste and **crisp** bite of asparagus is an excellent contrast to starchy potatoes. Wholegrain mustard adds a **sharp** complexity to the pair.

Mix mustard with an asparagus and new potato salad or serve roasted potatoes and asparagus side by side with a wholegrain mustard sauce. Alternatively, serve asparagus and potato salad alongside roast beef or salmon **marinated** in wholegrain mustard.

5 Eggs + béchamel

Asparagus topped with béchamel sauce is **simple** and delicious. Try adding poached eggs to the dish for a **rich** and **healthy** spring meal. Make a classic griddled asparagus, béchamel, and boiled egg dish or layer the sauce over poached eggs on a bed of prosciutto-wrapped asparagus.

You could add cheese to the béchamel recipe to create a Mornay sauce – another classic sauce that can really bring out the flavour of asparagus.

Béchamel sauce, one of the key mother sauces, is covered in the Building Blocks. Find the recipe on pp50–1.

Summer late June to August

Revel in the flavour combinations available to you in the summer months. Experiment with your recipes, making the most of the ripe fruit and juicy salad vegetables as they come into their very best. Soak up the delicious atmosphere of the festival season.

Here are three great food occasions to mark this glorious season:

The al fresco lunch (p370)
Ratatouille brioche tart Buttery brioche dough filled with seasonal stewed vegetables topped with baked quail's eggs

The Afternoon Tea (p376)
Mini sultana and almond scones Delicate scones served with fresh damson jam and clotted cream

The drinks party canapés (p382)
Thai-style crab–mangetout rösti Fried rösti with a crab, chilli, lemongrass, and coconut topping

What's in season?

At their best

Summer is a good time to marinate seafood or make salad dressings with chilli and fresh herbs. The wonderful local fruit available is astounding. Consider using it in both sweet and savoury dishes.

vegetables
artichokes
aubergine
beetroot
broad beans
chillies
courgettes
cucumber
fennel
kohlrabi
lettuce
  round, curly, Batavia,
  oakleaf, Iceberg, Lollo
  Rosso, Romaine
mangetout
new potatoes
pak choi
peas

pea shoots
peppers
rocket
runner beans
samphire
spinach
sugarsnap peas
sweetcorn
Swiss chard
tomatoes

fruit
apricots
bilberries
blueberries
cherries
crab apples
currants
damsons
dessert apples
elderberries
figs
gooseberries
grapes
greengages
loganberries
plums
raspberries

rhubarb
strawberries
tayberries

meat, poultry, and game
grouse
ptarmigan
snipe

fish and seafood
cod
crab
crayfish
haddock
halibut
herring
langoustines
lobster
mackerel
oysters
pollock
sea bream
scallops
sole
squid
whiting

Make it your own...
Al fresco lunch

A rocket salad will go beautifully with this brioche tart – find choice pairings over the page. Work up an appetite with picnic bites on pp374–5.

Serves 6
Ingredients

For the dough
350g (12oz) strong plain flour
1½ tsp fast-action dried yeast
3 eggs, beaten
125g (4½oz) unsalted butter, softened, plus extra for greasing

For the filling
3 tbsp olive oil
2 red onions, sliced
2 garlic cloves, finely chopped
1 aubergine, diced
3 courgettes, sliced
2 red peppers, diced
1 yellow pepper, diced
4 large tomatoes, diced
splash of red wine
1 tbsp tomato purée
½ tsp caster sugar
1 large bay leaf
salt and freshly ground black pepper
12 quail's eggs
grated Parmesan cheese, to serve

The main event
Ratatouille brioche tart

1 Smooth dough Sift 250g (9oz) of the flour, a pinch of salt, and yeast onto a work surface. Make a well in the centre and add the beaten eggs. With your fingertips, work the ingredients. Draw in the flour and form a smooth dough, adding 1 tbsp water. Knead the dough on a floured work surface, until it is very elastic: 10 minutes. Work in more flour, so that the dough is slightly sticky but peels from the work surface. Add the butter, squeeze to mix it into the sticky dough, knead for 3–5 minutes, adding the flour until smooth. Shape into a ball and leave covered in an oiled bowl to rise for a minimum of 1 hour.

2 Rich ratatouille Meanwhile, heat the oil in a large saucepan. Add the onion and fry, stirring, for about 3 minutes until softened but not browned. Add the garlic and prepared vegetables and fry, stirring, for about 5 minutes until softened. Stir in the wine, purée, sugar, bay leaf, and some salt and pepper. Bring to the boil, reduce the heat, and simmer for 15 minutes, stirring. Discard the bay leaf.

3 Buttery brioche base Butter a 30cm (12in) deep flan dish or a 28cm (11in) square ovenproof dish. Knock out the brioche dough. Flour a work surface, then roll out the dough to about 7.5cm (3in) larger than the dish. Lay the dough over the rolling pin and drape it over the dish. Gently lift the edges of the dough with one hand and ease it into the bottom and edge of the flan dish with the other hand. Press the dough evenly up the sides, from the bottom, to increase the height of the dough to just above the rim.

4 Golden crust Preheat the oven to 200°C (400°F/Gas 6). Spread the vegetable mixture evenly in the dough case. Fold the top edge of the dough rim over the filling. Let rise in a warm place until puffed up, about 30 minutes. Bake for 40 minutes until the brioche is golden.

5 Baked eggs Gently make 12 little wells all over the tart. Break a quail's egg into each. Return to the oven for about 5 minutes. Remove from the oven. Serve with some grated Parmesan.

John's Take on Al Fresco Lunch
Fill the extra-special brioche dough with other ingredient toppings. For an excellent picnic recipe, try a smoked bacon, shallot, and crème fraîche filling, scattered with fresh herbs.

Golden crust

Rich ratatouille

Baked eggs

Buttery
brioche base

5 ways with...
Rocket

A versatile ingredient, rocket can add a dash of heat to recipes such as the summer al fresco salad. Earthy, intensely peppery, and nutty, temper it with milder lettuce leaves.

Storing and preparing rocket

Origin
Native to Asia and southern Europe, rocket now grows well in all temperate zones around the world. True and wall rocket are salad greens with an earthy, nutty flavour that is only slightly bitter when the leaves are tender and young. As hotter weather arrives in late summer, it develops an aggressive, peppery heat.

Store
Keep rocket in the fridge for no more than 3 days. Freshness is best preserved if the leaves are wrapped in a moist kitchen towel or stored in a sealed container.

Prepare
Best eaten fresh, rocket is good in salads and in sandwiches, or as a topping or accompaniment to warm dishes. It can be cooked and added to pizza and vegetable frittatas. Try puréeing rocket and stirring it through soups, adding it to dipping sauces, or running it through pesto.

1 Blue cheese + pine nuts

Though both strong flavours, the **peppery** taste of rocket and the **pungency** of blue cheese complement one another very well, whereas the sweet **buttery** pine nut is a natural ally for creamy blue cheese.

The three together compose a lovely summer salad or can be served atop pizza or pasta dishes. Try adding grilled or fresh summer fruits, such as peaches, plums, or raspberries, to the blend for a touch of sweetness and a **brighter** flavour palate.

2 Tomatoes + olive oil

Like the blue cheese and pine nut pairing, rocket, tomatoes, and olive oil are all that are required for a **bright** summer salad or for **fresh**, summery pasta and pizza toppings. Try topping freshly sliced tomatoes and buffalo mozzarella with rocket pesto and a drizzle of olive oil for a **twist** on the classic Caprese salad.

Whether using heirloom, plum, cherry, or beef tomatoes, they're at their best in the summer months, so let them **shine** with just a gentle sprinkle of sea salt.

Gregg's Advice on Choosing Rocket

Check for the freshness of the leaves – they should be bright green with no blemishes and the ends should look freshly cut. Ensure the leaves aren't limp and lay mostly flat. The best leaves are average in length – avoid long, limp leaves as they won't taste the best.

3 Scallops + thyme

The sweet sea flavour and **succulent** texture of scallops is exquisitely **enhanced** by soft, peppery rocket and fresh thyme. Top seared scallops in a rocket and thyme pesto; place thyme-seasoned, grilled scallops atop a bed of fresh rocket; or toss them all together in linguine with a light **buttery** sauce.

This combination of flavours is surprisingly versatile. Try **wrapping** the scallops in pancetta for a more savoury flavour, incorporate a little chilli for some spice, or serve with grilled peaches for added **sweetness**.

4 Manchego + figs

For a rich and **complex** mouthful of flavours, rocket, Manchego cheese, and figs are a winning combination. The **bitter** spice of the rocket; the delicate **honey-sweet** taste of the figs; and the rich, creamy, **nuttiness** of the Manchego complement one another surprisingly well.

This flavour group can be enjoyed any number of ways, including in omelettes, frittatas, and sweet-savoury tarts; on pizzas, tartines, and crostini; or in salads and pasta dishes. Add **salty** prosciutto to the mix for an extra dimension of flavour.

5 Eggs + cherry tomatoes

Rocket, eggs, and cherry tomatoes lead the way to a **healthy**, fresh, and **delicious** summer breakfast. Whether in omelettes, frittatas, or quiches, or stacked atop English muffins and **drizzled** with hollandaise sauce, the combination tastes delightful.

For an evening meal suggestion, toss together a **quick** and tasty salad with rocket, cherry tomatoes, and soft-boiled quail's eggs, or top a light, buttery spaghetti with warm cherry tomatoes, fresh rocket, and a fried egg.

The al fresco table

A very special ratatouille tart is best served with light, delicately spiced salads and sides.

John's Presentation Tips
Halloumi should be griddled for texture, colour, and flavour. Baby squid goes crisp on the outside and deliciously soft on the inside – if using larger pieces, cut into smaller squares or strips, and then grill well.

Summer vegetable and rocket salad with halloumi
Prepare and chargrill 8 asparagus spears, following the method on pages 118–19. Repeat in batches with 2 small, sliced aubergines and courgettes, 1 yellow and 1 red pepper, cut in wedges, and 4 quartered baby artichokes or freshly prepared artichoke hearts. Toss together in a large salad bowl with 4 handfuls of rocket, 12 black olives, a small, sliced red onion, and a handful of chopped thyme. Drizzle with olive oil and lemon juice. Season and combine gently. Oil a sliced block of halloumi cheese and griddle or barbecue for a minute or two each side. Cut in strips and add to the salad.
See Chargrilled asparagus with hollandaise, pp118–19

Marinated chilli and preserved lemon olives
Put 300g (10oz) mixed black and green olives in an airtight container. Add 1 halved and chopped preserved lemon; 1 fat red and 1 fat green chilli, deseeded and chopped; 1 tsp dried oregano; a good grinding of black pepper; 1 tbsp red wine vinegar; 1 tbsp liquid from the preserved lemons; and 3 tbsp olive oil. Toss gently, cover, and leave to marinate for at least 8 hours, shaking the container occasionally. Toss with 1 tbsp finely chopped parsley and serve.
You could also try Hummus, pp106–7, with dips

Warm spiced calamari salad
Split 800g (1¾lb) small, cleaned squid and open flat.
Score in diamond shapes on the "inside". Trim tentacles.
Toss in 1 tbsp each chopped flat-leaf parsley and mint,
1 crushed garlic clove, 1 chopped red chilli, 1½ tsp
paprika, zest of 1 lime, 4 tbsp olive oil, and season well.
Chill for 30 minutes. Mix 2 handfuls each lamb's lettuce
and pea shoots, 1 small, sliced red onion, and 12 halved
cherry tomatoes. Dress with juice of 1 lime, 4 tbsp olive
oil, ½ tsp sugar, 1 tbsp each chopped mint and dill.
Barbecue the squid for 2 minutes each side, and mix in.
You could also try Salade niçoise pp250–1

Summer berry and elderflower fizz
Put 400g (14oz) mixed summer berries in
a shallow dish with 120ml (4fl oz) elderflower
cordial. Toss and chill for at least 30 minutes.
When ready to serve, spoon into wine glasses,
including the juice, and top up with chilled
sparkling wine such as Prosecco.
You could also try Strawberry fool, pp294–5

" Give me books, French wine,
fruit, fine weather and a
little music out of doors... "
John Keats

Make it your own...
Afternoon Tea

These light, delicate scones are best eaten warm with damson jam that bursts with fresh fruit flavour. They would also work with other fruits of the season such as sweet, rich cherries (see pairings over the page). Serve with divine sweet and savoury offerings – see pp380–1 for inspiration.

Makes 20
Ingredients

For the jam
225g (8oz) ripe damsons, halved, stoned, and chopped
2 tbsp caster sugar
2 tbsp port
1 tsp arrowroot
For the scones
115g (4oz) plain flour
2 tsp baking powder
1/4 tsp salt
30g (1oz) unsalted butter, cut in small pieces
2 tbsp ground almonds
few drops of natural almond extract
1 tbsp caster sugar
small handful of sultanas
approx. 5 tbsp buttermilk or plain yoghurt
To serve
clotted cream or unsalted butter

The main event
Mini sultana and almond scones

1 Juicy damson jam Place the damsons in a small pan with the sugar. Heat gently until the juice runs, stir, and simmer until the fruit is tender but still with some shape, about 3 minutes. Blend the port with the arrowroot. Stir into the fruit and bring just to the boil, stirring gently until thickened and clear. Remove immediately from the heat and leave to cool.

2 Sultana and almond batter Preheat the oven to 220°C (425°F/ Gas 7). Sift the flour, baking powder, and salt into a mixing bowl. Add the butter and rub in until the mixture resembles breadcrumbs. Stir in the almonds, almond extract, sugar, and sultanas, then gently mix in the buttermilk or yoghurt, using a round bladed knife, until the crumbs draw together to form a soft but not sticky dough. To get the lighest scones, don't work this dough any more than absolutely necessary.

3 Golden baked scones Turn the dough on to a lightly floured surface and shape into a cake. The rougher the dough remains, the lighter the scones will be. Pat the dough into a 1cm (1/2in)-thick round. Cut out 10 rounds with a 4cm (1 3/4in) pastry cutter, cutting additional rounds until all the dough has been used. Arrange the scones a little apart on the baking sheet. Bake for 10–12 minutes, until lightly browned and the bases sound hollow when tapped. Transfer to a wire rack to cool until warm.

4 Cooling clotted cream Split the scones and top with clotted cream or spread with butter. Add a dollop of the damson jam and arrange on a serving plate.

John's Take on Afternoon Tea
For miniature party-sized scones, use a napkin ring as a cutter, or try being playful with cutters in a few different sizes. The mini mouthfuls look fantastic with a dollop of cream and jam.

Golden baked
scones

Cooling clotted cream

Juicy
damson jam

Sultana and
almond batter

5 ways with...
Cherries

Sweet, succulent cherries are one of the flavours of summer. The seasonal fruit works with a delicious number of pairings – making it a versatile choice.

Cherry varieties

Bigarreaux
Hard-fleshed Bigarreaux are available in early June.

Bing
Sweet, juicy, and deep red in colour, Bing cherries are available from June to July.

Ferrovia
These large, juicy Italian cherries are firm to the touch and available from May to June.

Kordia
Large heart-shaped Kordia cherries are readily available in the UK. Dark red, sweet, and juicy with dense flesh.

Picota
Available from June to July, Picotas originate from Spain and have a strong, sweet flavour. Sold without stems.

Santina
Moderately sweet, Santina cherries are large, firm-fleshed, and very dark. They have an elongated heart shape, and are available from May to June.

Sweetheart
Available from June to August, Sweetheart cherries have a mild, sweet flavour with sturdy flesh. Large, bright red, and heart-shaped.

1 Duck + Port

Duck is best paired with **sharp, fruity** flavours that can cut through the **richness** of the meat. Cherries and Port do the job perfectly, and the three flavours complement one another well.

The best assembly of these ingredients is a recipe with roast duck or pan-fried duck breasts served with Port and cherry sauce. Try incorporating **citrus** as well for a more complex flavour palate.

Cherries can also be **mulled** in Port and used in sweet sauces, cocktails, or preserves.

2 Rhubarb + ginger

In a pie, biscuit, or crumble, the **sweet–tart** tang of cherries, rhubarb, and ginger makes for an ideal summer dessert, especially if served **al fresco** with a dollop of good-quality vanilla ice cream.

Consider adding crystallized ginger pieces into a meringue mix before baking. Serve the meringues with a **juicy** rhubarb and cherry coulis.

The three also combine well in **jams** and sauces to top anything from meats to meringues.

Gregg's Top Cherry Tip

Ninety-five per cent of cherries sold in the UK come from other countries. When they are in season, ensure you buy locally, or consider going cherry picking in farms to enjoy the juiciest British cherries.

3 Chocolate + chilli

Chocolate, chilli, and cherries work inexplicably well together, and their **harmony** is down to more than alliteration.

Sample this sweet threesome in cakes, mousses, tarts, **truffles**, and ice creams. Try making your own chocolate bars or truffles with chopped cherries and a pinch of chilli powder. Alternatively, dip cherries in **melted** chocolate and chilli for a sweet and **spicy** flavour explosion. This particular variation can be served cold as chocolate-covered cherry sweets or warm as chilli chocolate fondue.

4 Brandy + cream

Approach this threesome with a **luscious** brandy cream, which can be used to top any and all cherry desserts, from pies and tarts to crumbles and cakes.

Combining brandy and cherries in **ice cream**, or making a cherry–brandy **clafoutis** and topping with fresh cream are alternative, delicious ways to combine these ingredients. Be creative and experiment with the different flavours. Incorporate **brandied** cherries and cream in a coffee cake, in pots de crème, or even in cream-based cocktails.

5 Yoghurt + currants

The simplest and perhaps most delicious way to enjoy these ingredients is to mix them together in a **cooling** cherry and currant yoghurt.

Alternatively, bake the cherries and currants into any number of baked goods and top with cool yoghurt for a **refreshing** summer treat. A clafoutis may be one of the best ways to highlight this flavour mix, or for a delicious, on-the-go snack, make yoghurt-dipped **dried cherries** and currants.

The Afternoon Tea table

Serve sweet and savoury afternoon treats with the scones, making use of ripe summer pickings.

John's Presentation Tips

Combine tradition with your own modern twist by getting playful with presentation. Clean, tidy lines of finger sandwiches give a professional touch.

Mini white chocolate and blueberry éclairs

Make the choux pastry (see p300). Pipe 30, 5cm (2in) lengths onto 2 baking trays lined with baking parchment. Bake at 200°C (400°F/Gas 6) for 20 minutes until crisp and golden. Slit the side of each and bake a further 5 minutes. Cool on a wire rack. Fill with 175g (6oz) roughly crushed blueberries folded into 300ml (10fl oz) whipped cream. Melt 200g (7oz) white chocolate with 30g (1oz) unsalted butter and 2 tbsp double cream. Spread over the éclairs. Leave to set.
See Profiteroles with ice cream, pp300–1

Mini sweet cherry and pistachio brownies

Make the chocolate hazelnut brownie mixture (see p350), reserving 1 tbsp of the cocoa powder and omit the hazelnuts. Mix 100g (3¹/₂oz) quartered and stoned cherries with the reserved cocoa powder. Fold into the mix with 60g (2oz) roughly chopped, shelled pistachio nuts. Bake, cool, then cut into 28 little squares. Dust with extra cocoa powder.
See Chocolate brownies, pp350–1

Prawn, roasted pepper, and guacamole wraps

Grill a large red pepper until blackened all over. Put in a plastic bag to cool, then peel, deseed, and cut into thin strips. Mash 2 large, ripe avocados with 2 tsp lime juice, 1 chopped fresh red chilli, and some seasoning. Spread the guacamole over 3 large flour tortillas. Scatter over the pepper strips and 200g (7oz) small cooked, peeled prawns. Roll each up tightly, wrap in cling film, and chill. Trim ends, then cut each roll diagonally into 6 pieces.

You could also try Smoked mackeral pâté, pp108–9

Cucumber, watercress, and cracked pepper sandwiches

Peel and thinly slice $1/2$ cucumber. Sprinkle with 2 tsp white balsamic condiment. Chop a good handful of watercress, discarding the stalks. Mix with 200g (7oz) soft white cheese and add 1 tsp coarse cracked black pepper and a pinch of salt. Spread 8 thin slices of white bread with the cheese mixture. Add the cucumber and sandwich in pairs. Cut off the crusts, then cut each into fingers.

You could also try Brioche Nanterre, pp324–5

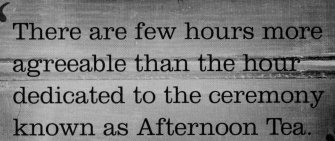

" There are few hours more agreeable than the hour dedicated to the ceremony known as Afternoon Tea.

Henry James

Make it your own...

Drinks party canapés

These moreish, easy-to-make little morsels make a perfect party centrepiece. Try them as part of the sensational party menu on pp386–7. Crab is a great friend to other flavours, as shown on the following pages.

Makes 20
Ingredients

For the rösti
500g (1lb 2oz) potatoes, peeled
4 spring onions, finely chopped
1 garlic clove, crushed
1 tbsp flour
salt and freshly ground black pepper
2 tbsp sunflower oil

For the topping
125g (4½oz) crab meat
30g (1oz) mangetout, trimmed and finely chopped
½ tsp grated ginger
½ tsp finely chopped lemongrass
1 thin red chilli, deseeded and finely chopped
2 tsp chopped fresh coriander
1½ tbsp coconut cream
½ tsp lime juice
½ tsp Thai fish sauce
micro coriander, to garnish

The main event
Thai-style crab–mangetout rösti

1 Grated potatoes Using a box grater, coarsely grate the potatoes onto a large plate. Immediately place the potatoes in the centre of a clean tea towel. Bring the corners of the towel together and squeeze over the sink to remove moisture.

2 Crunchy spring onion Place the grated potato in a large mixing bowl, add the spring onions, garlic, flour, salt, and plenty of black pepper, and mix together well.

3 Crisp and golden röstis Heat 1 tbsp sunflower oil in a frying pan over medium heat. Fry the röstis as shown below. Once the röstis are crisp and golden, remove from the pan with the fish slice and drain on kitchen paper. Repeat using the remaining oil and mixture, to cook a further 10 röstis. Drain and leave to cool.

4 Thai crab topping Mix the crab and mangetout together. Blend the remaining ingredients together and gently fold through the crab mixture. Chill until nearly ready to serve. Pile the crab mixture onto the röstis. Garnish with micro coriander or torn leaves.

Frying the röstis

Place a 4cm (1½in) pastry cutter in the pan and press in 1 tbsp of the potato mixture. Remove the ring. Using the cutter, shape and fry a further 9 röstis for 3–4 minutes on each side, pressing them down with a fish slice as they cook.

Gregg's Take on Canapés

It's fun to think about what foods can be scaled down to create tasty canapés. Röstis are a sturdy base for ambitious toppings. I enjoy creating röstis from half beetroot and half potato quantities. Colourful, delicious, and almost virtuous!

Crunchy spring
onions

Thai crab topping

Grated
potatoes

Crisp, golden
rösti

5 ways with...
Crab

Extensively paired with Asian-style flavours, as highlighted by the Thai-style rösti recipe, crab has a flavour of the sea that is well-matched with soft-flavoured ingredients.

Crab varieties

Blue crab
This is sourced in early summer from the West Atlantic, but can also be found in the waters surrounding Japan. It is often served whole as soft-shell crab, and is commonly used in crab cakes and dips.

Brown crab
Found in the North Sea, the North Atlantic, and the Mediterranean Sea, a surprising 70 per cent of brown crab are caught around the British Isles. Available from April until November, brown crab is known for its large, sweet, succulent claws. It is often used in traditional dressed crab recipes.

Snow crab (spider crab)
Fished from the Atlantic, Arctic, and Pacific Oceans between April and October, snow crab are often found as far north as Norway, Newfoundland, and Greenland, as far south as California, and as far east as Japan. Snow crab are primarily liked in cooking for their long, sweet, succulent legs.

1 Chilli + sweetcorn

Sweet crab and sweetcorn complement one another very well. The addition of chilli adds a **burst** of spice and an element of heightened complexity to the flavour blend.

These three items can be combined in any number of ways. The most familiar pairing of these ingredients is crab and sweetcorn **soup**, but they also taste great in crab and corn cakes with chilli **sauce**; or in a crab, sweetcorn, and chilli **salsa**. Try blending the three in a spicy variation on crab dip, or in a stuffing mixture for fresh summer vegetables.

2 Dill + new potatoes

The classic combination of dill and new potatoes pairs well with just about anything, but sweet and **succulent** crab seems to be an ideal match for the pair.

Try mixing the three **delicately flavoured** ingredients together in crab cakes, or in a simple salad dressed with lemon juice and mustard.

Flavour a smooth, **creamy** new potato mash with a chopped sprig of dill. Serve alongside simply prepared crab, and you'll find the flavours will really come into their own.

Gregg's Advice on Choosing Crabs

Pick crabs that feel heavy and don't have liquid sloshing around inside them. If you like white meat, buy a cock or male crab. It is better to buy the crab while it is still alive, but place it in a freezer at -18°C for at least 2 hours, so it becomes comatose before cooking.

3 Tomatoes + basil

Nothing says summer to the palate more than the sweet flavours of crab and tomatoes combined with fresh, **aromatic** basil.

Tomato–basil crab **bisque** is one way to sample these ingredients together, as is soft-shell crab stuffed with **tomato–basil coulis**. Layer slices of each ingredient on a baguette for a **fresh** summer sandwich.

Alternatively, top a traditional Caprese salad with a spoonful of fresh crabmeat, or top spaghetti with the three ingredients and toss in a light butter sauce.

4 Parsley + cream cheese

Parsley adds an element of **freshness** and complexity to the seamless mixture of **soft**, **mild** cream cheese and crabmeat. These ingredients are most commonly found together in crab dip, crab alfredo, and crab Rangoon, but feel free to **experiment** and devise a new way to serve this flavour blend.

Try stuffing Portobello mushrooms with a crab and cream cheese mixture, or create your own sushi roll.

Layer these ingredients between bread and serve as finger sandwiches at an outdoor summer gathering.

5 Lollo Rosso + cucumbers

Crab is an excellent addition to any salad and can transform an uninspiring starter into an elegant main dish. Lollo Rosso is a salad leaf that can hold its own. With a bold, slightly **nutty** flavour and **crisp** ruffled leaves, it provides a striking **contrast** with sweet succulent crab in taste, texture, and appearance. Fresh, delicate, and slightly **sweet** cucumbers bring out elements of both the crab and the lettuce and create a **harmony** between the two.

To create a fun rendition of this crab salad for summer parties, spoon a crab and cheese mixture into cucumber cups, garnished with a torn piece of Lollo Rosso.

Drinks party canapés

This spread of party bites looks incredible and complements a glass of fizz or a dry, white wine.

John's Presentation Tips
Canapés need to impress immediately. Try a mix of hot and cold canapés with different bases. Less is more when it comes to serving – better to refill platters often rather than serve tumbling piles of food.

Marinated queen scallops in pancetta with basil and baby plum tomatoes
Mix 2 tbsp olive oil, juice of ½ lemon, ½ tsp dried basil, 2 chopped green garlic cloves, a little salt, and lots of freshly ground black pepper in a plastic sealable container. Add 20 queen scallops and toss. Cover and chill for several hours or overnight. Wrap each scallop in ½ slice of thin pancetta. Fry in a hot non-stick pan, sealed sides down for 1 minute, turn and fry a further minute. Thread each on a cocktail stick with a basil leaf and ½ baby plum tomato. Serve warm or cold.
You could also try Courgette, broad bean, and pea quiches, pp218–19

Roasted aubergine and feta rolls
Roast an aubergine in the oven for about 45 minutes or until soft. Scoop out flesh and mix with 100g (3½oz) feta cheese, 1 tsp ground cinnamon, 2 tbsp chopped black olives, 1 tsp dried oregano, olive oil, and lemon juice. Brush 3 sheets of filo pastry with olive oil. Top each with a second sheet, and brush again. Cut each to make 8 equal pieces. Spread filling over centres of the squares. Fold in sides, roll up. Bake on an oiled baking sheet for 25 minutes until crisp. For the dip, mix 6 tbsp mayonnaise with 2 tbsp sun-dried tomato paste.
You could also try tiny squares of Spanish omelette, pp214–15

Minted crushed pea and lettuce crostini
Cut a part-bake baguette in 24 slices,
discarding ends. Fry in olive oil until golden.
Drain on kitchen paper. Melt 30g (1oz)
butter in a pan. Add 175g (6oz) shelled
fresh peas, 2 finely chopped spring onions,
1 shredded gem lettuce, and 1 tbsp
chopped fresh mint. Stir, cover, and stew
gently for 5 minutes until tender. Crush
with a masher. Cool. Stir in 3 tbsp crème
fraîche, season, and spoon onto the
crostini. Garnish with a mint sprig.
**You could also try this topping on
Blinis, pp326–7**

Tandoori chicken and peach chutney bites
Mix 1 chopped skinned peach with 1 tbsp
honey, 1½ tsp white wine vinegar, ½ tsp
grated ginger, 1 tsp curry paste, and 2 tbsp
ground almonds. Chill. Make a few slashes in
a chicken breast and marinate for 2 hours
in a mixture of 1 tbsp plain yoghurt, 1 tsp
tandoori paste, and 1 tsp coriander. Grill for
15 minutes, turning once until cooked. Cool,
slice, then cut in thin strips. Cut out 20, 6cm
(2¼in) rounds from chapattis. Spread chutney
on each and add the chicken. Fold sides over
the chicken, and tie with a chive stalk.
**You could also try Mini haddock and herb
fishcakes pp128–9**

Autumn
September to November

Delight in the changing colours as the crisp autumn weather arrives. Revel in the wonderful change in the produce available. Create delicious vegetable stews and fresh side dishes to accompany game recipes. Exploit the exciting fruit available with pairings of apples and blackberries or pears and plums.

Here are two great food occasions that are perfect opportunities for playing with autumn's key flavours:

The autumnal celebration (p390)
Pear and blackberry cake Light cinnamon sponge with zesty pear filling, topped with fresh fruit, and drizzled with cassis syrup

The brunch (p394)
Black pudding with leeks Deliciously rich black pudding is served with buttery leeks, caramelized apples, crisp bacon, and fried eggs

Gregg's Seasonal Recommendations

Winter squashes are star ingredients in autumn, and they needn't be reserved for Halloween – butternut squash makes a wonderfully bright purée, perfect for garnishing a baked mullet main course. Pears are fantastic, especially when flavour-matched as shown on pp392–3.

What's in season?

At their best
Squashes, beans, and green vegetables run the show.

vegetables
aubergine
beetroot
broccoli (calabrese)
brussels sprouts
butternut squash
cabbages
cavolo nero
celeriac
chillies
courgette
fennel
green beans
horseradish
kale
leeks
parsnips
peas
peppers
pumpkin
radishes
runner beans
squashes
sugarsnap peas

sweetcorn
tomatoes
wild mushrooms

fruit
apples
bilberries
blackberries
cranberries
currants
damsons
elderberries
fresh figs
grapes
loganberries
pears
plums
quinces
rosehips
sloes
strawberries

meat, poultry, and game
duck (wild)
goose
grouse
hare
lamb
partridge
pheasant
wild boar
woodcock

fish and seafood
brill
cockles
cod
crab
haddock
halibut
langoustines
mackerel
monkfish
mullet
mussels
oysters
pilchards
pollock
razor clams
sea bass
sea bream
shrimps
squid
turbot
whelks

Make it your own...

Celebration

Stacked with layers of autumn fruits, this cake has the "wow" factor. Make the most of juicy pears with the suggestions over the page.

Serves 12
Ingredients

6 eggs

340g (12oz) caster sugar

175g (6oz) butter, melted

1/2 tsp vanilla extract

400g (14oz) self-raising flour

1 tsp ground cinnamon

2 tbsp milk

1 large lime, half zest pared, half zest grated

450ml (15fl oz) double cream

250g (9oz) quark or creamy white soft cheese

4 tbsp icing sugar

4 small, ripe pears, peeled and cored

500g (1lb 2oz) plump, ripe blackberries, hulled, if necessary

5 small ripe plums cut into 6 pieces

50g (1³/₄oz) pomegranate seeds

4 tbsp crème de cassis

6 tbsp apple juice

1 tsp arrowroot

The main event
Pear and blackberry cake

1 Light cinnamon sponge Preheat the oven to 160°C (325°F/Gas 3). Grease two, 20cm (8in) round cake tins and line the bases with baking parchment. Put the eggs in a bowl with the sugar. Place the bowl over a pan of gently simmering water and beat with a hand-held electric whisk until thick and pale. Remove the bowl from the saucepan and add the melted butter and vanilla extract, whisking.

2 Sift the flour and cinnamon over the surface and gently fold in with a metal spoon, adding the milk to slacken slightly. Divide the mixture between the two prepared tins and level the surfaces. Bake in the oven for 40–45 minutes or until risen, golden and firm to the touch. Remove from the oven and leave to cool for 5 minutes, then turn out onto a wire rack and leave to cool.

3 Zesty filling Squeeze the lime juice. Whip the cream, cheese, icing sugar, and the grated lime zest until peaking. Set aside a quarter of the cream mixture for the top. Chop three of the pears and toss in 1 tsp lime juice. Fold through the remaining cream mixture.

4 Fruity topping Cut the remaining pear into neat slices, toss in a further tsp of lime juice, and set aside for the topping with a third of the blackberries, plums, and pomegranate seeds.

5 Cassis drizzle Blend the cassis with the apple juice and arrowroot in a small saucepan. Bring to the boil, stirring until thickened and clear. Remove from the heat and set aside to cool.

6 Split each cake in half. Top one piece with a third of the pear and cream mixture, then a third of the fruit not reserved for decoration. Repeat the layers then top with the last cake half. Top with the reserved cream mixture and fruit. Drizzle the cassis syrup over the fruit. Sprinkle with pared lime rind. Chill until ready to serve.

John's Celebration Cake Variation
Turn the luxury up a notch by leaving out the lime zest and soft white cheese and mixing the topping ingredients with 250g (9oz) melted dark chocolate and 2 tbsp crème de cassis.

Fruity topping

Zesty cream filling

Cassis drizzle

Light cinnamon sponge

5 ways with...
Pears

Perched atop the spectacular tiered autumnal cake, pears have their chance to shine. There are many more seasonal allies for pear, which suits both sweet and savoury recipes.

Cooking pears

Poach
Choose firm-fleshed pears for poaching. To cook, peel, slice in half, and remove the seeds. Place the pears in boiling water along with selected flavours such as sugar, vanilla, cinnamon, or nutmeg. Turning them occasionally, cook for about 20 minutes until tender. Remove with a slotted spoon.

Roast
Peel pears, slice in half, and remove the seeds. Toss the pears in a bowl of lemon juice and sugar, arrange in a baking tin, and place in an oven that has been preheated to 220°C (425°F/Gas 7). Roast for 25–30 minutes, turning occasionally, until soft and golden brown.

Grill or pan-fry
Cut the pears in quarters lengthways and remove the seeds. Heat a tbsp of butter in a heavy-based frying pan over medium-high heat. Arrange the pears on the hot pan when the butter has melted. Fry for 6–8 minutes, turning over half way. Remove from the pan when pears are slightly brown and soft.

1 Pheasant + fennel

Soft, **sweet**, and aromatic pears combined with **crisp**, **anise-like** fennel blend to create a bright, clean flavour with a delicate juicy crunch.

Perfect in salads, they also blend well with the **rich** game flavour of pheasant. Braise the three ingredients together in a **pot roast**.

Alternatively, stuff the bird with a pear and fennel filling, serve sliced pheasant breasts atop a pear and fennel salad, or drizzle pheasant breasts with a pear and fennel **sauce**.

2 Walnuts + goat's cheese

A pear, walnut, and goat's cheese salad is the perfect side dish to an autumn meal. The textures of **soft**, grainy pears, **crunchy** walnuts, and **creamy** goat's cheese combine well and are further enhanced by the addition of any **crisp** seasonal salad greens. The flavours are complementary too, as the slightly bitter taste of the walnuts is balanced by the sweetness of the pears and the gentle tang of goat's cheese.

If not in the mood for a salad, sample these flavours in a **sweet–savoury** tart, in an Italian crostata, or on a tartine with a little fresh rocket and honey drizzle.

Gregg's Guide to Choosing Pears

Pears ripen from the inside out and pass from rock-hard to woolly and unpleasant very quickly, so once perfectly ripe they should be eaten very quickly. A quick test to try is that the stalk on a ripe pear should yield gently if pressed.

3 Beetroot + celery

The sweet, **earthy** flavour of roasted beetroot is a natural match for the pear, and the **delicate** flavour of celery adds **freshness** and crunch to the blend.

A particularly **healthy** combination, a blend of these ingredients is high in B vitamins and amino acids. Combine them to make a **delicious**, nutrient-packed juice.

Alternatively, incorporate them in soups, salads, and tarts.

4 Ricotta + figs

Pears, figs, and ricotta share a number of characteristics, each possessing a delicate, **sweet** flavour and a soft, slightly grainy texture.

Perfect in baked goods like tarts, **crumbles**, and clafoutis, with a little creativity, these ingredients can be combined in any number of tasty treats. Try **poaching** the pears and figs in either vanilla or Marsala wine and serve them over ricotta. Alternatively, combine the pears and figs in a **tapenade**, layer with ricotta on crostini, and serve as canapés.

5 Grapes + pecans

Bright, juicy, and sweet, pears and grapes are natural allies in the fruit salad and beyond. Much like walnuts, with which they're each often paired, but quite a bit **sweeter**, the pecan complements them both. The combination of the three textures can be particularly pleasing as the soft **graininess** of the pear contrasts with the **crunch** of pecan and the crisp burst of juice from the grape.

These three combine well in any manner of salad, particularly over a bed of **crisp** greens, and taste even better with the addition of **creamy** Roquefort or gorgonzola.

Make it your own...

Brunch

Apples and leeks are perfect brunch partners to black pudding. Apples shine in many recipes – turn over the page for inspiration.

Serves 4
Ingredients

45g (1½oz) butter
2 leeks, trimmed
  and sliced
freshly ground black
  pepper
2 eating apples, peeled,
  halved, cored, and
  sliced
2 tsp light brown sugar
sunflower oil, for frying
4 thin smoked streaky
  bacon rashers, halved
8 large slices of black
  pudding
4 eggs

The main event
Black pudding with leeks

Black pudding If you've never tried black pudding before, this recipe is a great way to introduce yourself to it. Its mix includes oatmeal, so it is like a heavier sausage with a wonderful crumbly texture and a tangy aftertaste. If you prefer, replace black pudding with boudin blanc pork sausages – a delicious alternative.

1 Buttery leeks Melt half the butter in a small saucepan, add the leeks and fry, stirring, for 2 minutes. Cover the pan and sweat over medium–low heat for 5 minutes until soft but not brown. Season with black pepper. Remove from the heat and keep warm.

2 Caramelized apples Melt the remaining butter in a large non-stick frying pan, add the apple slices and sugar, and cook over medium heat, turning occasionally, for 5 minutes, or until softened and caramelized. Transfer to a plate and keep warm.

3 Crisp bacon and black pudding slices Wipe out the pan, and fry the bacon slices. Heat a little oil in the pan and fry the bacon strips for 2–3 minutes, or until cooked through, browned, and fairly crispy, turning once. Remove from the pan, drain on kitchen paper, and keep warm. Fry the black pudding slices in the pan over medium-high heat for 2–3 minutes on each side, or until slightly crisp and hot through.

4 Eggs sunny-side up Meanwhile, fry 4 eggs in a little oil in a separate frying pan. To serve, place slices of black pudding side by side on each plate, add a layer of apples, then leeks. Lay an egg on top, resting between the two, and top each with two bacon strips.

John's Presentation Suggestions
Use oiled egg rings when frying eggs, as it keeps their shape. Try adding a cheeky touch with bacon curls. Roll strips of bacon into rolls, and thread them onto skewers. Place the skewers under a grill for 4–6 minutes, turning occasionally, until crisp.

Crispy bacon

Eggs sunny-side up

Buttery leeks

Caramelized apples

Black pudding

5 ways with...
Apples

Caramelized apples, featured in our autumn brunch, can add a tart sweetness to many meals. Here are combinations that can help you to be more ambitious with the nation's favourite fruit.

English apple varieties

Bramley
Large cooking apples, Bramleys are green-yellow in colour and often irregular in shape. They are firm in texture and have acidic flesh that cooks quickly to a frothy pulp. Top choice for apple sauce and apple pie.

Cameo
Cameo apples are bright red and striped over with creamy orange. They are firm and crisp with an aromatic and sweet flavour. Popular for their firm skin but juicy flesh.

Cox
Widely said to have the nicest taste of them all, this quintessentially English apple has rosy skin and creamy flesh. Coxs are small in size with a sweet, acidic flavour. Look out for them in October, when the first crop appears.

The best of the rest

Large, tart New Zealand **Braeburn** apples have a clean, sweet flavour. For a more refreshing and even sweeter flavour, try Japanese **Fuji** apples. **Golden Delicious** from the USA and creamy Australian **Pink Lady** apples are also common favourites.

1 Cheddar + quince

The flavours of apple and cheddar are perfectly **harmonious** in even their simplest forms, served side by side on a cheese board with a dab of quince jelly. The full-bodied, **creamy** tang of cheddar stands in delicious contrast to bright, crisp apples, particularly varieties with a little **tartness**. Cooked quince naturally **enhances** the flavour of the apples and makes for a **stronger**, more delicious flavour pairing. These flavours can be enjoyed in an apple and quince pie, tart, or cobbler with a cheddar crust.

2 Cabbage + sultanas

The unexpected blend of apples, cabbages, and sultanas manages to find its way into all manner of gently altered traditional dishes. Sultanas add a **sweet** and **fruity** twist to traditional braised red cabbage and apples. Cabbage is an ideal substitute for celery in a Waldorf salad, and apples and sultanas together can **enliven** any standard cabbage slaw.

Each of these ingredients can be quite versatile, so use a bit of **creativity** to come up with a unique way to feature these fresh autumn flavours.

Gregg's Advice on Choosing Apples

Choose unblemished fruit with firm, unwrinkled skin. There should be a faint aroma around the stem – try pressing this area lightly with your finger. Colour has little to do with flavour as sometimes vivid, waxy skins can conceal woolly, tasteless flesh.

3 Partridge + brandy

A classic autumnal dish, partridge with brandy and apples is both **warming** and **comforting**. The richness of the game and the tart flavour of cooking apples complement one another well. Brandy brings out the flavours of each and adds a layer of **depth** and complexity.

Prepare and serve **brandied** apples alongside the meat, roast the bird with a brandied apple stuffing, or layer the apples on top for a traditional fruited partridge.

4 Walnuts + demerara

Apples and walnuts are the stars of many an autumn cake, tart, and cobbler. Considered seasonal **staples** by many, they even appear together in various salads and pasta dishes, on pizza and in risotto.

Of course, nearly any sugar can be used for the dessert pairings of these two ingredients, but the delicate **toffee** flavour and subtle **crunch** of demerara sugar is the ideal match for any warm and **aromatic** apple and walnut treat.

5 Nutmeg + honey

Nothing says autumn like the lingering **aromas** of nutmeg, apples, and honey wafting in from a warm kitchen. The flavours combine in a perfect **marriage** of sweetness and **spice** and exude the essence of the season.

Irresistibly **perfect** in cakes, crisps, and crumbles, they also combine well in sweet–savoury dishes. Serve apples with nutmeg and honey alongside a honey-baked ham, with butternut squash, and in **crisp** seasonal salads.

Winter December to early March

Bring some comfort to the winter months with some warming and nourishing feasts. Make the most of seafood available with hearty fisherman's stews. Use the season's ripe offerings as your guide.

The season is peppered with chances for the home cook to impress. Here are three occasions, perfect for promoting the season's best:

The romantic Valentine's dinner for two (p400)
Venison with port–cranberry sauce Pavé of venison served with port and fresh cranberry sauce and a celeriac and potato gratin

The winter warmer to spice up a frosty evening (p404)
Red turkey curry with pak choi Thai red curry spiced with ginger and chilli served with tender pak choi and delicate jasmine rice

The night in with friends on New Year's day (p408)
Beef, beetroot, and Stilton burgers Served with a stack of roasted root vegetable chips and a horseradish relish

Gregg's Seasonal Recommendations
Flavoursome vegetables and meat are in abundance – vibrant cabbages and squashes taste so delicious, you'll want them with everything. Serve often overlooked celeriac with simple pairings to allow its delicate flavour to sing. See pp402–3 for some examples.

What's in season?

At their best

Winter is a time to cook rustic vegetables and gamey meat. It is also the perfect season for seafood.

vegetables
beetroot
brussels sprouts
butternut squash
cabbage
  savoy, red, white
cauliflower
cardoon
cavolo nero
celeriac
celery
chicory
endive
  curly, escarole
kale
horseradish
Jerusalem artichokes
leeks
parsnips
potatoes
pumpkin
radicchio

radishes
romanesco
salsify
swede
Swiss chard
turnips
wild mushrooms

fruit
apples
  cooking, dessert
cranberries
medlars
pears
quinces
rhubarb

meat, poultry, and game
duck
goose
grouse
guinea fowl
hare
lamb
partridge
pheasant

ptarmigan
quail
rabbit
snipe
turkey
veal
venison
woodcock

fish and seafood
abalone
brill
clams
cockles
cod
coley
crayfish
dab
haddock
halibut
langoustines
mullet
mussels
oysters
razor clams
sole
squid

Make it your own...

Valentine's Day meal

This stunning, romantic dish is simpler than it looks to prepare and will really get the pulses racing. Try celeriac with the exciting pairings overleaf.

Serves 2
Ingredients

½ small celeriac, peeled and sliced

1 tbsp lemon juice

1 large potato, peeled and sliced

large knob of butter for greasing

salt and freshly ground black pepper

1 garlic clove, finely chopped

60g (2oz) Gruyère cheese, grated

200ml (7fl oz) double cream

1 egg, beaten

2 tbsp redcurrant jelly

120ml (4fl oz) beef stock

1 bay leaf

60g (2oz) fresh cranberries

1 tbsp olive oil

2 tbsp port

knob of butter

2 thick venison loin steaks

flat-leaf parsley sprigs, to garnish

purple-sprouting broccoli, to serve

The main event
Venison with port–cranberry sauce

1 Creamy gratin To make the gratin, preheat the oven to 180°C (350°F/Gas 4). Place the celeriac in cold water with the lemon juice added. Par-boil the potato slices for 2 minutes. Add the celeriac slices and boil 2 minutes more. Drain. Liberally butter an 18cm (7in) square shallow baking tin. Lay half the vegetable slices in the tin, mixing up the potato and celeriac. Season and sprinkle with half the garlic and cheese. Repeat the layers. Whisk the cream and egg together. Pour over the vegetables. Bake in the oven for 30 minutes or until set and lightly golden on top. Cover with foil. Reduce the oven to 150°C (300°F/Gas 2).

2 Sweet–sharp cranberry sauce Meanwhile, dissolve the redcurrant jelly in half the stock in a small pan. Add the bay leaf. Boil rapidly for 2 minutes until reduced by half and syrupy. Add the cranberries, reduce the heat, and simmer for 2 minutes until soft but still holding their shape. Remove from the heat.

3 Juicy venison pavé Wipe the meat, rub all over with the oil, and season well with pepper. Heat a griddle pan or non-stick frying pan. Cook the steaks quickly for 1 minute on each side to brown. Wrap the meat side by side in foil and stand the parcel on an ovenproof plate or baking sheet. Keep the pan for finishing the sauce. Cook the steaks in the oven for 10 minutes, then remove immediately.

4 Deglaze the venison pan with the remaining stock and port, stirring and scraping up any sediment. Boil rapidly for a minute or two to reduce by half. Add to the cranberries. Add the butter, and cook over low heat, gently stirring until the butter is incorporated. Taste and season as necessary. Discard the bay leaf.

5 Remove the gratin from the oven, cut it in slices, and arrange on two warm serving plates. Carve the venison steaks in thick slices and arrange to one side. Spoon the sauce over. Garnish with parsley and serve with **tender broccoli**.

John's Take on the Valentine's Day Meal
The full-flavoured, tender steaks are laced with a juicy port and cranberry sauce. Let the sauce reduce and don't stir, just swirl the pan every so often so that the berries won't burst. These strong but delicious berries add a sharp note to this rich meat.

Creamy gratin

Tender broccoli

Juicy venison pavé

Sweet–sharp cranberry sauce

5 ways with...
Celeriac

A largely underrated ingredient, celeriac has thick, rough skin that conceals white flesh with a refreshing, crisp, and lightly herbal flavour.

Storing and preparing celeriac

Store
Store in the refrigerator before use.

Prepare
Begin by removing both ends of the root with a sharp knife and removing the tough skin with a potato peeler. A fair amount of the vegetable may be discarded before you reach the succulent flesh underneath. Celeriac discolours quickly, so after cutting to size, place it in a bowl of cold water with a bit of lemon juice or white wine vinegar to preserve it. You could prepare to eat raw by cutting sticks for crudités, or grating into a salad.

Cook
If boiling, celeriac requires about 20 minutes until it reaches the best texture. After boiling, you could purée and mix with an equal amount of mashed potato. If roasting, cook for 40 minutes in a medium-high preheated oven.

1 Potatoes + mustard

Though closely related to celery and with a similar, albeit milder, slightly **nutty** flavour, celeriac is often treated as a member of the potato family and is commonly prepared with potatoes. Celeriac potato mash and celeriac potato gratin are two delicious examples of this natural **harmony**. The heat of mustard adds a kick and a depth of flavour to this starchy, mild pair.

For a larger **burst** of flavour, choose ground English mustard. For a milder dish, use wholegrain, American, or German mustard.

2 Cream + lemon

Cream and lemon may seem like unnatural allies, however they're both often found in some of the best dishes featuring celeriac.

Cream brings out the **soft**, starchy texture of this root vegetable. Lemon adds a bright, **tart** freshness, enhancing the natural flavour and preventing the dish from becoming too heavy or bland. Sample this threesome in a cream of celeriac soup, a celeriac dauphinoise, or in a classic French celeriac remoulade.

Gregg's Advice on Choosing Celeriac

Celeriac combines the taste of parsley, parsnip, and celery. Choose roots that are the size of a small grapefruit. They should feel heavy for their size and firm to the touch, especially at the top where the leaves emerge.

3 Honey + apple

It can be easy to forget that celeriac is closely related to celery, and that as such it pairs **superbly** with apples. Sample this pairing in a celeriac and apple salad or slaw with honey–mustard vinaigrette.

Combine the two in a celeriac and apple gratin, or in a celeriac and apple soup, with a touch of honey for **sweetness**. The honey also serves to provide balance between the tartness of the cooking apples and the **earthiness** of the celeriac.

4 Squash + mascarpone

The sweet, **buttery** flavour of butternut squash pairs exquisitely well with **delicate**, nutty celeriac and with rich, **creamy** mascarpone. These delectable winter ingredients can also be found together in soups, tarts, mashes, and gratins. One favoured way to sample this threesome is in a celeriac, butternut squash, and mascarpone parmigiana.

Alternatively, use mascarpone as a **condiment** for roasted winter vegetables containing celeriac and butternut squash.

5 Swede + double Gloucester

Not unlike celeriac, with its fine texture and **subtly sweet** flavour, swede is another in the root vegetable family to routinely find itself in traditionally potato-based dishes. Slice, layer, and bake for a celeriac, swede, and potato gratin, or boil and mash.

As an alternative, you could also chop, coat in olive oil, and roast with other winter vegetables for a **nutritious** and appetizing winter medley. Any of these variations benefit substantially from the addition of grated or melted single or double Gloucester cheese and the **rich**, nutty, and creamy flavour and texture it imparts.

Make it your own...

Winter warmer

Here's a tasty Thai-style curry to use up the turkey and get the taste buds tingling. Turkey is in abundance in the festive season. Find out more flavour pairings for this surprisingly tender meat on pp406–7.

Serves 4

Ingredients

For the gratin
225g (8oz) jasmine rice
2 tbsp sunflower oil
6 chestnut mushrooms, sliced
4 tbsp Thai red curry paste
1 tsp grated fresh root ginger or galangal
1 tsp dried chilli flakes
1 large garlic clove, finely chopped
400ml can coconut milk
1 tbsp chopped fresh coriander
2 tsp Thai fish sauce
350g (12oz) cooked turkey, cut in bite-sized pieces
salt and freshly ground black pepper
2 pak choi, shredded

To garnish
1 carrot, pared
handful of coriander leaves, roughly chopped
1 tsp crushed dried chillies
lime wedges

The main event
Red turkey curry with pak choi

1 Delicate jasmine rice Put 375ml (13fl oz) water in a large saucepan with a pinch of salt and bring to the boil. Add the rice, stir, bring back to the boil, reduce the heat, cover tightly, and simmer gently for 20 minutes. Remove from the heat and leave to stand for 5 minutes, then remove the lid and stir gently with a fork.

2 Nutty chestnut mushrooms Meanwhile, heat 1 tbsp of the oil in a saucepan. Add the mushrooms and stir-fry for 2 minutes.

3 Spicy curry Add the curry paste, ginger, chilli, and garlic then blend in the coconut milk and stir in the coriander, fish sauce, and turkey. Bring to the boil, reduce the heat and simmer gently for 10 minutes until the turkey is tender. Taste and season, if necessary.

4 Juicy pak choi Meanwhile, heat the remaining oil in a frying pan and stir-fry the pak choi for 1 minute to wilt. Stir into the cooked curry. Blanch the carrot in boiling water for 1 minute. Drain.

5 Spoon the rice into bowls. Spoon the curry over and garnish with the pared carrot, coriander, crushed chillies, and a lime wedge.

How to pare carrot

Curly carrot ribbons can be easily created with the help of a vegetable peeler. Wash the carrot, then peel long strips lengthways. Place the ribbons straight into a bowl of fresh lemon juice to keep them from going brown prior to use.

John's Winter Warmer Variation
Try shredded kale or savoy cabbage leaves instead of pak choi, and wilt for an extra 2 minutes as the leaves will be tougher. If you find the curry gets too spicy, add a little more coconut milk or yoghurt to temper the spice.

Spicy curry

Juicy pak choi

Curly carrot ribbons

Nutty chestnut mushrooms

5 ways with...
Turkey

Turkey is leaner than chicken, and when cooked correctly with the right pairings, it can be just as succulent.

wing

crown / breast

thigh

leg

Cooking cuts of turkey

The average size of a whole turkey is 5.5kg (12lb) but smaller birds are sold outside of the festive season. Good breeds to look out for are Norfolk black, Kelly bronze, and Cambridge bronze.

Buy from reliable merchants such as local butchers, farmer's markets, or farm shops. Some supermarkets can also give you advice about where the bird was reared and whether it was treated humanely.

The dark (leg) meat has more fat and is more succulent than the white (breast) meat.

Roasting – whole bird; crown (cooks a little quicker and is easier to carve); boneless breast joint; roll; legs

Braising and stewing – diced breast; diced thigh and leg; wings

Frying – breast steak; diced breast or leg

Grilling – breast steak

Barbecued – breast steak; leg; marinated wing

1 Cranberry + fontina

The tartness of cranberries is tempered by the delicate, nutty flavour of fontina cheese and the mildly **gamey** taste of turkey. Whether in a panini, a Monte Cristo, or a toastie, these flavours combine best in a sandwich. The ooze of melted fontina, with the **succulence** of turkey breast and the **juiciness** of cranberry sauce between the two crisp pieces of toasted bread is an ideal use of Christmas leftovers. These ingredients also combine well in wraps, salads, and turkey burgers.

2 White wine + mushrooms

One of the most delicious ways to serve turkey is with a **creamy** mushroom and white wine sauce. The mushrooms provide a savoury **earthiness** to the delicate flavour of the bird, while white wine adds **brightness** and enhances the depth of flavour.

Combine the wine and mushrooms with cream and butter for a **comforting** cream sauce for whole roast turkey, as a condiment for turkey burgers, or for linguine and chopped turkey breast. Alternatively, use the mushrooms in a turkey **stuffing** and spoon white wine gravy over the top.

John's Advice on Choosing Turkey

Choose turkey that has a creamy white colour. Grade A turkeys have plump breasts, perfect skin, and will be fresh from imperfections such as cuts, bruises, or broken bones. Avoid meat that looks watery as it will probably taste that way.

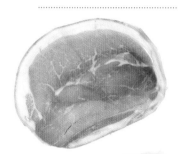

3 Ham + Emmental

A classic sandwich with turkey, ham, and Emmental, served warm in toasted bread, is meaty, oozy, a little **crispy**, and the ultimate winter comfort food. The sweetness and succulence of ham pairs naturally well with turkey, and the **delicate**, nutty tang of Emmental cheese enhances the flavour of each, without overpowering the taste of the meat. Combined with eggs in a turkey, ham, and cheese omelette, these flavours continue to warm and comfort. Served cold in a salad, they seem to take on a whole new flavour profile.

4 Shallots + apples

The delicate flavour of turkey is naturally **enhanced** by the contrasting bite of shallots and **sweet-tart** taste of apples. An apple and shallot stuffing, glaze, or sauce for roasted turkey is a delicious way to combine these complementary ingredients.

Alternatively, **blend** the apples and shallots with turkey mince when preparing turkey burgers for a seamlessly incorporated blend of flavours, or top a turkey and apple salad with a shallot vinaigrette.

5 Leeks + bacon

The flavour of turkey is quite **versatile**, and among the many elements that enhance its flavour are the mildly **sweet**, onion taste of leeks and the distinct **smoky** crisp of bacon.

This flavour combination can be enjoyed any number of ways. Incorporate the **flavours** in a savoury pie, or combine the leeks and bacon in a cream sauce to **drizzle** over turkey-topped fettuccine or turkey-stuffed cannelloni. Alternatively, fill the cavity of a whole turkey with leek and bacon stuffing before roasting.

Make it your own...

New Year's Day meal

This rich and nutritious dish is sure to wake up even the most jaded of partied-out palates. Vibrant, earthy beetroot is delicious with beef – find more pairings for the superfood over the page.

Serves 4
Ingredients

1 small onion, grated
2 beetroot (about
   175g/6oz), peeled
   and grated
400g (14oz) lean
   minced steak
salt and freshly ground
   black pepper
1 tsp dried oregano
1 tbsp milk
75g (2½oz) Stilton
   cheese, crumbled
1 large potato,
   scrubbed
1 small sweet potato,
   scrubbed
2 large carrots, peeled
1 large parsnip, peeled
3 tbsp sunflower oil
   plus extra for
   brushing
pinch of coarse sea salt
To serve
8 tbsp mayonnaise
1 tbsp grated
   horseradish
4 burger buns, split
handful of crisp lettuce
1 small red onion, sliced
1 large tomato, sliced

The main event
Beef, beetroot, and Stilton burgers

1 Succulent burgers Put the grated onion and beetroot in a large bowl. Add the steak, season well, and add the oregano, milk, and crumbled Stilton. Mix well together with your hands until thoroughly combined.

2 Divide the mixture into 4 equal pieces. Shape each piece into a patty about 12cm (5in) diameter (depending on the size of your burger buns). Flatten firmly with the palm of your hand. Make a small hole through the centre of each with your finger to help prevent shrinkage. Chill for at least 30 minutes.

3 Crunchy veggie chips Preheat the oven to 200°C (400°F/Gas 6). Prepare the chips. Cut all the vegetables in halves widthways, then in chunky chips. Place in a large baking tray and toss in the sunflower oil. Bake towards the top of the oven for about 50 minutes until golden and cooked through, turning once. Sprinkle with a little coarse sea salt.

4 Meanwhile, brush the burgers with the oil and place on an oiled baking tray. Add to the oven when the chips have been cooking for 30 minutes. Bake for 15–20 minutes.

5 Relish with a kick Mix the mayonnaise with the horseradish. Spread a little on the cut sides of the buns. Put the remainder in small dishes to serve as a dip for the vegetable chips.

6 Juicy salad Put the bases of the buns on plates. Top each with a little shredded lettuce. Add the burgers, then the onion slices and tomato slices. Top with the bun "lids". Press down firmly with your hand and serve with the root chips and the horseradish dip.

John's Take on the New Year's Day Meal
For an extra-special "oomph", you could brush the lid of each bun with a little beaten egg and a sprinkling of ½ tsp of crushed cumin seeds and ½ tsp crushed coriander seeds. Bake them in the oven for a few minutes before serving.

Crunchy veggie chips

Succulent burger

Relish with a kick

Juicy salad

5 ways with...
Beetroot

Beetroot can add a subtle kick to a dish, as with the hearty beef burgers, but it also works well when prepared with other simple flavour pairings.

Preparing beetroot

Roast
Remove the green stems, wrap the beetroot in foil, and place on a baking tray. Place it in a 170°C (340°F/Gas 3) oven for 1–2 hours, varying according to the beetroot size. It is fully cooked when easily pricked with a knife. Rinse under cold water and remove the skin fully before serving.

Boil
Any size of beetroot can be cooked by boiling, but it works best for smaller ones. Remove the stems and submerge in salted boiling water for about 25 minutes. The beetroot is cooked when easily pricked with a knife. Rinse under cold water and remove the skin fully before serving.

Grate
Top, tail, and peel raw beetroot, and grate the flesh for a nutritious addition to soups or salads.

Juice
The gentle sweet flavour of beetroot suits blends of vegetable juice. Wash the root and the leaves thoroughly, remove the stems above the root and chop into small pieces. Put both the root, and the leaves through the juicer.

1 Orange + goat's cheese

The gentle **tang** of soft goat's cheese is the perfect match for **rich**, earthy beetroot.

Combined with sweet, **juicy** oranges and seasonal greens, they compose a classic winter salad and incorporate diverse and **complementary** tastes to create a bright, **fresh** flavour profile. The combination of sweet–tart oranges, earthy roasted beetroot, and creamy goat's cheese can also blend deliciously in **sweet–savoury** tarts, soups, or gratins, and can be mixed with couscous, quinoa, or risotto for a heartier grain-based meal.

2 Vodka + crème fraîche

Roasted beetroot is often served with something cool and creamy to subtly **enhance** its best qualities. Crème fraîche is the thickest, creamiest cream and is the perfect complement to the flavour and texture of beetroot. Vodka's traditional use in the kitchen is to extract and enhance the flavours of the ingredients with which it is combined. Thus, like cream, it can be used to bring out the **richness** and **sweetness** of roasted beetroot. Combine the vodka and crème fraîche to top roasted beetroot, or blend the three ingredients in a classic Russian borscht. Try adding complementary smoked salmon for another dimension to the flavour palate.

Gregg's Advice on Choosing Beetroot

The leaves of a fresh beetroot should be glossy and fresh, and the roots themselves should feel hard, with no mould, cuts, or abrasions on the surface. Smaller roots are likely to be more tender than older ones, which may have more of a woody taste.

3 Paprika + haddock

The gently **warming** spice of paprika adds an entirely new flavour dimension to dishes traditionally containing beetroot, but the two flavours play off each other well. The **delicate**, sweet flavour of haddock is an ideal intermediary to play these ingredients against one another in an earthy, **warming** winter dish.

Poach haddock in a paprika–cream sauce and serve alongside roasted beetroot. Top a haddock timbale with paprika and beetroot dressing or incorporate the ingredients in anything from soup or salad to risotto.

4 Sprouts + horseradish

Beetroot and brussels sprouts are two of the best winter roasting vegetables, and the sweet, **nutty** flavour of perfectly **roasted** brussels sprouts is a good match for the taste of beetroot.

Combine these vegetables with hot, peppery horseradish for a strong **kick** of flavour. Believe it or not, the natural **sugars** brought out in the roasting process will hold their own against the contrast of the pungent, **fiery** root.

5 Cabbage + cider vinegar

Similar to the sweet–savoury flavour of brussels sprouts when gently cooked, cabbage is a natural complement to sweet, earthy beetroot. Cider vinegar, which is milder, more **fragrant**, and less acidic than other varieties of vinegar, and which has a bright apple flavour, brings out the flavours of both and complements their sweetness, without stealing the show. Combine these ingredients in soups, salads, and curries. Alternatively, meld the flavours by **braising** beetroot and red cabbage in cider vinegar and serve as a vegetable side.

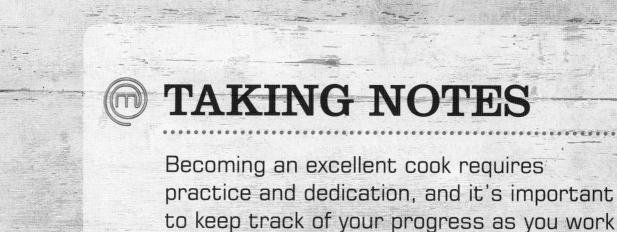

TAKING NOTES

Becoming an excellent cook requires practice and dedication, and it's important to keep track of your progress as you work through the course. Record everything you learn from your cooking experiences – and be sure to include the highs and the lows!

The key techniques

As you practise the techniques (pp22–43), keep a note of anything you discover that will help you to improve in skill and confidence.

Roasting Frying
temperatures timings
Stewing Poaching fish
fruit
ingredients Baking
measurements

The mother sauces

It may take a few attempts to perfect the classic sauces (pp44–65).
Note down anything that helps you to streamline the process.

Tomato Espagnole
consistency roux
Béchamel Hollandaise
texture
colour Velouté
variations

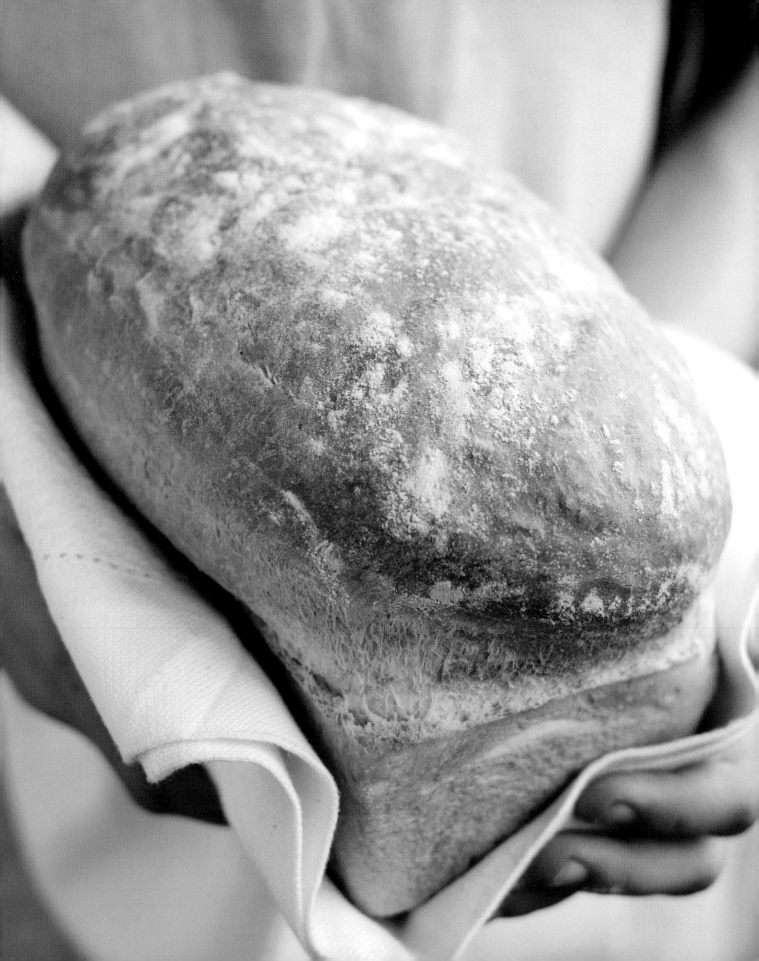

Building blocks

The key staples

Did your bread rise? Was your rice fluffy? Did your pie have a soggy bottom? Take notes to help to improve your key staples (pp66–87).

....
....
....
....
....
....
....
....
....
....
....
....
....
....
....
....
....
....
....
....
....

Rice *methods* Salad *dressings*
Pasta Bread *flavourings*
colourings *shapes* Pie *fillings*

....
....

Make it your own

Give recipes your own twist. Keep a record of how recipes change with replacement ingredients. What worked and what didn't? Capture presentation ideas that take your cooking to the next level.

Flavour pairings

Get creative with your flavours! Take cooking inspiration from everything around you (the seasons, recipes, menus at your favourite restaurants), to create your own flavour pairing ideas page.

Family favourites

Family and friends will enjoy sampling your delicious recipes as you work through the book. Keep track of any that are a great success or adaptations that you make to suit allergies or preferences.

Technique index

Refer to this helpful technique index for recipes that require a little extra know-how or expertise.

Preparation

Dairy
butter, softening 275
buttermilk alternatives 328
caramel, making 283
chocolate, melting 286
cream, whipping 278
crème pâtissière, making 310
custard, making 292
eggs
  clarifying with egg whites 100
  separating 215
  testing for freshness 39
fools, making 294
ice cream, making 297
meringue, making mixture 307

Grains, pulses, and pasta
chickpeas, cooking dried 107
couscous, preparing 185
pasta, making homemade 74–5

Meat and seafood
chicken
  boning a thigh 158
  spatchcocking 163
  stuffing breasts 164
crab, shelling 152
fish
  curing in salt 116
  pin-boning 123
  skinning 123
gammon, glazing 202
lamb, trimming rack of 187
livers, trimming 111
mussels, de-bearding 142
prawns, de-veining 145
pâté, pressing 113
rabbit, jointing 172

Vegetables
asparagus, trimming 119
avocados, stoning 114
beetroot, grating 410
cabbage, chopping 252
celeriac, trimming 402
chillies, de-seeding 240
citrus fruits, zesting 291
clams, shucking 98
dried fruit, soaking 332
garlic, chopping 49

leeks, trimming 257
lemon, juicing 108
potatoes, mashing 124
mushrooms, rehydrating 191
onions, chopping 49
peppers, chopping 264
rocket, puréeing 372
salad, preparing 76–9
spinach, washing 230
tomatoes, peeling 48
walnuts, shelling 331

Cooking

Baking 40–43
biscuits 40
  sizing 345, 353
bread 84–87
  testing for "doneness" 319
  working dough 320
brioche, making 325
cakes 40–43
  retaining moisture 340
  rolling up Swiss rolls 346
cookies 40
  sizing 353
crumble topping 269
en papillote 140
fish 130
macaroons, shaping/baking 338
pastry techniques 80–3
  blind baking 272
  choux pastry 300
  "hot-water" pastry 210
  lining tins with filo 216
  making a pie 80–3
  rolling out puff pastry 150

Dressings
Caesar salad 246
herb vinaigrette 78
niçoise dressing 251
soured cream 252

Frying 32–5
asparagus 366
blinis 326
deep-frying 147
fish, pan-frying 133
in butter 207
pancakes 280
pears, pan-frying 392

rösti 382
steak 34–5
tuna 139
stir-frying 225

Grilling
hazelnuts, toasting 262

Poaching 36–9
eggs 38–9
fish 134
pears 392

Roasting 24–7
asparagus 366
beef 188
chicken 25–7
pears 392
pork 197
poultry 428
resting roast meat 24

Sauces
béchamel 50–53
bolognese 226
espagnole 62–5
hollandaise 54–7
mayonnaise 57
mint 363
mornay 52
Napoli 230
pesto 232
port-cranberry 400
tomato 46–9
velouté 58–61

Simmering
asparagus 366
eggs, soft-boiling 127
lentils, cooking 243
lobster, cooking live 155
par-boiling 259
pasta, cooking 72, 226
pulses, cooking 243
rice, cooking 68–71
  cooking rice pudding 277
risotto rice, cooking 236

Stewing 29–31
browning meat 28

Stocks
court bouillon 135
fish 104
meat 180
vegetable 95

Essential information

This at-a-glance reference guide covers the practical information you need – from measurement conversions to appropriate times and temperatures.

Measurements

There are many variables in cooking, so certain recipes may take less time or longer. All recipes have been tested, and the cooking times given are as accurate as possible, but learn to rely on your instincts for doneness.

• Use the measurements stated, especially when baking.
• Use measuring spoons. The recipes refer to a level spoon, unless otherwise stated.
• Use a measuring jug for liquids, and take the measurement looking at it from eye level.
• Never mix metric and imperial.

Conversion charts

LINEAR MEASURES

3mm	($1/8$in)	2.5cm	(1in)	10cm	(4in)	20cm	(8in)	30cm	(12in)
5mm	($1/4$in)	5cm	(2in)	12cm	(5in)	23cm	(9in)	46cm	(18in)
1cm	($1/2$in)	6cm	($2^1/2$in)	15cm	(6in)	25cm	(10in)	50cm	(20in)
2cm	($3/4$in)	7.5cm	(3in)	18cm	(7in)	28cm	(11in)	61cm	(24in)
								77cm	(30in)

WEIGHTS

10g	($1/4$ oz)	85g	(3oz)	250g	(9oz)	750g	(1lb 10oz)	2kg	($4^1/2$ lb)
15g	($1/2$ oz)	100g	($3^1/2$ oz)	300g	(10oz)	800g	($1^3/4$ lb)	2.25kg	(5lb)
20g	($3/4$ oz)	115g	(4oz)	350g	(12oz)	900g	(2lb)	2.5kg	($5^1/2$ lb)
25g	(scant 1oz)	125g	($4^1/2$ oz)	400g	(14oz)	1kg	($2^1/4$ lb)	2.7kg	(6lb)
30g	(1oz)	140g	(5oz)	450g	(1lb)	1.1kg	($2^1/2$ lb)	3kg	($6^1/2$ lb)
45g	($1^1/2$ oz)	150g	($5^1/2$ oz)	500g	(1lb 2oz)	1.25kg	($2^3/4$ lb)		
50g	($1^3/4$ oz)	175g	(6oz)	550g	($1^1/4$ lb)	1.35kg	(3lb)		
60g	(2oz)	200g	(7oz)	600g	(1lb 5oz)	1.5kg	(3lb 3oz)		
75g	($2^1/2$ oz)	225g	(8oz)	675g	($1^1/2$ lb)	1.8kg	(4lb)		

VOLUME MEASURES

1 tsp		75ml	($2^1/2$ fl oz)	240ml	(8fl oz)	500ml	(16fl oz)	1.4 litres ($2^1/2$ pints)
2 tsp		90ml	(3fl oz)	250ml	(9fl oz)	600ml	(1 pint)	1.5 litres ($2^3/4$ pints)
1 tbsp (equiv. to 3 tsp)		100ml	($3^1/2$ fl oz)	300ml	(10fl oz)	750ml	($1^1/4$ pints)	1.7 litres (3 pints)
		120ml	(4fl oz)	350ml	(12fl oz)	900ml	($1^1/2$ pints)	2 litres ($3^1/2$ pints)
2 tbsp		150ml	(5fl oz)	400ml	(14fl oz)	1 litre	($1^3/4$ pints)	3 litres ($5^1/4$ pints)
3 tbsp		200ml	(7fl oz)	450ml	(15fl oz)	1.2 litres (2 pints)		
4 tbsp or 60ml (2fl oz)								

Roasting meat and poultry

All of the recipes have been tested on a gas ring hob and an electric oven – for a fan oven, reduce the temperature by approximately 10°C. If in doubt, it may be wise to invest in an oven thermometer.

Meat Cuts of meat can vary, so use this as a general guide and add an extra 450g (1lb) of weight to your joint for cooking time if it weighs less than 1.35kg (3lb). Preheat the oven, use a meat thermometer (inserted into the thickest part of the cut, away from any bones) for an accurate internal temperature, and always allow the meat to rest.

MEAT		OVEN TEMPERATURE	COOKING TIME	INTERNAL TEMPERATURE
Beef	Rare	180°C (350°F/Gas 4)	15 mins per 450g (1lb)	60°C (140°F)
	Medium	180°C (350°F/Gas 4)	20 mins per 450g (1lb)	70°C (160°F)
	Well-done	180°C (350°F/Gas 4)	25 mins per 450g (1lb)	80°C (175°F)
Pork	Well-done	180°C (350°F/Gas 4)	25 mins per 450g (1lb)	80°C (175°F)
Lamb	Medium	180°C (350°F/Gas 4)	20 mins per 450g (1lb)	70°C (160°F)
	Well-done	180°C (350°F/Gas 4)	25 mins per 450g (1lb)	80°C (175°F)

Poultry Use these times as a guide, bearing in mind that the size and weight of each bird vary. Be sure to preheat the oven before cooking your bird(s), and always check that the bird is fully cooked before serving.

POULTRY		OVEN TEMPERATURE	COOKING TIME
Poussin		190°C (375°F/Gas 5)	12 mins per 450g (1lb) plus 12 mins
Chicken		200°C (400°F/Gas 6)	20 mins per 450g (1lb) plus 20 mins
Duck		180°C (350°F/Gas 4)	20 mins per 450g (1lb) plus 20 mins
Goose		180°C (350°F/Gas 4)	20 mins per 450g (1lb) plus 20 mins
Pheasant		200°C (400°F/Gas 6)	50 mins total cooking
Turkey	3.5–4.5kg (7–9lb)	190°C (375°F/Gas 5)	2$\frac{1}{2}$–3 hrs total cooking
	5–6kg (10–12lb)	190°C (375°F/Gas 5)	3$\frac{1}{2}$–4 hrs total cooking
	6.5–8.5kg (13–17lb)	190°C (375°F/Gas 5)	4$\frac{1}{2}$–5 hrs total cooking

INDEX

Entries in roman indicate recipes.
Entries in *italic* indicate specific
cooking skills, techniques, and
expertise.

INDEX

439

Cookery Editor Norma MacMillan

Project Editor Martha Burley
Project Art Editor Collette Sadler
Editorial Assistant Christopher Mooney
Design Assistant Jade Wheaton
Managing Editor Dawn Henderson
Managing Art Editor Christine Keilty
Jacket Design Assistant Rosie Levine
Senior Jacket Creative Nicola Powling
Pre-Production Producer Raymond Williams
Senior Production Controller Jen Lockwood
Creative Technical Support Sonia Charbonnier
Art Director Jane Bull
Publisher Mary Ling

DK India
Senior Editor Dorothy Kikon
Senior Art Editor Balwant Singh
Assistant Editors Tina Jindal and Ekta Sharma
Art Editors Ira Sharma and Zaurin Thoidingjam
Managing Editor Glenda Fernandes
Managing Art Editor Navidita Thapa
DTP Designers Rajdeep Singh, Sachin Singh, and
Manish Chandra Upreti
CTS/DTP Manager Sunil Sharma

Commissioned Recipe Photography Will Heap
Photography Art Direction and Prop Styling Sonia Moore
Food Stylist Jane Lawrie
Food Stylist Assistant Paul Jackman

Printed and bound L.E.G.O. S.p.A., Italy

Acknowledgments
Shine would like to thank
David Ambler, Laura Biggs, Martin Buckett, Jo Carlton, Bev Comboy, John Gilbert, Jessica
Hannan, Lori Heiss, Ozen Kazim, Jodie King, Ben Liebmann, Maya Maraj, Mark Nash, Lou
Plank, Lyndsey Posner, Franc Roddam, Karen Ross, Rosemary Scoular, John Torode, Sophie
Walker, and Gregg Wallace.

Dorling Kindersley would like to thank
Clare Nielsen-Marsh, Laura Nickoll, Tia Sarkar, and Katie Bone for editorial help; Rachel Ng,
George Nimmo, and Tom Morse for production help; Anne Harnan for recipe testing; Carolyn
Humphries and Jane Lawrie for recipe writing; Claire Cross for proofreading; Vanessa Bird
for indexing; Alan Buckingham for images p369 (cb) and p389 (cb); Max Moore for hand
modelling; Le Creuset for the casserole dish loan; Backgrounds Prop Hire London and China &
Company for prop hire; and Lasco Salvage Merchants for wooden surfaces and props.

" **Condiments are like old friends** – highly thought of, but often taken for granted.

Marilyn Kaytor, food journalist and author

The belly rules the mind.

Spanish proverb

... no one is born a great cook, one learns by doing.

Julia Child

One cannot think well, love well, sleep well unless one has dined well.

Virginia Woolf

food should be prepa

Swedish proverb

This will change your **life!**

John Torode

One of the very nicest things about life is the way we must regularly stop whatever it is we are doing and devote our attention to eating.

Luciano Pavarotti